The Phantom of Ben Het
Vietnam: The Missing Chapter

> To My brother Dennis
> "Vietnam, 67-68 —
> a comrade in arms"
> 4/29/03
> "Freedom is not Free!"

THE PHANTOM OF BEN HET

Vietnam: The Missing Chapter

[signature: John W. Lamerson]

by

John D. Lamerson

Credits:

Cover Art: John D. Lamerson
Cover Design: Barbara A. Swanson, Graphics West, Inc.
Cover Art Computer Enhancement: Helstrom Studios
Text Maps and Graphics: Deborra Dodson
Production and Composition: Graphics West, Inc., Colorado Springs, Colorado
Editor: Sharon Green, Graphics West, Inc.
Printer: Publishers Press, Salt Lake City, Utah

Copyright © 2001 by Lamerson Publishing
All rights reserved. Published 2001.
Printed in the United States of America

Published by
Lamerson Publishing
Website: www.lamersonpub.com

No part of this book may be reproduced or transmitted in any form or by any means, electronic or mechanical, including photocopying, recording, or by any information storage and retrieval system without permission in writing from the publisher. For information contact: Lamerson Publishing, 5102 Galley Rd. Lot 327-A, Colorado Springs, CO 80915 or e-mail One55mm@aol.com

ISBN: 0-9711424-0-8
        0-9711424-1-6 (paperback)

Library of Congress Cataloging-in-Publication Data

Lamerson, John D.
  The Phantom of Ben Het
  Vietnam: The Missing Chapter
  John D. Lamerson
      p.   cm.
  ISBN 0-9711424-0-8
  1. History   2. Vietnam War   3. Military History

2001 133006

CIP

DEDICATION

This book is dedicated to my wife, Mavis, and our four daughters, Donna Sue, Tina Marie, Julie Ann, and Shery Renae, who have always been there for me. I also wish to honor the military service of my younger brother, Jerry L. Lamerson, Capt. U.S. Marine Corps, retired, who served in Vietnam during the early part of my tour. And, finally, this is in memory of my oldest brother, James V. Lamerson, Chief Master Sergeant, U.S. Air Force, who served in Thailand during the Vietnam war.

CONTENTS

Preface   ix
Acknowledgments   xv
Introduction   xvii

PROLOGUE 1

CHAPTER 1   A Soldier's Duty 5

CHAPTER 2   Setting the Stage 10

CHAPTER 3   The 24th STZ and the Enemy B-3 Front. 19

CHAPTER 4   A Red Leg in The Nam. 27

CHAPTER 5   Operation Dan Quyan 38 A: Phase I 34

CHAPTER 6   7th USAF TAC Air Support: Dan Quyan 38 A . 46

CHAPTER 7   Dan Quyan 38 A: Phase II 53

CHAPTER 8   The Siege of Ben Het: Part I 65

CHAPTER 9   The Siege of Ben Het: Part II 81

CHAPTER 10   The Siege of Ben Het: Part III 99

CHAPTER 11   The Siege of Ben Het: An Unpredictable Conclusion 112

CHAPTER 12   The Last Straw 129

CHAPTER 13   The Siege of Ben Het: An Analytical Review 146

CHAPTER 14   Aftermath: Part I 163

CHAPTER 15   Aftermath: Part II 184

CHAPTER 16 Ben Het: The Final Chapter 197

CHAPTER 17 Summation 201

EPILOGUE The Phantom of Ben Het 205

GLOSSARY 209

BIBLIOGRAPHY. 219

PREFACE

> *Ben Het at night is a scene that is at once beautiful and fascinating, weird and horrible. Dali, Goya, Bach, The Beatles, Hemingway and Zanuck would understand. Flares hang in the sky, casting milky, light purple shadows. A plane drones and circles overhead, periodically spitting streams of fiery tracers at enemy positions.*
>
> B. Drummond Ayers, Jr.
> June 30, 1969
> *New York Times* News Service

The main battles during the Vietnam War were fought on the periphery, away from the television camera lenses and the eyes of the rest of the world. Big unit war, offensive operations, were limited to only a few significant battles.

One such battle that immediately comes to mind is "The Battle of the Ia Drang Valley," which was located in South Vietnam's Central Highland Pleiku Province and was fought during November of 1965. In this epic battle, the 1st Battalion of the 7th Cavalry, U.S. 1st Cavalry Division (Air Mobile) was pitted against a surrounding force of 2,000 North Vietnamese Army Regular Infantry Soldiers. The Americans held their own, but three days later a sister battalion only two and one-half miles away was chopped to pieces by another newly arrived NVA Infantry Regiment to the bloody battleground. These two actions together constituted one of the most savage and significant battles of the entire Vietnam War. It was believed that North Vietnam's General Vo Nguyen Giap planned to cut South Vietnam in two. His plans were stopped cold.

In November 1967, Giap's multiregimental forces once again entered South Vietnam's Central Highland Province of Kontum. This time however, General Westmoreland, the MACV commander, ordered nearly 16,000 Allied troops to be deployed to head off the four NVA Regiments that were threatening the area. The Allies declared the ensuing battle that raged around the city of Dak To and the hamlet of Ben Het a great victory; however, the objective of the attacking force has never been determined. One point I wish to make is that the NVA 66th Infantry Regiment took part in both of the battles mentioned above. In the annals of American warfare, the battle above is recognized as "The Battle of Dak To."

I do not wish to discuss other battles at this time, because, I want to focus on the May–June 1969 "Siege Of Ben Het." Once again the security of Kontum and Pleiku Provinces was under a threat from the NVA. Generals Giap and Dung once more sent multiregimental forces across the borders into SVN. This time, however, no large Allied units were deployed to stop them. In addition to the 66th NVA Regiment comprising part of the enemy force, a new NVA Infantry Regiment was introduced to the Allies. The NVA 28th Infantry Regiment was allegedly formed by using two leftover battalions from the 1968 "Siege of Khe Sanh." It is believed that these two regiments were less than half the total enemy attack force threatening the mountain outpost. Without any Allied Infantry support, U.S. Artillery and Air Support saved the day. The enemy was beaten back once more, but no official determination has ever been declared as to the intent of the NVA for fighting "The Siege of Ben Het."

I have my own hypothesis, which is that NVA battle plans included not only the creation of a "Southern Dien Bien Phu," but also a plan to cut South Vietnam in two, as originally planned by Giap in 1965. The battle for Ben Het served as a full dress rehearsal for a battle yet to come.

During the March 1972 Easter weekend enemy offensive dubbed Nguyen Hue by the NVA, the North Vietnamese Army once more struck in the Central Highland Provinces of Kontum and Pleiku. The equivalent of three NVA Divisions harassed the South Vietnamese forces and laid siege to seven firebases west of the provincial capital at Kontum, while other Communist troops cut the main supply route, Highway 19, to the coastal town of Qui Nhon. They also inflicted heavy casualties on a South Korean Division that tried to reopen the road. But here at least <u>air support was possible and B-52 strikes inflicted enormous casualties on the NVA 28th Regiment.</u>[1]

"War is death and destruction. The American way of war is particularly violent, deadly, and dreadful. We believe in using 'things', artillery, bombs, massive firepower to conserve the lives of our soldiers. The enemy on the other hand, to make up for his lack of 'things' expended men instead of machines and therefore, suffered enormous casualties."[2]

The casualties alluded to by General Weyand represented the price that the North Vietnamese were willing to pay in order to win the "War of Attrition" that they had chosen as a tactic to buy them time. Time to build their foot-bound army into a modern fully-mechanized one. As an

American soldier, and highly trained in the use of "things," I found it within the purview of my duty to kill as many of the massed enemy force threatening me and my comrades as I could. To do so required that I employ all the "things" available to me in the U.S. Arsenal of Weaponry.

I challenge anyone interested in the History of the Vietnam War to read my compelling story.

John D. Lamerson
MSG U.S. Army (Ret.)

John D. Lamerson, after the Siege of Ben Het, July 1969

Notes

1 Tim Page and John Pimlott, eds., *Nam: The Vietnam Experience 1965–75*, (New York, Barnes & Noble, Inc., 1995), 493–94.
2 Harry G. Summers, Jr., *On Strategy: A Critical Analysis of the Vietnam War*, (New York: Dell Publishing Co., 1982), 69–70.

AUTHOR'S NOTE

The Phantom of Ben Het

"Coming from the air, from land and from the sea, American firepower was the great equalizer in Vietnam. It could punish enemy troops when they dared mass into large units and extricate isolated American units from the most dangerous situations. American firepower could convert nighttime into day, turn jungle covered terrain into charred fields, and give American combat troops a firepower edge even when badly outnumbered" (*America Takes Over*, 46).

The Phantom of Ben Het is based on the use of American firepower in the capacity alluded to above. I can only add one word when it comes to describing American firepower in Vietnam: "Awesome"!

ACKNOWLEDGMENTS

I wish to acknowledge the following individuals who helped me in the writing of "The Phantom of Ben Het" by reviewing draft type manuscripts followed by critiques. These critiques kept me on track in the production of my final book length manuscript:

Dr. Richard P. Hallion, The Air Force Historian HQ USAF/HO 500 Duncan Ave. Box 94 Bolling AFB, DC 20332-1111	Extensive Review/Critique
Dr. Wayne Thompson, AFHSO, a colleague of Dr. Hallion	Extensive Review/Critique
Kenneth R. Bailey Colonel, U.S. Army Retired 62 Wilikoki Place Kailua, Hawaii 96734	Extensive Review/Critique
M.E. Morris Captain, U.S. Navy Retired Author: *The Last Kamikaze* 2242 Glenwood Circle Colorado Springs, CO 80909	Extensive Review/Critique
Donald B. Bunn Captain, U.S. Navy Retired 5845 Wilson Rd. Colorado Springs, CO 80919-3356	Editing/Critique
Lisa Dobbles USAF Academy Graduate Class of 99, maiden name (Lisa Meier). 556 Carter Grove Charleston, SC 29414-9014 Active Duty at Charleston AFB, SC	Editing & Critique/Research

Note: All of the people mentioned above are familiar with my book manuscript content and all have agreed that it is a valuable work. My intent now is to make the manuscript available to students of history, political science, military intelligence, etc. so that they can use the material as a research document. I make note here that at the present time, there appears to be no commercial market for written works on The Vietnam War.

Every effort has been made to ensure that required permissions for all material were obtained. The editor and Graphics West, Inc., cannot take responsibility for any errors or omissions. Please contact Lamerson Publishing concerning any errors or omissions.

Grateful acknowledgment is made to the following to reprint previously published and unpublished material:

Chris McGee and Nicole Van Natter at the USAF Museum for the use of all the airplane photographs in this book.

INTRODUCTION

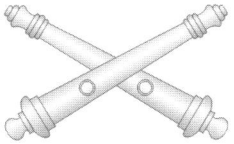

Go tell the Spartans, thou who passeth by, that here obedient to their laws, we lie.

Epitaph inscribed by unknown author
at Thermopylae, Greece

As a result of the Tonkin Gulf Resolution signed by President Lyndon B. Johnson on 5 August 1964,[1] America allied herself with South Vietnam in the war against the Communist regime of North Vietnam. America was deeply enmeshed in the war by the time I volunteered for a tour of duty with the U.S. Army in November 1968. My involvement in that war, the subject of this book, provides a missing chapter in the annals of that war. This book focuses on the withdrawal of the North Vietnamese Army (NVA) from the Ben Het battlefield, which commenced on or about 27 June and was complete by 2 July 1969.

The pivotal point in America's war with North Vietnam did not come about due to any major or decisive battle or battles. The fact is, a pivotal point was reached in late March or early April 1967 when President Johnson decided it was time to de-emphasize General William C. Westmoreland's "big unit war" and emphasize pacification. Johnson then decided to begin looking for alternative solutions to the war that did not require more troops. One alternative was to give the pacification program a giant boost. A second was to upgrade the training and equipment of the South Vietnamese Army (ARVN) and get them more involved in the ground war.

To energize the pacification program, he assigned Ellsworth Bunker to Vietnam as the new United States ambassador and appointed Robert Komer, a civilian, as Westmoreland's deputy in charge of pacification. He gave the job of energizing the South Vietnamese Army to General Creighton Abrams, who became Westmoreland's Deputy Commander in charge of "Vietnamization."[2] It is noteworthy to add that the term "Vietnamization" had not yet been coined.

On 3 July 1968, General Abrams took over command of MACV (Military Assistance Command Vietnam). After a major shift in

American policy, Abrams took charge with no expectation of further manpower and with instructions to turn the war over to the Vietnamese as quickly as possible.[3] On 3 September 1968, I, as an Army Sergeant First Class, married and with four children, made an inexplicable decision. I volunteered to serve in Vietnam under my secondary MOS (Military Occupational Skill), which was 13Z50 FA (Field Artillery) Cannon, and Rocket Senior Sergeant. My application was readily accepted. My departure date was set for Halloween, 31 October 1968.

Meanwhile, the 1968 presidential candidate, Richard M. Nixon, was alluding to a "secret plan" to end the war in Vietnam. Of course Nixon really had no such plan. Nevertheless, he was elected on 5 November 1968 and took the oath of office on 20 January 1969. Nixon and his new cabinet went right to work as they searched for solutions to the great problems facing them. Henry Kissinger, Nixon's National Security Advisor, conducted a very important and high-level survey of all of the U.S. government's defense groups that were involved in the war. The results of the survey became the basis for NSSM-1 (National Security Study Memorandum). There were two separate groups surveyed: Group "A" included MACV, CINCPAC, JCS, and Embassy Saigon; Group "B" included OSD (Civilian Office of the Secretary of Defense), CIA, and Secretary of State.

The survey was completed by mid-February and, of those surveyed, MACV was the most pessimistic in reference to the more important questions. MACV recognized that a war of attrition was virtually unwinnable. Assuming that the enemy casualties remained at the all-time record highs of 1968 (largely a result of the full-scale Tet attacks), "it would take thirteen years to exhaust the [North Vietnam] manpower pool." But MACV warned, "It is unlikely that the high enemy loss rates of January–June 1968 could be maintained." And as for the hope that ARVN could completely replace American servicemen, MACV predicted, "It could not now, or in the foreseeable future, handle both VC and sizable NVA forces without U.S. combat support." Concluding, NSSM-1 seemed to indicate that a military victory was unattainable unless the American commitment of troops doubled or tripled.[4] President Nixon, who had no alternative plan, had little choice but to ignore MACV and move forward at full speed with the emerging "Vietnamization" process.

Meanwhile, in January 1969, Lieutenant General William Peers, U.S. Army, Commanding General of First Field Force, Vietnam (I FFORCEV), reached a verbal agreement with Major General Lu Lan, Commanding General of II Corps, Army of the Republic of Vietnam

(ARVN), for the ARVN assumption of responsibility for northern Kontum Province. The basis for the IFFORCEV proposal was to free a U.S. brigade of the 4th U.S. Infantry Division for employment:

- as a reaction force for any contingency in the Highlands,
- as a striking force to be employed within II Corps Tactical Zone (CTZ),
- for deployment outside II CTZ on order of COMUSMACV,
- or, to assist the pacification program in Binh Dinh Province.

The agreed effective date for the changeover was 1 February 1969. Thus, a situation was established for the first significant test of the emerging "Vietnamization" policy.[5] Under the new policy, the U.S. would continue to support the ARVN with air, artillery, and combat engineers.

To gain a better perspective on the North Vietnamese position, we must turn back the calendar to the year 1953. General Van Tien Dung, leader of one of the Vietminh's first Divisions and Army Chief of Staff, along with General Vo Nguyen Giap, was given the task of organizing the Vietminh military arm. The years of combat that followed made both generals firm believers in the thesis that while guerrilla tactics could prolong a war and limit losses, the key to victory was the use of regular Army forces capable of waging major battles.

It was said that, while working in the shadows of Giap, "Dung, if not the actual author of Giap's plans, was the most responsible for carrying them out. He orchestrated battlefield maneuvers and marshaled the necessary supplies, arms, munitions, and men. He was also the prime mover in transforming the NVA (North Vietnamese Army) into a modern military machine between 1968 and 1972."[6]

During their first major encounter with the Americans in the battle of the Ia Drang Valley in 1965, the NVA learned a most valuable lesson. They learned that with violent and close-in fighting on battlefields of their choice, and with timing of their choice, they could greatly diminish the effects of American firepower superiority.[7] This is not to say that American firepower was rendered impotent as is noted by Giap's own revelations. In early January 1969, Giap admitted to Italian news correspondent, Oriana Fellaci, that his method had cost him 600,000 VC/NVA soldiers in the war to date.[8] MACV had determined that due to Tet 1968 enemy battlefield losses, there was little chance that the enemy would be strong enough to go back on the offensive in the foreseeable future. MACV had made a serious miscalculation. The VC had taken the brunt of the big Tet losses, while the NVA was still a very potent fighting force, as the record will prove.

An Allied intelligence source revealed that an enemy propaganda lecture was conducted in eastern Khanh Hoa Province on 4 May 1969, urging the villagers to prepare for an offensive that would encompass all of South Vietnam. This offensive would bring success in the Paris Peace Talks and would be instrumental in ending the war by August 1969. Another agent reported that a 5 May propaganda lecture in a hamlet northeast of Kontum City told of <u>four NVA regiments</u> that had entered Kontum Province to liberate Kontum City. Sensor indicators, particularly intelligence reports (IR), showed increased activity in western Kontum Province.

During the period of 4–10 May 1969, enemy activity greatly increased in the Ben Het, Dak To, and the Tan Canh area of Kontum Province. Enemy patrols were encountered at short distances from allied installations and attacks-by-fire were received on many of these installations. The IR activity greatly increased in the "Rocket Ridge" area southwest of Dak To. Significant ground attacks began on 8–9 May 1969.[9] Thus, Phase I commenced for the ARVN counteroffensive, which was dubbed Dan Quyan 38A.

During the remainder of May, the ARVN ground forces, supported by tactical air and Arc Light (code name for B-52) strikes, were able to take command of the key terrain south of Ben Het and aggressively seek out and engage the VC/NVA.[10]

In late May and early June, it appeared the South Vietnamese had won the battle. The VC/NVA forces were seemingly withdrawing westward toward the Cambodian border. The ARVN units began to return to their camps, having fought aggressively the preceding month, and having inflicted severe casualties upon the enemy—figures provided showed 1,162 enemy dead.

During the first part of June, enemy activity in the immediate vicinity of Ben Het increased. The camp under continuous ABFs (Attack by Fire) began to receive small-arms/automatic weapons (SA/AW) fire from enemy troops located a short distance from the perimeter. The camp's defenders detected enemy units close-in, with increasing regularity, as it became apparent that the VC/NVA were massing in preparation for an assault.[11]

In early June, the ARVN forces drew back into population centers nearby and the VC/NVA closed in on Ben Het. The South Vietnamese did not counterattack and the siege tightened.

The defense force at Ben Het consisted of about 440 Civilian Irregular Defense Group (CIDG), 25 U.S. SF and ARVN SF advisors, one ARVN tank platoon, and 180 U.S. Artillerymen (Red Legs).

There was a mixture of artillery cannons (totaling twelve) inside the camp. There were also one 81mm mortar tube and one 106mm jeep-mounted recoilless-rifle, plus the two ARVN tanks. The camp found it necessary to depend on air power for the bulk of its defensive firepower.

The tactic of using air power to defend an isolated camp was a standard one that reduced friendly casualties by using ordnance instead of troops to destroy a massed enemy.

As early as February 1969, the 7th Air Force had mounted an interdiction program against the numerous roads and trails leading into South Vietnam (SVN) from the enemy border sanctuaries. This program, the Seventh Air Force Special Interdiction (SASI), prevented the enemy from having road access into their chosen battleground.

As the fighting at Ben Het continued during June, charges were made that U.S. troops inside the camp were needlessly exposed, possibly as "bait" for a trap. There was a widely publicized complaint to members of the U.S. Congress. There were also hints that the Americans connected with the defense of the camp were disgusted with the South Vietnamese for not coming out and fighting. The VC/NVA inflamed the situation by keeping Ben Het under attack by fire and code naming the siege "Dien Bien Phu."

The NVA created an "enigma" by making a sudden withdrawal from the Ben Het battlefield. The Allied command initially expressed surprise at the mystery surrounding the enemy's sudden withdrawal. However, after a few day's time, even though the battle was never joined by the ARVN forces, they were declared the victors in a joint communiqué by the U.S. and ARVN commands.

I knew the answer to why the NVA made a sudden withdrawal, but no one thought to ask. I was burned-out due to combat fatigue, having worked an average of 18 to 20 hours per day during the preceding ten straight days of the siege and was still in a bit of a fog. I did not get a single wink of sleep the night of 24–25 June. So, during my "one-on-one" briefing by the Deputy Commander of MACV, I did not even think to bring up the subject of why the enemy had withdrawn. I was just happy to know that a withdrawal had taken place. But now, following years of research on "The Siege of Ben Het" and other relevant subject matter, I believe that I have discovered the true intent of the enemy in reference to "The Siege." This is my hypothesis.

Notes

1. Stanley Karnow, *Vietnam: A History*. (New York: Penguin Books, 1986), 374.
2. Samuel Zaffiri, *Westmoreland: A Biography of General William C. Westmoreland*. (New York: William Morrow and Company, 1994), 290.
3. Clark Dougan, Stephen Weiss, and the editors of Boston Publishing Company, *Nineteen Sixty-Eight*, a volume of *The Vietnam Experience*, (Boston: Boston Publishing Company, 1983), 149.
4. Edward Doyle, Samuel Lipsman, and the editors of Boston Publishing Company, *Fighting for Time*, a volume of *The Vietnam Experience* (Boston: Boston Publishing Company, 1983), 29.
5. U.S. Air Force, Air War College, *Tactical Air Support and the Battle of Ben Het: A Professional Study*, by Thomas M. Crawford, Jr., No. 4029 (Air University: 1970), 4.
6. Clark Dougan, Stephen Weiss, and the editors of Boston Publishing Company, *The Fall of the South*, a volume of *The Vietnam Experience*, (Boston: Boston Publishing Company, 1985), 15.
7. 4. Edward Doyle, Samuel Lipsman, and the editors of Boston Publishing Company, *America Takes Over*, a volume of *The Vietnam Experience* (Boston: Boston Publishing Company, 1982), 70.
8. Clark Dougan, Stephen Weiss, and the editors of Boston Publishing Company, *The Fall of the South*, a volume of *The Vietnam Experience*, (Boston: Boston Publishing Company, 1985), 15.
9. U.S. Air Force, Air War College, *Tactical Air Support and the Battle of Ben Het: A Professional Study*, by Thomas M. Crawford, Jr., No. 4029 (Air University: 1970), 7.
10. U.S. Air Force, CHECO Division, *The Siege of Ben Het*, prepared by Ernie S. Montagliani, (1 October 1969), 8.
11. Ibid., 10.

PROLOGUE

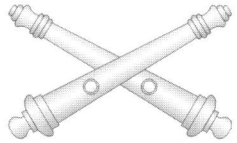

The little bullet with my name on it did not concern me nearly as much as did those big bastards addressed to "whom it may concern."
John Lamerson

As an ordinary soldier placed in extra-ordinary circumstances, I found myself playing a key role in one of America's most epic battles of the Vietnam War. I arrived in South Vietnam in early November 1968. But after only one month, even though enlisted and wearing the rank of Sergeant First Class (E-7), I was appointed to a duty position normally assigned to a commissioned officer in the grade of Captain (03).

During my first seven months of duty, I served six of them as the S-2 (Intelligence Officer), assigned to a heavy gun battalion, 6th Battalion, 14th Artillery. I was a member of the battalion gunnery staff. While still in that position at the end of May, I was given a special combat mission. My orders were clear: "Pack up your S-2 Section's equipment for movement to Ben Het. You are directed to set up a targeting section in conjunction with the relocated Battalion Forward TOC (Tactical Operations Center)." Our mission was to support ARVN Forces of the 24th STZ (Special Tactical Zone), as they mounted a counter offensive operation against the NVA Forces located in Northwestern Kontum Province.

In combat situations, orders often get changed in midstream. That was the case in this particular situation. The NVA made plans of their own. They moved right in behind the ARVNs, who had withdrawn their forces back into the population centers of Dak To and Tan Canh, and prepared to surround and isolate Ben Het using siege tactics. In so doing, NVA forces were able to interdict Highway 512 between Dak To and Ben Het. This action prevented our battalion gunnery team from traveling to Ben Het as planned, which was to be by way of convoy. We were forced to divide up and sortie in aboard a Huey Slick (Bell UH, utility helicopter, one in a series, as opposed to Huey Gun Ship, Huey Dust-off, etc.) that had been placed at our disposal for the insertion mission. The situation became sticky, since Ben Het was under constant enemy artillery bombardment. The helicopter-landing pad at Ben Het's Main Hill was zeroed in by enemy gunners, and the camp's small (abandoned) airstrip lay outside the perimeter wire in an area now under enemy control. Being the last key member of our battalion "Phantom Gunnery Team" to insert into Ben Het, my arrival was marred by a barrage of enemy mortar fire. The Huey Slick pilot, taking no chances on getting his chopper hit by the red-hot chunks of shell shrapnel flying through the air, took off, leaving me and the two RTOs (radio telephone operators) accompanying me stranded in the open and still under an ABF (attack by fire). Shaken, but unharmed in the ordeal, I was finally able to reach the safety of the 5th USSF A-Detachment TOC.

Lieutenant Colonel Kenneth R. Bailey, my battalion commander and now the chief artillery gunnery officer at the camp, briefed me on the latest changes to our gunnery mission at Ben Het. Our arrival had been kept at low key. (We were to never receive official recognition for our part in "the Siege of Ben Het.") That is the reason I have referred to our gunnery team as a "Phantom Gunnery Team."

Changes to our mission were as follows:

1. Lt. Col. Bailey was assigned the mission of coordinating all fires in the defense of Ben Het.
2. Our gunnery team would share the TOC at Ben Het with the SF (Special Forces) A-Team and we were attached to them for rations and quarters.
3. In addition to setting up a targeting section, I was directed to set up an artillery observation post in an exposed SF observation tower that stood near the main entrance to the TOC.

My artillery observation team consisted of only myself and an RTO, whereas artillery observer parties normally are made up of three men. They are the Forward Observer the Reconnaissance Sergeant, and the RTO. But we did not have a man to spare for the job of Recon Sgt.

My subsequent occupation of the observation tower at Ben Het posed a great threat to the NVA gunners of the 40th NVA Artillery Regiment. The NVA gunners, provoked by the fact that I was directing counter battery fire against them, saw my blatant disregard for their marksmanship abilities as a "vulgar middle finger gesture." Unable to knock me off my perch with intense cannon and mortar fire, the NVA employed close-in infantry snipers to get the job done. Failing in their mission to dislodge me from my post, the NVA enabled me to stick around for the duration of the battle. In so doing, they sealed their own fate. While I, on the other hand (serving in the duty position of the S-2 and working in close cooperation with the 7th USAF Air Liaison Officer), was able to coordinate a single "knockout" blow that resulted in the defeat and sudden withdrawal of the massed regimental infantry forces of the NVA that seemed to be assured of a spectacular victory. A victory of such proportions that the effects would resound all the way to the Paris Peace Talks, where they were expected to influence the outcome and bring about an early end to the war.

The Allied command in Vietnam used the defeat of the NVA at Ben Het as an example of South Vietnam's readiness to move forward with the American plan to Vietnamize the war. Vietnamization called for ARVN forces to assume responsibility for the ground fighting, while still receiving air, artillery, and engineer support from the Americans. What Allied commanders failed to reveal to the American public and to the Vietnamese people was the fact that ARVN troops never rejoined the battle at Ben Het. Once he had withdrawn his troops from the battlefield, the South Vietnamese Field Commander failed to initiate counteroffensive operations against the enemy. Colonel Nguyen Ba Lien, the ARVN Field Commander, by his own admission used the American and CIDG (Civilian Irregular Defense Group) defenders at Ben Het as bait for a trap. Lien's plan was to use a long-excepted American practice of creating a killing field where enemy forces could be drawn to mass and where superior American firepower could destroy them. Lien, who had been directed to keep casualties down before further being ordered to withdraw his troops, saw no wrong in following the American tactic of using fire power instead of troops to defeat a massed enemy. What the Allied command failed to consider was, with the withdrawal of U.S. ground troops would eventually go the U.S. fire support elements. The NVA, on the other hand, knew that time was their ally. With the eventual withdrawal of all American forces, the NVA would be left in a position of having the battlefield advantage necessary to win their war with the South.

"The Siege of Ben Het" merely served as a full-dress rehearsal for a larger and more decisive battle yet to come. As for the American involvement, Vietnamization did not prevent the loss of many more American lives before we extracted ourselves and proved to the world what we knew following "the Siege of Ben Het." The ARVN was not prepared to get the job done without the support of U.S. ground troops.

Three decades following "the Siege of Ben Het," I use ten years of research and personal experience to present my own hypothesis as to the actual intentions of the NVA at Ben Het. I have uncovered supporting evidence that indicates that the NVA, under General Dung's guidance, was prepared to test their newly acquired mechanized warfare capability. Dung planned to use his reorganized 325 C Infantry Division, reinforced by the 202nd Armored/Artillery Regiment to spearhead an attack that would culminate with the capture of Kontum and Pleiku border provinces. Giap and Dung reasoned that this victory would place them in a position of strength, which could be used to North Vietnam's advantage at the Paris Peace Negotiations. The fall and capture of Ben Het would have opened the gate that was blocking the roads leading east to Dak To, Tan Canh, and then south to Kontum and Pleiku Cities. Giap and Dung knew that once Pleiku City fell into their hands, a run down Highway 19 to the coast would be possible. By reaching Qui Nhon, the South would be cut in two. A quick "peace" could then be negotiated, leaving North Vietnam in a position of great military strength. For the North, it would be a dream come true.

CHAPTER 1

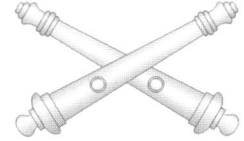

A Soldier's Duty

*I would lay down my life for America, but I
cannot trifle with my honor.*
John Paul Jones
September 7, 1776

Duty, honor, and country all played an important part in the decision that I made in early September 1968. Making the decision to volunteer for duty in Vietnam was not an easy one. In September 1968, as the married father of four little stair-stepped daughters and a wife who was not yet a citizen of the United States, I had to study all of my options before acting. I had full knowledge of the perils that I was opening myself up to if I acted on an uncontrollable urge to serve in Vietnam. I was reluctant to discuss the subject with my wife, yet somehow got up the courage to do so. She was less than thrilled and, though apprehensive, she reluctantly rendered her approval of my decision to volunteer.

Prior to taking final action, I sat back, carefully replaying in my mind all that I knew about Vietnam. I then made a conscious decision that volunteering for duty in Vietnam was the right choice for me to make. I submitted my paperwork on 3 September. I carried a critical Military Occupational Skill (MOS) that pretty well exempted me from duty in Vietnam. My younger brother, Jerry, a U.S. Marine and married with children, was already serving over there. This fact further exempted me from duty in Vietnam. In order to legally circumvent the Army policy, I was permitted to sign a waiver that freed me to go.

The Army personnel people took very quick action on my request for duty in Vietnam. I received my alert for reassignment to Vietnam just three working days following the submission of my paperwork. My battalion Sergeant Major, CSM Hawthorne, 44th Pershing Missile Battalion, received conformation by telephone and passed the unofficial word along to me. I received the official word on 9 September. I was to attend a two-week jungle warfare training school right there at Fort Sill. The training, though interesting, would prove to be quite useless. I was scheduled to depart Fort Sill, Oklahoma, on 31 October 1968. My most important concern was for my family's well-being and safety during my long (one-year) absence. My wife, Mavis, had never held a driving license and was not qualified to drive. Getting her a driving license became our number one priority during the preparation stage.

On 30 October, Mavis passed her driving test and was issued an Oklahoma State driver's license. Not realizing the insensitivity of the act, I treated the family to a movie at the local drive-in, on my last night home. The featured movie was *The Green Berets,* starring John Wayne. The publicity for the film states: "They had to be the toughest fighting force on earth—and the men who led them had to be just a little bit tougher."[1] The kids were not interested in such a movie and were soon fast asleep. My wife was disturbed by all of the blood and gore depicted in the movie and sobbed in silence as I selfishly indulged myself. I did try to comfort her following the movie by rationalizing about the fact that those Green Berets belonged to an elite group. "Hell," I said, "I am a Red Leg artilleryman. There is no way that I will ever face anything like what was depicted in that movie." How wrong I was. Deep down, I really did know that my life would be in great danger over in Vietnam.

I could recall when the French fought the Viet Minh in the late Indo-Chinese War, during which time I was finishing up a four-year enlistment in the U.S. Air Force. I was stationed in England at the time the French were defeated at Dien Bien Phu. We GIs felt that the action in Indo-China would have our futures tied to Indo-China. I was discharged from the Air Force on 4 August 1954.

I reentered military service during July 1955. I had been highly trained by the USAF as a small arms specialist. I thought that the Army Ordnance Corps was the right place for me to be in the U.S. Army. When asked about my career preference, I answered "Big Guns." "OK," said the personnel clerk, "You are assigned to the 509th Field Artillery Battalion, 3rd Armored Division. They are located at Fort Knox, Kentucky." Nearly a year later, the 3rd Armored Division gyroscoped to West Germany during June 1956. Gyroscope was the Army program for rotating major troop units in Europe.

I had not heard anymore about Vietnam until after being assigned to Fort Lewis, Washington, in 1960. Our Army training was being conducted and centered around preparation for wars in the jungles of Southeast Asia. The Army placed emphases on counterinsurgency operations and guerrilla warfare.

I think that it was late 1962, when an old Army buddy serving with me in the 30th Artillery Battalion at Fort Lewis approached me in reference to volunteering for duty in Vietnam. "Come on Sergeant Lamerson, go with me to personnel and check up about volunteering for advisory duty in Vietnam." I said to Sergeant Mills, "I ain't lost nothing in no f—-ing Vietnam. Hell no, man. I've got two kids." Sergeant First Class Rufus Mills, a WW II ex-Marine artilleryman, continued in his quest to convince me to go with him for the purpose of volunteering for advisory duty. "Come on Sarge," he continued with his persuasive rhetoric, "Man, that is good duty." His words fell on deaf ears.

It was January 1965. Stationed back in West Germany since 1963, I was now the senior enlisted instructor of the 155mm (millimeter) branch of the U.S. Army School, Europe. I was with the Weapons Assembly Department. Forward assembly of nuclear artillery ammunition was the subject matter taught at the school.

I was interested in Vietnam because our American armed forces were on the verge of being deployed there. I signed up for a University of Maryland course of instruction. The subject was American Foreign Affairs. I selected Vietnam as the subject of choice for my term paper/report. The U.S. Army Lt. Col. teaching the course made an attempt to discourage me from picking the subject. "Too controversial," he explained. "You will have a tough time with that as your subject." I ignored his remarks, completed my report, and received an A+ grade. I had read the late Bernard Falls' *The Two Vietnams* as part of my resource and research material. I also read other books. I am not sure in which book I read the following: "Legionnaires!" shouted the French General to the tough and bearded men-for-hire standing before him. "You have come here to die! I will now take you to where one goes to die." So the men plodding off, spread out into the swamplands of the Red River Delta where many dutifully died. The year was 1886. Frenchmen dutifully died in Vietnam over the next 70 years.

After killing 500,000 Vietnamese and losing only one of their men for every ten of the Vietnamese that they killed, the French achieved no better than a stalemate. Following the fall of Dien Bien Phu, Falls, a Frenchman himself, warned the West about getting involved in a war in Southeast Asia, especially Vietnam. Not understanding the perils that would befall them, the Americans ignored Falls' warnings. I was fully on the side of my country on the Vietnam issue. I had reasoned that with our nation's power and military know-how, victory was assured.

As I prepared to leave my family and travel to Vietnam where I would join in the American war, I realized that in October 1968, Vietnam was still a land of death and pain, a place where men were sent to die. I had momentary second thoughts about my decision. However, for me it was still a matter of honor and duty; so, without hesitation or further mental reservations, I loaded my travel bags into the car. Accompanied by my wife and four children, I drove to the Lawton, Oklahoma, Municipal Airport. It was Halloween, 31 October 1968.

I drove to the airport because my wife, Mavis, was still a very nervous driver. As my family and I said our good-byes on the tarmac, the tears shed by my beautiful young wife and four little daughters brought a lump to my throat. It was time for me to board the big jet airplane that sat there on the tarmac. Once aboard, I located a seat next to a window over the wing. I could look back out to the edge of the tarmac, where I had just left my family standing. I could see Mavis standing there flanked on the left by our four little girls. They, too, were all looking up toward the airplane, their tear-filled eyes were searching as they tried to steal one last glimpse of me before the plane made its departure. The picture of them standing there like that was indelibly burned into my memory and would haunt my thoughts all the time I was away. The big jet engines coughed to life and our pilot taxied the plane out to the end of the runway. Following the few moments of traditional preflight warm-up, the big ship rumbled down the runway and we were soon airborne. The first leg of my journey to Vietnam took me to Sea-Tac airport in Washington State. I was required to process further at Fort Lewis, Washington.

Sergeant First Class Painter and I, who were Army traveling companions, deplaned upon arrival at the airport. We picked up our luggage and then hailed a local cab. Once inside the taxi, I instructed the driver to take us to downtown Seattle and drop us at a hotel of his recommendation. Once checked into a hotel for the night, we hit the streets for the purpose of finding a suitable restaurant. After dining, we hit the streets again. We walked a block or two before we spotted a friendly looking cocktail lounge. We entered "Dante's Inferno," a most friendly little place where we sat down and ordered drinks. I especially got a kick out of one bar patron who was dressed in a Halloween costume. His costume was in the form of a barrel and from a tap located near the bottom of the barrel, he was dispensing pee-colored apple cider into small plastic cups and handing them out to the happy customers. After a couple of drinks, we retired to our hotel rooms. Back in my room, I turned the TV on to the late evening news. President Lyndon B. Johnson was featured as he made the announcement to the world that he had ordered the cessation of all America's bombing of North Vietnam. I was very displeased with his decision.

The next day, Sergeant Painter and I bought bus tickets to Fort Lewis. After we reported in, we were assigned temporary lodging and then released for the weekend. On Monday, we finished our out-processing and were bussed to McChord AFB where we boarded a giant DC-10 for our trip to Vietnam. By the time our plane landed in Vietnam, Richard Nixon had been elected to the presidency of the United States of America, and was now the commander in chief.

As I stepped off the plane at Cam Ranh Bay, South Vietnam, I muttered to myself, "Who opened the damn furnace door?" Having spent ten years during my military career to date on foreign soil, I was not affected by cultural shock. However, I was not prepared for what I can best describe as "the American military subculture" that was so prevalent in Vietnam.

Note

1 *The Green Berets*, prod. and dir. by Ray Kellogg and John Wayne, 135 Min., Warner Bros., 1968, videocassette.

CHAPTER 2

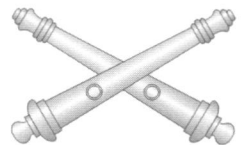

Setting the Stage

When duty whispers low, thou must —you must reply, I can.
Ralph Waldo Emerson

I arrived at Cam Ranh Bay, South Vietnam, in early November. As I recall, it was either the 4th or 5th of the month. Within a couple of days, I was processed out and then flown by C-130 up the coast to Nha Trang. Following an overnight stay at the IFFORCEV artillery unit headquarters, the IFFORCEV Artillery Personnel Center reviewed my records prior to assigning me to the 52nd Artillery Group, located at Artillery Hill in Pleiku City, Pleiku Province. Pleiku was a provincial capital and the headquarters for the ARVN (South Vietnamese Army) II Corps Combat Tactical Zone (CTZ).

I was relieved upon learning that I would be traveling to Pleiku by air. Had I been assigned to go by road, it would have meant traveling by convoy. The route would have taken me north to Qui Nhon, another coastal city, and from there the convoy would travel west up highway 19 to An Khe. At An Khe, I would have had to catch the next convoy to Pleiku. That leg of my journey would have taken me west over the Mang Yang Pass. It was in this mountain pass that the Viet Minh ambushed and annihilated French Mobile Group 100 during the French Indo-China War. In 1968, it was still known to the American GIs as "ambush alley." I felt fortunate to be flying.

I boarded a C-123 at Nha Trang. We had en route stops at Qui Nhon and An Khe before the plane landed at Hensel Field, located just outside of Pleiku. Hensel Field was part of the U.S. 4th Infantry Division's Camp Enari. Once I deplaned, there was a U.S. Army First Lieutenant who herded me toward an overloaded Huey Slick. It was sitting there on the tarmac with its rotor blades turning and its engine at the idle. I was pulled aboard just seconds before the Huey pilot revved up the engine and took off. "Huey Slick," was the nickname for the

UH-1 series assault support, multipurpose helicopter. The word "Slick" meant that it was not carrying weapons. The M-60 machine guns attended by door gunners were primary defensive weapons and did not classify the aircraft as armed.

Flying at low altitude, no more than three to four hundred feet above the ground and cross-country, the Huey pilot headed for Pleiku Air Force Base (AFB). En route, I could see the peasant farmers as they tilled and worked in the rice paddies below, while others walked along the main roads. I became very nervous as I noticed their garb. They were dressed in black silk pajamas, all wore cone-shaped straw hats, and some wore sandals. "Damn!" I swore under my breath. "VC!" I expected the door gunners to open fire, but they just sat there appearing stone-faced and showing no interest what-so-ever in the people below.

I suddenly understood why I had not yet been issued a weapon and ammunition. "Hell," I couldn't identify the enemy from the "friendlies." Right then and there, I came to know that there had been major flaws in the jungle warfare training school program that I had attended prior to coming to Vietnam. Once I reached Pleiku AFB, my eyes were opened wider as I tried to communicate with several different minor airport officials.

Everyone, including Americans, seemed to speak a foreign language. I was being introduced (informally) to what I can best describe as "Nam Speak." Nam Speak refers to thousands of acronyms, nicknames, code names, brand names, names of significant events, campaigns, technical terms, and one hell of a lot of other slang used by the American armed services serving in Vietnam. All newcomers could have used a yet unpublished book by Linda Reinberg. In her book, *In the Field: The Language of Vietnam,* Reinberg offers an A-to-Z guide to almost 5,000 terms from the extraordinary vocabulary used by the American GI in Vietnam. Eventually, I was able to obtain the information I needed. There would be a shuttle bus that I could catch.

I traveled by shuttle bus to Artillery Hill. The bus stopped at the main gate, just outside the compound. Struggling with my bags, I made it to the guard shack where I asked for directions to the 52nd Artillery Group Headquarters building. It was very close by, and still struggle with my bags, I headed for the building entrance. It was hot. I was dead tired and thirsty. As I entered the building, I asked someone for directions to the Command Sergeant Major's office. His desk was located in the middle of an open area within the building. I sat my bags down, approached his desk, and introduced myself. He shook my hand, welcoming me aboard and asked to see my Military 201 personnel file, which I was hand carrying. As he reviewed my file, he took a moment out to direct me toward the unit's mess hall. "When you get back from chow, I'll have you a duty assignment," he informed me.

I went to evening chow. Knowing no one, I sat and ate alone. Following my after-dinner Camel cigarette, I returned to the CSM's desk. "You have been assigned to the 6th Battalion, 14th Artillery. Your unit Sergeant Major is on his way over here to pick you up." I retrieved my personnel file from the CSM, picked up my bags once more, and headed toward the door. Outside now, I stood there, having another cigarette. A jeep drove up and rolled to a stop. The Command Sergeant Major of the 6/14 climbed out from behind the wheel, stepped out of the jeep, and came around to the passenger side. He introduced himself, helped me put my gear in the back, and we both mounted the jeep for the trip down the hillside to the 6/14 Battalion Headquarters building. "Just leave your bags in the jeep," he instructed me. "I'll get the Headquarters Battery First Sergeant over here to pick you up." First Sergeant Shelton came right over. He helped me as I retrieved my bags from the jeep. He led me over to the battery orderly room. He called for a supply clerk, and instructed him to issue me bed sheets and pillowcases before sending for one of the battery's platoon sergeants. When the platoon sergeant arrived, he introduced himself, and then asked me to follow him. With my gear in tow and him carrying my bedding, he led me to a building called, "The Senior NCO Hootch."

By this time, it was already very late in the evening. The sergeant showed me to my assigned two-room, cubicle-style quarters. I put down my gear and he placed my pillowcase and set of sheets on the Duncan Phyfe Hollywood-style bed before turning to me to speak. Grinning from ear to ear, the sergeant pointed to the Duncan Phyfe set of drawers standing against the plywood wall of the cubicle. "Not bad for a combat zone, huh, Sarge?" he said. "Come on. I'll show you the rest of the place." He led me to the far end of a poorly lit corridor. "In here is the bath and shower," he said, as he led me through an open doorway. The small bathroom contained a small sink with wall-mounted mirror above it, and next to that was a standard commode. Both the sink and commode were porcelain. The bathroom had cold running water. "Now over here is the shower," he said, as he pulled the shower curtain open. Hanging down was a section of standard rubber garden hose that was clamped shut on the end with a set of vise grips. "You will only be allowed enough water to wet yourself down, after which you must shut the water off, soap up, and rinse yourself off, being careful to use no more hot water than is absolutely necessary. You see, the water tank is outside and is open on top. Our water is heated by the sun. The supply is very limited. All of our water comes from the top of the hill and is gravity fed in to us by way of a jury-rigged pipeline. When you brush your teeth, don't swallow the water, it's unsafe for human consumption." The sergeant then stepped back and grinning from ear to ear again he proudly announced, "We of the 6/14 don't burn our shit." (He was alluding to the SOP [Standard Operating Procedure] of having a daily work detail pour diesel fuel on the unit's human waste and setting fire to it.)

I was dead tired from the long day of travel, followed by all the in-processing. I asked the sergeant for directions to the unit mess hall. I was making sure that I knew where to head come morning. I thanked the sergeant for the "cook's tour" of the hootch, excused myself, and returned to my assigned cubicle. I made up my bed and arranged the mosquito netting on the handmade frame that someone had constructed and attached to the bed, before crawling inside and fastening the net shut. As I settled into the comfortable bed, I was sure that I would sleep soundly throughout the night. I was wrong. Sometime around midnight, a 155-mm (millimeter) gun battery from the 1/92 Artillery Battalion opened fire. Boom! Boom! Boom! They continued to fire all night long. In fact, the firing continued until dawn. I lay wide-awake most of the night.

Just before dawn, still groggy from lack of sleep, I pulled myself out of bed before heading to the bathroom. I was the first in the hootch to arise. After a quick cold shave, followed by a tooth brushing session, I returned my shaving gear to my cubicle before heading to the mess hall. Following the consumption of a healthy breakfast, I headed for the unit orderly room. I was told to go get my 201 file and report to the battalion personnel office. After signing in and leaving off my personal 201 file, I was instructed to report to the battalion Sergeant Major. I was faced with several days of in-processing before being assigned to a duty position. In due course, I was welcomed into the battalion as the new battalion Intelligence Sergeant. Master Sergeant Payne, who was finishing his tour, gave me a detailed briefing prior to turning that part of the intelligence section over to me.

At this point, I shall discuss the unit history or combat record since its arrival in Vietnam. The battalion, 6th Battalion 14th Artillery, was designated as a heavy battalion. That is to say, it was a composite unit armed with 8-inch howitzers, and 175mm guns, each of which were mounted on a common-type gun carriage. The full tracked M-107 gun carriage, when fitted with either an interchangeable 8-inch howitzer tube (gun barrel) or a 175mm-gun tube (barrel) was then designated as a self-propelled (SP) gun or howitzer M-107. It is important to note that the 175mm-gun tube had a life of only 400 rounds and then had to be replaced. However, by July 1969 the 175mm-gun tube life was increased to 1200 rounds with the introduction of a newly designed tube.

The 6/14 War Bonnets had been in Vietnam since 23 October 1965. They had racked up an impressive record since their arrival. For example, on 6 November 1968, just as I had arrived in country, the battalion fired its 200,000[th] round in support of Free World Military Forces in the II Corps Tactical Zone. The official record shows that by close of business on that day, the total rounds fired represented 110,498 175mm rounds and 89,702 8-inch rounds.[1]

The battalion had been activated under MTOE (modified table of organization & equipment) 6-435G. Its mission was to provide "General Support Artillery [to United States, Republic of Vietnam Armed Forces]" and to respond "to calls for fire from all free world military forces in II Corps Tactical Zone."[2]

One of the unit's greatest achievements was realized when its mission was to provide fire support for operation MacArthur. Operation MacArthur began on Veterans' Day, 11 November 1967. On 13 November 1967, a battalion forward command post departed Artillery Hill for Dak To to provide necessary command and control for "the Battle of Dak To." This displacement greatly aided in controlling artillery fires in that region. In conjunction with Operation MacArthur, on 19 through 23 November 1967, Battery C fired continuously on hostile positions west of Dak To in support of the 1st Brigade, 4th Infantry Division, and the 173rd Airborne Brigade, with the following results:

> 50 to 100 VC/NVA were KIA (killed in action). Both Batteries B and C were involved from 15 November through 23 Dec. firing continuously in support of ground operations in the vicinity of Fire Support Base # 1.[3]
>
> On 25 June 1968, the battalion command post at Dak To, displaced to Fire Base Mary Lou (vicinity of Kontum) with the mission of providing fire control for all 52nd Artillery Group units located in the area.[4]

On 21 September 1968, the battalion command post located at LZ Mary Lou (vicinity of Kontum) was relocated at Artillery Hill, Pleiku, to assume control of Pleiku sector defense. Concurrently, a liaison section was sent to 3rd Armored Cavalry (ARVN) that had the responsibility of road security between Pleiku and Kontum, RVN (Republic of Vietnam).5

During my first ten days to two weeks in Vietnam, I had been in-processing, and training with the 4th Infantry Division. I had not been given a duty assignment.

> On 21 November 1968, the battalion reestablished a tactical command post at LZ Mary Lou to effect closer coordination of artillery support for the 2nd Brigade, 4th Infantry Division, 24th Special Tactical Zone (ARVN), Kontum Province. The battalion exercised operational control over the following units in the Kontum area: two 155mm batteries from the 1st Battalion 92nd Artillery, and Battery C, 6th Battalion, 14th Artillery.6

This latest mission change was the basis for my battalion commander making the decision to assign me to the duties of the battalion Intelligence Sergeant. We were still committed for keeping our main TOC at Pleiku open, while continuing to man the forward TOC in Kontum. My assigned duties primarily kept me in Pleiku. I was required to fill in for the battalion S-2 in his absence, which was expected to be often due to our dual mission. All of these new changes were slated to occur within less than three week's time.

On 10 December 1968, the battalion was assigned the mission of organizing and establishing a combined fire support coordination center (CFSCC) in the vicinity of Kontum in conjunction with the 24th Special Tactical Zone (ARVN), Kontum Province, and 4th Infantry Division.7 At this point, a decision was made that would prove to have significant impact on me for the remainder of my tour of duty.

Lt. Colonel Kenneth R. Bailey of Lancaster, Pennsylvania, a graduate of West Point and my battalion commander, assigned me to the position of the battalion S-2. My rank was Sergeant First Class. The battalion S-2 position is traditionally filled by a senior commissioned officer in the rank of captain, since he is a member of the battalion staff. The Colonel briefed me on my duties and explained to me that my duty assignment was not temporary; attempting to set my mind at ease, he also explained to me that I would be afforded full support from the battalion staff and subordinate unit commanders and their staffs. Since our battalion was preparing for a January 1969 Command Inspection, Colonel Bailey requested that I pay close attention to detail in reference to my particular areas of responsibility. In part, my duties included overseeing the battalion's sector of the Artillery Hill perimeter defense system. I was responsible for coordinating all battalion forward observation missions, which included briefing and debriefing the commissioned officers or acting sergeants that were Forward Observer Team leaders. They were responsible for leading an artillery reconnaissance section's Forward Observation Team on artillery support missions. I was also responsible for coordinating all battalion aerial observation support missions. I was placed on unit orders as the S-2, Chemical control officer and the S-5 officer, (Civil Affairs). I was also the official Classified Documents control officer. To enhance the operation, I attended a First Field Force Vietnam Intelligence Seminar held in Nha Trang. The seminar attendees came from all over II Corps Tactical Zone, and included South Koreans and ARVNs, as well as U.S. and other Allied forces' representatives. However, much of the disseminated information was not practical for use in the Central Highland Provinces. Upon my return to Pleiku, I applied the useful information to our unit's operation, while disregarding the other useless information.

On the day before Christmas 1968, the 30,000th name was added to the mounting toll of America's war dead in the Vietnam War.[8]

The CFSCC (Combined Fire Support Coordination Center) at Kontum City became fully operational on 15 January 1969. It was under the control of the 6th Battalion, 14th Artillery. The CFSCC was located in the TOC of the 24th Special Tactical Zone (STZ) and representatives were provided by the 24th STZ (221st) ARVN Artillery Battalion: 6th Battalion, 14th Artillery, and 4th Battalion, 42nd Artillery (4th Infantry Division). In addition, a targeting section was established in conjunction with the CFSCC.[9] 6/14 Artillery was also tapped for supplying two commissioned officers to perform as liaison officers. The overall drain on my battalion's commissioned officers is the main reason that I was assigned to the duties of the S-2; we were critically short of commissioned officers. My nearly 18 years of service provided me with a wealth of experience that the young 1st and 2nd lieutenants lacked. The experience that I possessed made me the most qualified man for the job. Taking the proverbial bull by the horns, I stepped into the job and did it well. On 20 January 1969, the battalion received a satisfactory rating in the Command Inspection conducted by Headquarters IFFORCEV Artillery.[10]

As for the North Vietnamese Army, General Giap admitted to Italian reporter, Oriana Fallaci, that by early January 1969 his methods had cost the North Vietnamese 600,000 men and an end to the war was not yet in sight.[11] I shall present evidence in a later chapter that supports my hypothesis that the NVA by NLT (no later than) early 1968 were sending large numbers of cadre personnel to Russia for training at their armor and artillery schools. Here they learned how to operate and employ Soviet and Chinese tanks, long-range artillery, large caliber anti-aircraft guns, and a variety of missiles. This training would be used to expedite the formation of newly designated spearhead "mobile strike forces" capable of challenging the Allied superior mobility forces. It is my belief that the NVA 325 C Division, which was deployed for the purpose of fighting around Khe Sanh during the 1967 so called "Hill Fights," stayed on for the purpose of joining in the 1968 siege of Khe Sanh. Following the siege of Khe Sanh, the 325 C Division deployed to South Vietnam's Central Highlands, where key maneuver elements were positively identified as the ones that clashed with U.S. Fourth Infantry Division maneuver elements on 9 or 10 May of 1968. I believe that operating in the vicinity of NVA Base Area 609 in Northeastern Cambodia and Southeastern Laos (in the tri-border area), they formed a fully mechanized Armored/Artillery/Infantry Division. There is evidence to support this and I believe that the NVA, under Giap and Dung's leadership, were anxious to test this newly created mobile strike force in their upcoming Spring/Summer Offensive of 1969.

With our command inspection out of the way, I was able to focus on my new job assignment as the battalion S-2 (Intelligence Officer). Since we were so short on commissioned officers, I suggested to Lt. Col. Bailey that he allow me to attend a two-week aerial observation school being conducted by the 209th Aviation Company (Headhunters) 17th Aviation Group at Camp Holloway, vicinity of Pleiku City. "I can fly aerial support missions myself when no one else is available," I reasoned. Colonel Bailey agreed to allow me to attend the two-week course; however, I would be required to commute to and from the school on a daily basis during the duration of the course. My other duties were demanding and would still have to be completed each day.

It was during

> …January 1969, that Lieutenant General William Peers, U.S. Army, Commanding General of First Field Force, Vietnam (IFFORCEV), reached a verbal agreement with Major General Lu Lan, Commanding General of II Corps, Army of The Republic Of Vietnam (ARVN), for the ARVN assumption of responsibility for Northern Kontum Province. The basis for the IFFORCEV proposal was to free a U.S. brigade of the 4th U.S. Infantry Division for employment as the following:
>
> —as a reaction force for any contingency in the Highlands,
> —as a striking force to be employed within II CTZ,
> —for deployment outside II CTZ on order of COMUSMACV,
> —or, to assist the Pacification Program in Binh Dinh Province.

The agreed effective date for the change over was 1 February 1969. Thus a situation was established for the first significant test of the emerging "Vietnamization" Policy.[12]

Notes

[1] DA Headquarters, 52nd Artillery Group, APO 96318 to Commanding General, U.S. Army Vietnam, APO 96375, letter, 8 August 1968, *Recommendation for Meritorious Unit Commendation,* Department of the Army, section 2, paragraph ee.
[2] Ibid., Introduction, paragraph 2.
[3] Ibid., section 2, paragraph f–g.
[4] Ibid., section 2, paragraph v.
[5] Ibid., section 2, paragraph cc.
[6] Ibid., section 2, paragraph gg.
[7] Ibid., section 2, paragraph hh.
[8] Clark Dougan, Stephan Weiss, and the editors of Boston Publishing Company, *Nineteen Sixty-Eight,* a volume of *The Vietnam Experience,* (Boston: Boston Publishing Company, 1983), 185.
[9] DA Headquarters, 52nd Artillery Group, APO 96318 to Commanding General, U.S. Army Vietnam, APO 96375, letter, 8 August 1968, *Recommendation for Meritorious Unit Commendation,* Department of the Army, section 2, paragraph pp.
[10] Ibid., section 2, paragraph qq.
[11] Clark Dougan, Stephan Weiss, and the editors of Boston Publishing Company, *The Fall Of The South,* a volume of *The Vietnam Experience,* (Boston: Boston Publishing Company, 1985), 15.
[12] U.S. Air Force. Air War College, *Tactical Air Support and the Battle of Ben Het: A Professional Study,* by Thomas M. Crawford, Jr., No. 4029 (Air University: 1970), 4.

CHAPTER 3

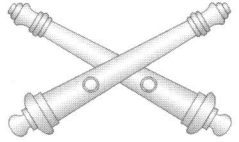

The 24th STZ and the Enemy B-3 Front

There must never be allowed to exist, mistrust, dissension, nor disloyalty among those destined to fight together.
Author Unknown

The ARVN 24th STZ (Special Tactical Zone) "was created in June 1965, when the ARVN 22nd Infantry Division moved out of Pleiku and Kontum Provinces into Phu Bon, Phu Yen, and Binh Dinh. The 22nd left behind a single regiment, the 42nd ARVN Infantry, to provide security in the newly created STZ.

The 24th STZ was both an operational area and a command, with headquarters in Kontum City. As an operational area it encompassed both Pleiku and Kontum Provinces."[1] By 1969, the 42nd AFVN Regiment was recognized as a good fighting unit, even by U.S. standards. The U.S. 4th Infantry Division still operated in special areas of the STZ. However, the 24th STZ, as a command, exercised operational control (OPCON) over all ARVN forces in the area.

The 42nd ARVN Regiment was commanded by Lt. Colonel Dinh The Thoai.[2] The 24th STZ was commanded by ARVN Marine Colonel Nguyen Ba Lien. In effect, the verbal agreement between General Peers and General Lu Lan during January 1969, created a new sector of control by ARVN forces for the defense of the Ben Het/Dak To area located in Northwestern Kontum Province.

During 1968, U.S. Army Engineers from the 299th Engineer Battalion located at Dak To assisted the U.S. 5th Special Forces A 244 Detachment in building a permanent SF/CIDG Camp at Ben Het (Special Forces/Civilian Irregular Defense Group).[3] Earlier, during the Battle of Dak To in 1967, Ben Het was designated as Fire Support Base (FSB) 12. The new camp (built in 1968), when completed, sat astride a main NVA/VC infiltration route and was closely monitored by Allied patrols in an attempt to preclude the enemy from launching a surprise attack en masse from their Cambodian sanctuaries. With the creation of Ben Het Camp, the NVA were prevented from moving sizable forces into the border province of Kontum without being detected.

The Tri-Border of South Vietnam lies in the rugged mountainous area of the Central Highlands where the borders of Laos, Cambodia, and South Vietnam join together at a common map location. Highway 512 enters South Vietnam from Laos just north of the tri-border junction and a scant six miles from Ben Het. See Figure 3-1. Another road, identified by the American forces as "Bravo Road," entered SVN from Cambodia just South of the tri-border junction and intersected with Highway 512 approximately three to four kilometers from Ben Het between the border area and the camp. Enemy forces could use these and other roads and trails in the tri-border area to infiltrate arms, men, and equipment by road convoys into South Vietnam from their large base of operations. Enemy Base Area 609 was located just across the borders of Cambodia and Laos. The Ho Chi Minh Trail terminated at Base Area 609 by 1965. Now in 1969, the Sihanouk Trail's northernmost terminus was also located in the vicinity of enemy Base Area 609.[4]

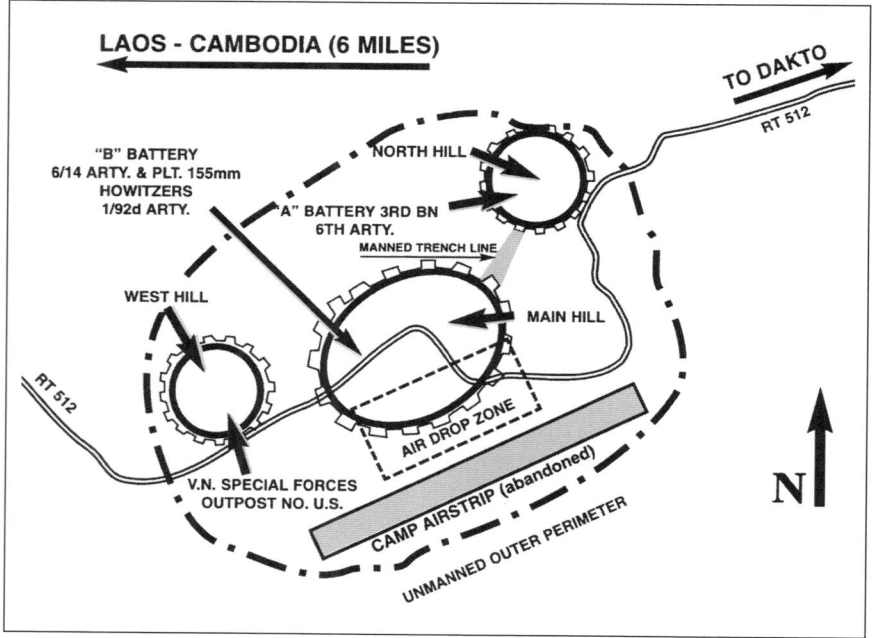

FIGURE 3-1   Map of Ben Het in relation to the tri-border junction. Courtesy of the *Daily Intelligencer Journal,* Lancaster, PA, June 28, 1969.

Toward the end of December 1968, intelligence reports of the movement of enemy forces into the northwestern area of II Corps presaged an end to the lull in fighting. The 24th NVA Regiment was suspected of having reinfiltrated into South Vietnam and was thought to be operating from a base area in the Chu Pa Mountains, northwest of Pleiku. Colonel Lien, CO, 24th STZ confirmed this information through a Hoi Chanh (Viet Cong Defector). To counter this threat a combined ARVN/U.S. Operation (Binh Tay/MacArthur) was planned for January in the Chu Pa area. The mission was to defeat the enemy in the base area and to destroy their supplies. The operation was initiated on 4 January 1969, as ARVN battalions on a reconnaissance in force mission began making daily contact with elements of the 24th NVA Regiment.

In the next phase of the operation, ARVN battalions provided a blocking force while U.S. battalions from the U.S. 4th Infantry Division air assaulted into the area and began sweeping in an effort to drive the enemy out of his dug-in positions and toward the ARVN forces. The combined ARVN/U.S. operation was successful and preempted the enemy spring offensive. The operation ended on 28 February 1969 with the withdrawal of the enemy into Cambodia. ARVN forces captured or destroyed over 300 tons of material and supplies and killed over 500 NVA. I make note here of the fact that 6/14 Artillery supported the above operation with an Artillery Forward Observation Team. Due to the length of the operation, the team ran out of C-rations and had to forage for food. They supplemented their meager rations with bamboo shoots. The team returned to Pleiku. I debriefed the enlisted team leader who complained about the ration situation. I then visited the U.S. 5th Special Forces compound there in Pleiku where I made a deal with an Australian Major to trade captured enemy weapons in exchange for Lurp (nickname for LRRP—Long Range Reconnaissance Patrol) rations, which we were not authorized to draw for our people. My observers appreciated my successful arrangement.

A phase of the enemy plan for his spring/summer offensive called for the interdiction of Highway QL14N between Pleiku and Kontum Cities during March and April. However, the 3d ARVN Cavalry Squadron, moving with lightening speed, thwarted two attempts at ambushes along the highway and killed 63 NVA. Here again, I wish to make note of the fact that (once again) 6/14 Artillery Forward Artillery Observers accompanied the ARVN Cavalry forces. First Lt. Warner, a battalion FO, and the enlisted Recon. Sgt. earned awards for valor during one of those operations. Both men were basically cited through my office for performing identical acts of bravery. The lieutenant received the Silver Star and the other man the Bronze Star with "V". With II Corps forces spread thinly throughout the area of operations by mid-April, the enemy revealed the objectives of his offensive with heavy attacks by fire in the Dak To area.[5] However, prior to that time, action during Operation Binh Tay/MacArthur involved elements of the 7th USAF.

During February 1969, the following action occurred near Ben Het: A mission to support a LRRP (Lurp) Patrol that had come under heavy enemy attack and required extraction support was being flown by a flight from the 633rd out of Pleiku. Meanwhile the CIDG Camp at Ben Het was being "hammered" by an enemy 100mm field piece. Tac Air was called.

> Upon reaching the target area, the FAC [Forward Air Controller] relayed the target information to the Spads [A1E, Skyraider, WWII-type fighter-bomber, used for close air support in Vietnam] and a battle plan was formulated. Since there were many 37mm and 23mm gun positions defended by numerous .50 Caliber weapons, it was determined that multiple passes would be required to accomplish the task. Col Corey quickly determined the optimum attack heading and led his flight to the attack. The flight struck again and again with maximum utilization of ordnance. So accurate was their delivery of weapons that on the first pass, one 23mm gun and its supporting defense was destroyed. Repeated passes were made through a hail of fire until all ordnance except the 20mm canon aboard the Spads had been expended. Three more passes were made by the flight utilizing the 20mm guns and finally all hostile fire ceased. The flight was credited with destroying two 23mm guns and damaging two 37mm guns and command of the air situation which was instrumental in subsequent destruction of the 100mm field piece that had been plaguing Ben Het.[6]

Following the above quoted action, the NVA Artillery changed the caliber of the weapons that they would use to bombard Ben Het. They now deployed 85mm field pieces. An NVA Artillery Regiment, identified by Allied Intelligence as the 40th, moved into the tri-border area. The 40th NVA Artillery Regiment introduced the Russian built 85mm field gun into the B-3 Front. (To my knowledge, no pictures of this weapon are available.) They positioned their long-range field pieces in mountain caves on the forward slopes that faced toward the east. These emplacements were reinforced with huge steel doors that were designed to be opened only during firing. The caves were expertly camouflaged in order to prevent detection by Allied air observers. Another tactic used by the NVA cannoneers was to sight their guns through V-cuts in the mask, forward of their gun positions. ("The mask" alludes to hills or mountaintops that prevent ground observers from seeing the terrain beyond them.) The 85mm field gun was a flat trajectory-firing weapon, which limited its use when firing the long-range fire required against Ben Het. For their fire to clear the hilltops and mountains between the NVA gunners and their Ben Het target, the enemy had to settle for a restricted field of fire by employing the V-cut tactic. Ben Het, during February 1969, began to receive daily bombardment from the 85mm field guns of the 40th NVA Artillery Regiment.

Even though the enemy weapons proved difficult to locate with pinpoint accuracy, our artillerymen at Ben Het knew their approximate locations, which were across the Cambodian border. U.S. Forces were prevented from sending American fighting men into the field to seek out and destroy the enemy gun positions threatening the security of Ben Het.

Since 1965, U.S. Forces in South Vietnam's Central Highland Provinces had been plagued by NVA "regular hard hats" who systematically executed attacks against them, while using the Cambodian sanctuaries as bases of operations. By 1969, U.S. Forces continued to obey a policy that prevented them from taking any offensive ground action against the enemy Cambodian or Laotian border sanctuaries. The policy which had been in effect since 1965 is explained in the book, *We Were Soldiers Once ... And Young,* by Lieutenant General Harold G. Moore (Ret.) and Joseph L. Galloway.

> This was the last major action in the Ia Drang Campaign. For the next five days, Colonel Lynch's soldiers and the cavalry scouts of the 1st Squadron, 9th Cavalry patrolled widely, screening the Western part of the valley up to the Cambodian border with little or no contact. On 27 November 1965, the last cavalry unit still in the field returned to home base in An Khe. ...
> The last units of Brigadier General Chu Huy Man's B-3 Front crossed into Cambodia. They were beyond reach now. They would reinforce, regroup, rest, and rehabilitate their surviving soldiers, and then at a time of their choosing in the spring of 1966, reenter South Vietnam and resume their attacks. Major Norm Schwarzkopf watched them go and was disgusted (Schwarzkopf was an advisor to the ARVNS) with the policy that permitted the creation of North Vietnamese sanctuaries across the border in supposedly neutral Cambodia. [It is apparent that the ARVN obeyed the MACV policy as well as the U.S. Forces.] ... Not long after this, orders came down ... that we were never to speculate or suggest to any reporter that the North Vietnamese were using Cambodia as a sanctuary or that they were passing through Cambodia on their way to South Vietnam.[7]

It is important to note that An Khe, located halfway between the border area and SVN's coast, was located in NVA Military Region 5, not in the B-3 Front.

By 1969, nothing about the policy had changed, except that it was common knowledge that the enemy was using Cambodia as a base area of operations. Not known by IFFORCEV men in the field in the vicinity of Ben Het/Dak To in February 1969, was the fact that multidivisional NVA forces were massing just across the border in Laos and Cambodia. Using Enemy Base Area 609 as a base of operations, these divisional units were poised to strike in strength against Allied military installations located within the reaches of their tentacles, just across the border of South Vietnam. Some of the regimental maneuver elements of these enemy divisions were combat-seasoned, having fought in The Battle of the Ia Drang, the 1967 Battle of Dak To, and even at Khe Sanh in 1967–1968. Now they sat there at full combat strength, ready to infiltrate across the South Vietnamese (SVN) border once more for the purpose of launching a major 1969 enemy offensive operation. The NVA Military Command had been planning the 1969 Spring/Summer Offensive for many months. The battleground had been selected and prepared. NVA forces would, upon orders, occupy their prepared fighting positions. In the vicinity of Dak To and Ben Het, enemy fighting positions had been prepared months in advance. Caches of food, water, ammunition, and weapons awaited the arrival of the troops. NVA Generals Giap and Dung had carefully laid their plans to strike a surprise "knockout" blow that they hoped would bring about an early negotiated peace settlement at the Paris Peace Talks. However, U.S. forces occupying Ben Het should have been tipped off as to what lay ahead, when on the night of 3 March 1969, NVA forces struck.

Five infantry-escorted Russian built PT-76 light amphibious tanks identified as being from the 17th tank Company, 202 Armored Regiment (NVA), supported by artillery fire and tear gas shelling, launched an attack against Ben Het. See Figure 3-2.

The garrison at Ben Het, which was temporarily reinforced by U.S. Army medium tank crews from the 1st Plt. B/1/69th Armor, along with Special Forces led, native rocket crews, and further reinforced by U.S. Artillery men from Battery B, 6/14 (Heavy), Artillery Battalion dueled the approaching enemy armor successfully and prevented a close assault. The North Vietnamese retreated after losing two tanks in a "firestorm" of exploding rockets, anti-tank mines and U.S. Army tank cannon fire. It is important to note that this action represented the only clash of the entire Vietnam War between U.S. and NVA armor. United

FIGURE 3-2 Russian built PT-76 tank captured at Ben Het, March 3, 1969.

States news reporters had gotten wind of the fact that the enemy was receiving all their supplies through Sihanoukville, via the new Sihanouk Trail located in Cambodia. A small article that was published in a small western newspaper during June 1969, stated that Allied intelligence reports indicated the enemy was still using the Ho Chi Minh Trail to send troops to South Vietnam and to send supplies to troops in the northern vicinity of I Corps, the DMZ, and the SVN Ashau Valley Base areas.

As a long-experienced soldier, trained in armored and mechanized warfare, I was keenly aware of the NVA's newly acquired capability to switch over from their traditional foot-bound army to a fully mechanized one. I was in contention with the Allied intelligence people who seemed content to completely ignore this apparently new threat.

Almost instantly, following the assumption of control of the Ben Het/Dak To area by the 24th STZ, the enemy made their first move. There had been a lull in the enemy activity in the area following the 3 March attack on Ben Het until a swift build-up in early May 1969 was confirmed by ARVN, Mobile Strike Forces (MSFs), and Montagnard elements screening Ben Het to the west. After the MSFs detected the enemy and initiated several small contacts, about 6 May ARVN infantry and ranger battalions were moved up to launch the offensive actions for which they were trained. This move reflected a change in tactics. The offensive operation was code-named "Operation Dan Quyan 38 A," which had officially begun on 1 May 1969.[8] The stage had been set for what was to become unofficially known as "The Siege of Ben Het."

Note: Before moving on to the May–June 1969 fighting, it is important that I expand on the February through May 1969 timeframe. (The fighting during May overlaps with the following events or situations). I also make note here to the fact that the U.S. Army never once referred to the fighting during May–June 1969 as "The Siege of Ben Het." Following the action, they dubbed it as "The Battle of Dak To/Ben Het." In so doing, the U.S. Army was able to cover up the truth about who the real victors were at Ben Het. One would certainly expect that the U.S. Army would welcome the credit for such an "unprecedented" victory. However, the Allied command had other fish to fry.

Notes

[1] "ARVNS Constrain enemy in Dak To area," *The Army Reporter*, 7 July 1969, 3.
[2] Ibid., 3.
[3] See Map of Ben Het Camp on page 20.
[4] Terrence Maitland, Peter McInerney, and the editors of Boston Publishing Company, "Map on Infiltration/Interdiction," in *A Contagion Of War*, a volume of *The Vietnam Experience*, (Boston: Boston Publishing Company, 1983), 133.
[5] U.S. Department of Defense, *Senior Officer Debriefing Report: December 1968 to December 1969*, (Washington: 1970), 24.
[6] U.S. Air Force, *History of the 633rd Special Operations Wing*, vol. III, (January–March 1969), 23.
[7] Lt. Gen. Harold G. Moore (Ret.) and Joseph L. Galloway, *We Were Soldiers Once ... And Young*, (New York: Random House, 1992), 314–315.
[8] U.S. Air Force, *History of the 633rd Special Operations Wing*, vol. I, (April–June 1969), 14.

CHAPTER 4

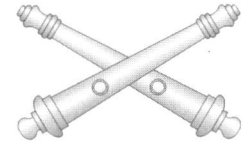

A Red Leg in The Nam

*I am a soldier. I fight where I am told to,
and I win where I fight.*
General George S. Patton, Jr.

The 52d Artillery Group, headquartered at Artillery Hill in Pleiku City, was responsible for providing general fire support to all Free World forces deployed in the II Corps CTZ (Combat Tactical Zone) in the zone's border provinces. The bulk of the general artillery support by the group was provided to ground forces deployed throughout the Pleiku and Kontum border provinces.

The 52d Artillery Group gun battalions were deployed as follows: The 3d Battalion 6th Artillery maintained a forward TOC (Tactical Operations Center) at the "Oasis," an Artillery Fire Support Base (FSB) located some 25 miles southwest of Pleiku City. All Group Artillery gun tubes (barrels) located within the 3/6 Artillery AO (Area of Operations) were OPCON (under operational control of) to the 3/6. That is to say, all firing by those guns was at the direction of 3/6. The 1st Battalion. 92d Artillery. maintained a forward TOC at Dak To, which was located in northwestern Kontum Province. All group gun tubes in the 1/92 were OPCON to 1/92. The 6th Battalion 14th Artillery maintained their forward TOC at landing zone (LZ) Mary Lou, located in the vicinity of Kontum City, Kontum Province. All group gun tubes in their AO were OPCON to 6/14. All three of the group's gun battalions were required to maintain separate main TOCs at Artillery Hill in Pleiku City. Too, all three collocated their headquarters and service batteries, along with the 52d Artillery Group Headquarters Unit that also maintained a main TOC there. Together, these rear echelon units maintained the perimeter defense post at Artillery Hill. Each separate unit was assigned a sector of responsibility on this circular line of defense upon which had been constructed fortified guard bunkers. We "Red Legs" (U. S. Field Artillery soldiers) were very capable in the area of perimeter defense of our FSBs. However, constant maintenance of field fortifications, weapons, and ammunition had to be closely supervised in order to maintain the highest level of combat readiness. As the battalion S-2, that type of supervision came under the purview of my domain.

Following my first inspection of our battalion's sector of perimeter defenses at Artillery Hill, I realized that we had some serious shortcomings to correct. I had to confer with the two rear echelon battery commanders in order to get the ball rolling, which I did. It was now time for me to commence a schedule of line battery visits for the purpose of inspecting their respective sectors of perimeter defenses as well as several other areas of responsibility, e.g., storage and destruction of Classified Document Logs, which was accomplished to enhance control in accordance with the various regulations and SOP (Standard Operating Procedures). I was also the battalion chemical control officer and the S-5 officer (S-5 referred to Civil Affairs, which played a major roll in "The Pacification Program").

My first visit to A Battery 6/14 was a memorable one. The morning of my arrival, members of the Special Forces A-Team had bagged a tiger weighing 500 pounds, which they had put on display there at Camp Plei Djereng . Our A/6/14 175mm gun/8-inch howitzer battery was collocated with the Special Forces. I carried with me a standard issue, waterproof bag, which was filled with protective gas mask spare parts. I made a few brownie points with the unit as I made on-the-spot corrections and repairs during the chemical equipment portion of my inspection. I found most everything else to be in order, which I reported to Lt. Colonel Bailey. Lt. Col. Bailey and I took time to attend the debriefing of A Battery in reference to the results of a First Field Force Vietnam (IFFV) Artillery conducted gunnery proficiency test. The critique of the inspection/gunnery test was scheduled to be conducted at the A Battery mess hall. The chief inspector/tester was a full colonel. Addressing our group while shuffling through a bunch of related paper work, the colonel commenced his opening statement. Ka-Boom! A 175mm gun opened fire. The noise and after shock was horrific. The little mess hall building vibrated violently from the shock waves, and pots and pans hanging on the walls rattled loudly. Patiently, the colonel waited for everything to settle down before making a second attempt to speak. Ka-Boom! The gun fired for the second time, and again, the colonel waited before trying to continue. After waiting through several more Ka-damn-Booms, the colonel snatched up his pile of papers, stuffed them in a briefcase, and stomped out of the mess-hall. One of the junior test team officers sheepishly explained that the results would be mailed at a later date. Lt. Colonel Bailey was scheduled to fly back to Pleiku, while I was scheduled to spend the night.

Following evening chow, the first sergeant and I had a nice long visit. As we discussed the war, the first sergeant pointed out a mountainous range in the distance that he referred to as the Chu Pong massif. He explained to me their significance. "The Chu Pongs overlook the Ia Drang Valley, where the NVA and the First Cavalry Division (Airmobile) elements fought it out in 1965. Some of those same NVA Infantry Regiments are still up there hiding out in Cambodia, just a step away and across the border. They can come back at any time and place of their choosing. We must always keep our guard up."

I slept with the troops of the firing battery that night. Their bunker was deep and heavily fortified. The smells of stale body odors and earthen bunkers laced with mildew permeated the air; it would take some getting used to.

The following morning I learned that one of the battery vehicles, an M-8 ammunition carrier which was full tracked, was scheduled to be airlifted back to Pleiku for Army ordnance repairs. A CH–54 Helicopter (nicknamed SkyCrane by the GIs) was on its way in to pick the load up. The battery had been notified to remove the tracks from the vehicle, which I noticed had been done. Soon, the big CH–54 SkyCrane was hovering over the vehicle while cannoneers hooked up the load slings. The signal was passed to the pilot that all was ready. The pilot revved the engine and made an attempt to get the load off the ground. Failing to do so, after making two or three attempts, the pilot set the big bird down. Climbing out of the chopper, he stomped over to the vehicle and peered into the rear cargo bed. Screaming at all concerned, he directed, "Get them god-damn f—-ing tracks out of there." Stomping back to his chopper, he climbed back aboard and was soon able to lift the air load back to Pleiku.

I also returned to Pleiku aboard one of our organic Light Observation Helicopters (LOHs), which were nicknamed "Loaches" by the GIs. Our battalion TOE (Table of Organization and Equipment) allowed my battalion a fleet of six LOHs.

My next scheduled visit to one of our line batteries took me to Kontum City, Kontum Province, approximately 30 miles due north from Pleiku. C battery was collocated with the headquarters element of the U.S. 4th Infantry Division's 2d Brigade at LZ Mary Lou. Also located at the LZ were our battalion's two special sections. The M-10 Directional Ground Radar Site, which was led by an Army warrant officer, and the battalion Meteorological Weather Section, also led by a warrant officer, were there. Our battalion's forward TOC was located at LZ Mary Lou. As the S-2, it was my duty to insure that the two special sections were being maintained properly and were receiving the necessary supplies with which to work. I also wanted to observe the forward TOC during operations. I now turned my attention to the required inspection of C Battery. I repeated my performance of making on-the-spot repairs of the unit's chemical equipment before I inspected the other areas.

Following the completion of my work at LZ Mary Lou, I was once more scheduled to spend the night. Following the evening meal, I went to the C Battery first sergeant's hootch, where we sat and discussed the business of war. As we sat there, each sipping on a cold can of beer (alcoholic beverages other than 3.2% beer were prohibited on FSBs and we were rationed to two cans per day while in the forward areas), the battery's 175mm guns commenced firing their night-firing program. It was already pitch-black dark by that time. Ka-Boom! The first volley sent shock waves reverberating throughout the compound. The only light we had in the first sergeant's hootch was provided by a small candle that he had setting next to his bed on some type wooden box. The shock waves from the first round of 175mm fire blew the candle out. The first sergeant re-lit the candle with a match from a C-ration packet lying next to the candle. He explained to me that his unit's 10-K generator was on the fritz and on its last legs. Ka-Boom! The gun fired again and he once more re-lit the candle as before.

I told the sergeant that I would see what I could do about getting them another generator. Meanwhile the guns kept firing and he kept re-lighting that damned pissy little candle. I said, "Sarge, I think I'd find a better emergency lighting system." Soon I turned in for the night. During the night, all hell broke loose on the perimeter. It turned out to be a tiger in the wire that was setting off a number of trip flares. The various guard posts opened fire on the big cat; however, it got away clean.

Returning to Pleiku, I put a bug in the ear of our battalion thief, a sergeant who was an expert on procuring equipment and supplies through the illegal supply system. "I need some 10-K generators," I said, and he replied with a question. "How many do we need?" "Six," I answered. Two or three days later, he returned from a trip to Qui Nhon. In the back of a five-ton truck he had brought back ten, spanking new, 10-K generators. I got one for the Battalion TOC and we issued each of our five batteries one. The sergeant used the other four for trading material. The one organic gun battery left for me to visit was collocated with another USSF A-Team, west of Dak To. We Red Legs simply referred to the place as Ben Het.

Ben Het was the site of an old American FSB used by the 173rd Airborne Brigade as a base of operation during the 1967 Battle of Dak To. At that time, it was identified as FSB 12. One of the four NVA infantry regiments threatening the area during that battle was the 66th. Lt. Col. Bailey and I traveled to Ben Het by Loach. We were on our way to visit B Battery that was collocated with the A-244 detachment of the 5th U.S. Special Forces at the CIDG (Civilian Irregular Defense Group) Camp.

We were put down onto the small airstrip that ran from east to west and lay along the southern perimeter of the camp. Being untenable (that which cannot be defended), the airstrip lay outside of the camp's perimeter wire. A jeep was sent out of the camp to pick us up. Upon landing, I noticed the rusting hulk of an old American cargo plane's fuselage lying next to the southern edge of the runway. A relic of the past, it seemed to signal a warning to the newcomers at Ben Het: a rusting monument to those brave Americans who had bled, suffered, and died during the bloody fighting in 1967. Although now quiet, Ben Het was still a foreboding place, a place that gave me a very uncomfortable feeling. I wanted to get on with the business at hand and get out.

Lt. Col. Bailey, following a short visit with the B Battery commander, returned to Pleiku on the same Loach that flew us there. I stayed on to conduct my scheduled work and inspections. I had already been informed that I would receive transportation back to the rear via one of the Huey Slicks that came into the camp on a daily basis. I finished my work by the COB (Close of Business).

No more choppers were due in that day, so once more I did an overnighter. That night, I had another long visit with the unit first sergeant. We sat sipping our daily ration of beer as we talked about the NVA. Looking to the west, we could see the mountainous terrain that encompassed the Tri-Border area of South Vietnam six miles away. We both knew that out there somewhere were multi-regimental forces of the enemy who hated our presence at Ben Het and who wanted to destroy our big guns that were interdicting their precious supply routes.

Our big guns only represented an insignificant threat to the NVA as compared to the threat posed by our total artillery and air firepower delivery systems. This awesome firepower threat never seemed to stop the NVA, which can be explained by their philosophy as stated by North Vietnam's Prime Minister, Pham Van Dong. In 1967, he stated, "We have been fighting for our independence for four thousand years. We have defeated the Mongols three times. The United States Army, strong as it is, is not as terrifying as Genghis Khan."[1] We knew that they respected but did not shy away from doing battle against the Americans, despite our awesome firepower. We knew that at a time and a place of their choosing, they would strike again in overwhelming force. We hoped that it would not be during our watch. But we were tough, tenacious, and just as determined to beat the enemy as they were to beat us.

I consider First Sergeant Earl Hodge, a huge black man, to be one of the finest NCOs that I've ever had the pleasure of knowing. I found myself, once more, sleeping in a bunker with a bunch of the cannoneers. When asked the next morning by First Sergeant Hodge how I had slept, I kidded with him. "Well, it would not have been so bad except for the rats who held a division parade above my head during the night." Rats were a problem and they were carriers of the dreaded rabies disease. One bite and you were required to undergo a series of painful rabies shots. Hodge advised, "There's a Huey Slick on its way. Get your gear together, and a jeep with a driver will take you back down to the airstrip where you can hitch a ride to Pleiku."

Even though I was in the field, I was dressed for the rear area. I was wearing heavily starched jungle fatigues and spit-shined boots. My hair was cut in the GI style with white sidewalls. Not required to wear a steel helmet, I was wearing a baseball cap. To the average field soldier, I presented the typical look of a REMF (Rear Echelon Mother F----r). As I stood on the airstrip waiting for the Huey Slick, I suddenly caught the sound of a chopper approaching from the west. I knew from the sound that it was not a Huey. I looked west and spotted an unmarked, older style CH–34 that was painted more of a dark OD (olive drab) than U.S. Army OD. The pilot of the CH–34 set it down on the runway about 25 to 30 meters from where I was standing. The pilot did not shut the chopper engine down; he put it at the idle. When I saw his passengers dismount from the chopper, I recognized the dozen men to be members of an elite SOG (Studies and Observations Group) team. In addition to his regular gear, each man carried a string of seven Army-issue canteens.

It became apparent that they were after water. Off they went down to the camp's water point that was somewhere near the west end of the airstrip. When they returned minutes later, they came down the road from the direction of the camp's main gate. To get back to the awaiting chopper, they had to parade right by my position. These men looked tough. They were dirty and sweaty, and they had the looks of hunted men. Their eyes were fixed in a cold stare. No facial expressions were noted except for the fact that they sneered at me in passing. I could tell they were looking at me in disgust and considered me to be a typical

REMF. Re-boarding the chopper, they were soon airborne. I watched as the CH–34 traveled west once more, and I knew that those men were headed back to hell, a place of death and pain where some were sure to die. I was left with a feeling of guilt as I heard the Huey Slick coming for me.

As I crawled aboard, a door gunner asked me my destination. "Artillery Hill in Pleiku," I answered, and the door gunner notified the pilots. In the due course of time, the chopper landed at Camp Holloway. The door gunner turned to me and said, "Looks like they forgot you, Sarge," and both door gunners got off, removing their weapons (M-60s) and ammo. They stepped aside as the chopper pilot revved the engine up before taking off and heading north once more. Over Dragon Mountain, the pilot performed some unauthorized acrobatics before realizing that I was still aboard. I was forced to hang on for my life as I clung to the center post because the seats had been folded away. The pilot and copilot finally recalled my destination, and flew me on to the airstrip at Artillery Hill where I happily exited the chopper.

Back in Pleiku, I assumed my primary duties once more. I soon realized that the conduct of the war was changing.

Note

1 Edward Doyle, Samuel Lipsman, and the editors of Boston Publishing Company, *America Takes Over*, a volume of *The Vietnam Experience*, (Boston: Boston Publishing Company, 1982), 136.

"CHI-COM" Ammunition 75mm on the left, and 57mm on the right for the Recoilless Rifle

CHAPTER 5

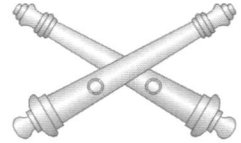

Operation Dan Quyan 38 A

Phase I

... You can't run an army without profanity; and it has to be eloquent profanity. An army without profanity couldn't fight its way out of a piss-soaked paper bag.
General George S. Patton, Jr.

May 1969

The first Allied intelligence reports indicating a possible NVA Spring/Summer offensive revealed that the NVA, infiltrating a divisional-size infantry force into the northwestern part of Kontum Province, were poised and ready to strike. Intelligence reports indicated that the NVA forces were reinforced with artillery, engineers, and sappers, as well as having an armored capability. These enemy forces posed a direct threat to isolated Allied camps and fire support bases in the vicinity of the tri-border area. (The Tri-Border was the point on the map where the Laotian, Cambodian, and South Vietnam borders intersect. See the map in Figure 5-1.)

Intelligence reports identified the 18th NVA Infantry Regiment, the 24th NVA Infantry Regiment, the 28th NVA Infantry Regiment, and the 66th NVA Infantry Regiment as the four regiments making up the bulk of the enemy force. Of these four regiments, the 24th and 66th were veterans of the 1967 Battle of Dak To.

The 18th Regiment had been at Khe Sanh and the 28th Regiment was reported to be a newly formed regiment comprised of two battalions left behind by the 325 C NVA Division following the Siege of Khe Sanh in 1968. Main maneuver elements of the 325 C Division had been positively identified when they clashed with elements of the 4th U.S. Infantry Division on 9–10 May 1968 near Ben Het. This demonstrated

CHAPTER 5: Operation Dan Quyan 38 A ♦ **35**

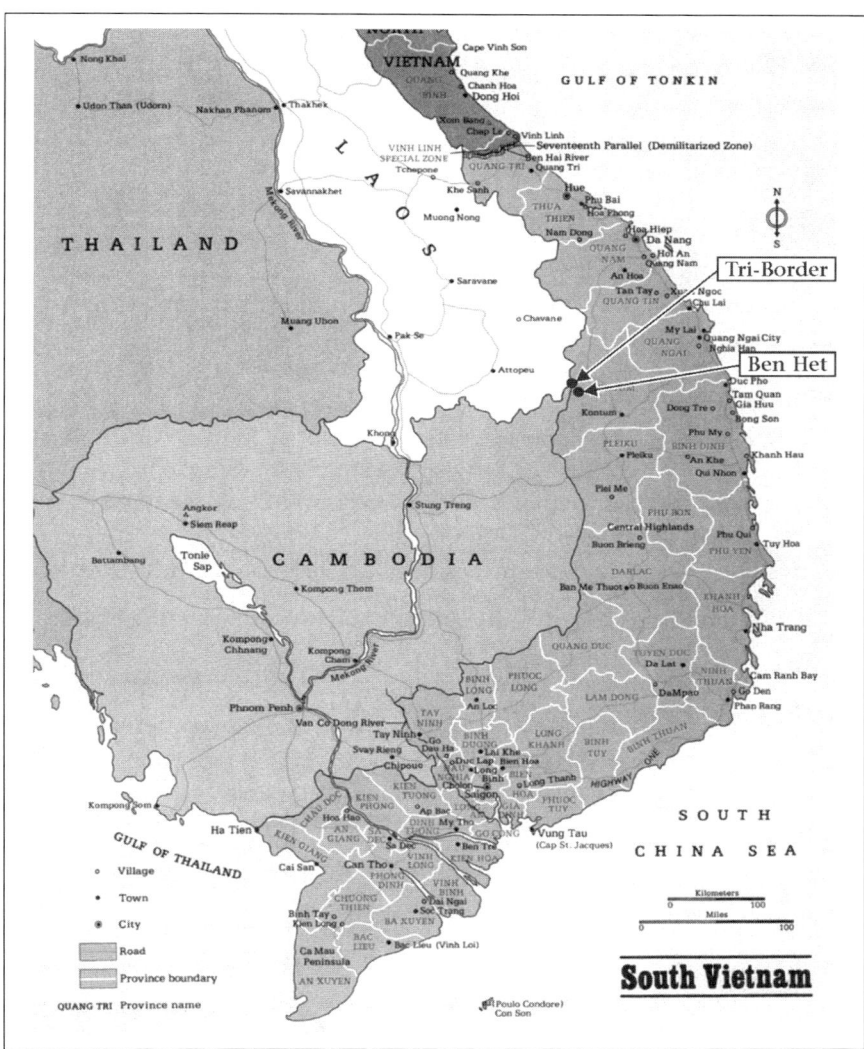

FIGURE 5-1 Map of Tri-Border indicating junction of Laos, Cambodia, and South Vietnam and the location of Ben Het.

a renewed interest by the NVA in the tri-border area. The mention of the 18th NVA regiment now in the area provoked the question of where the 325 C Division was now located. With the 40th NVA Artillery Regiment identified as supporting this new enemy offensive force, one could not help but wonder if it were possible that the NVA were prepared to launch a multidivisional attack on the Ben Het/Dak To area. If so, was it possible for Allied forces to blunt such an attack?

Presaging the 1967 Battle of Dak To, General Westmoreland deployed 16,000 US/ARVN troops to northwestern Kontum Province to cope with the four NVA regimental-size forces that threatened the area.[1] Actually, the fourth regiment was held in reserve. Samuel Zaffiri comments, "To counter the three enemy regiments on their way there, he ordered sixteen thousand men from the 4th Infantry Division, the 173d Airborne Brigade, the 1st Cavalry Division, and the ARVN Division to move to Dak To immediately." As to Allied firepower during The Battle of Dak To, "The Air Force executed nearly three thousand sorties and the artillery batteries at Dak To fired over 170,000 rounds."[2]

Here we were, only one-and-one-half years after the Battle of Dak To, facing some of the same veteran regiments of that action as part of an even larger potential threat with a far smaller defensive force. To verify in part the size of the 1969 NVA Force, I quote the following excerpts from an interview provided by Major William Yenke, the Pleiku Sector ALO (Air Liaison Officer), II Corps on 13 July 1969.

> I had a briefing at DASC Alpha before I started working with Lt. Col. Thomas (outgoing 24th STZ ALO). They said (Intelligence) that BH (Ben Het) was to be attacked by three VC/NVA Regiments and two more elements of another.
>
> To the South of Dak To is a long ridge called Rocket Ridge, where they always shot ABFs from. They intended to shell Ben Het/Dak To from Rocket Ridge, interdict Highway 512; and take Ben Het. They were going to stage ambushes along the road between Kontum and Dak To and Ben Het and blow bridges. Once the roads were sealed, they were going to move the 66th and 28th Regiments over. They were going to make a pincer attack... one from the northwest and one from the southwest on Ben Het.[3]

Note: VC/NVA indicates that the enemy force contains some VC maneuver elements. In this case, at least one VC Battalion was identified as being on the scene as part of the attack force. See Figures 5-2 and 5-3.

To meet the threat, ARVN Marine Colonel Nguyan Ba Lien, 24th STZ Commander, ordered crack ARVN ranger battalions into the hills south and west of Ben Het. These ARVN troops were the elite of the ARVN forces and they took little time before having their first encounters with enemy patrols. They were soon engaging NVA main force units and were able to identify elements of the 28th and 66th NVA Regiments as the opposing force. The following quotations from the October 69 CHECO Report verify this information:

CHAPTER 5: Operation Dan Quyan 38 A ♦ **37**

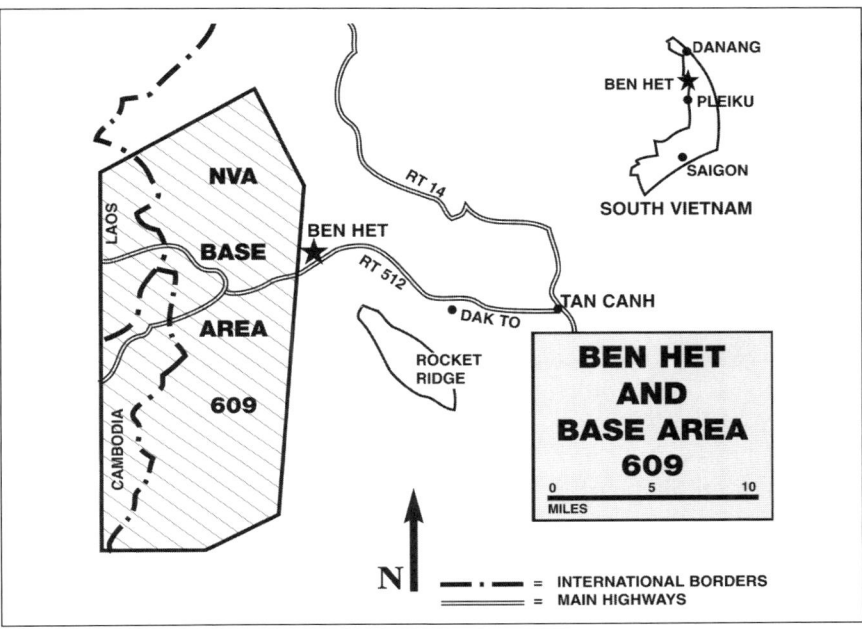

FIGURE 5-2 Ben Het and the Base Camp area.

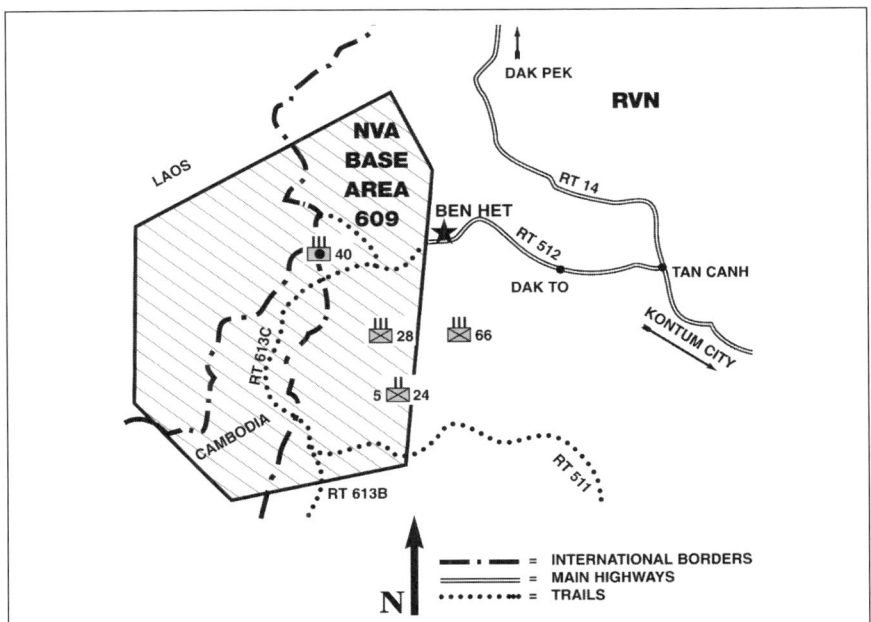

FIGURE 5-3 North Vietnamese Army base area.

During the first week in May, enemy activity greatly increased in the western part of the 24th STZ. VC/NVA patrols were encountered at short distance from Allied installations and attacks-by-fire became daily occurrences against Ben Het, Dak To, and fire support bases (FSBs) throughout the zone.

Major enemy units were detected moving into the hills to the South of Highway 512, which ran from the Cambodian border eastward through Ben Het and Dak To.[4]

Note: Highway 512 actually ran eastward from the Laotian border.

However, it intersected with a road identified by the 7th USAF as Bravo Road, which did run eastward from Cambodia and intersected with 512 only 3 or 4 kilometers west of Ben Het, as shown in Figure 5-4. Keep this information in mind as I later explain details in reference to a hypothetical situation that may have existed.

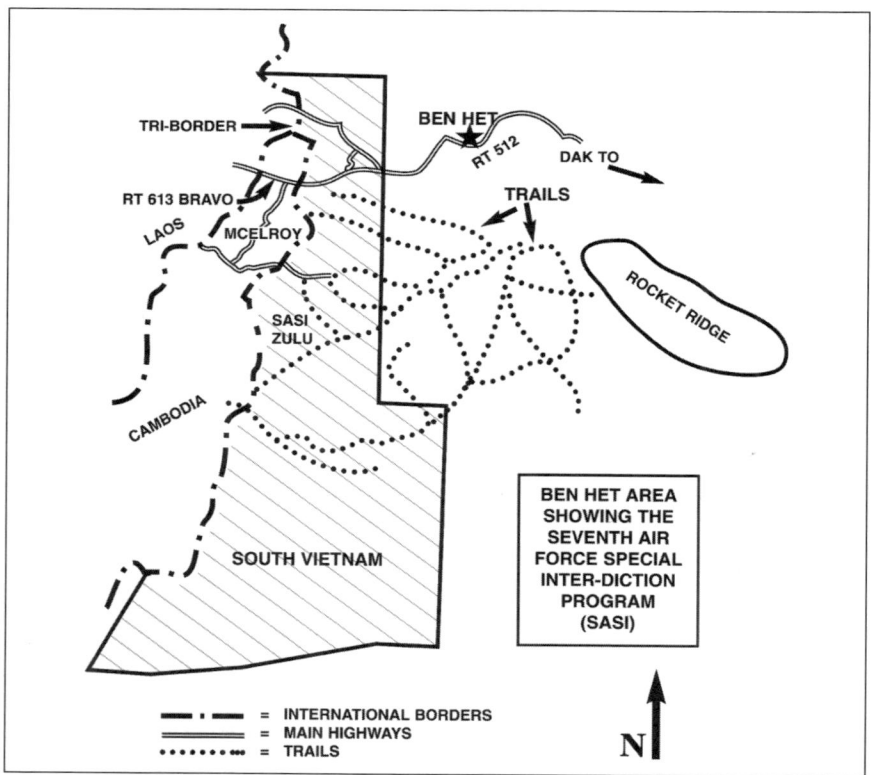

FIGURE 5-4 Ben Het area showing the 7th Air Force Special Interdiction Program (SASI).

The VC/NVA initially deployed the 28th and 66th Infantry Regiments, supported by the 40th Artillery Regiment, in a semi-circular fashion to the South of Highway 512 in preparation for the assault. See Figure 5-5.

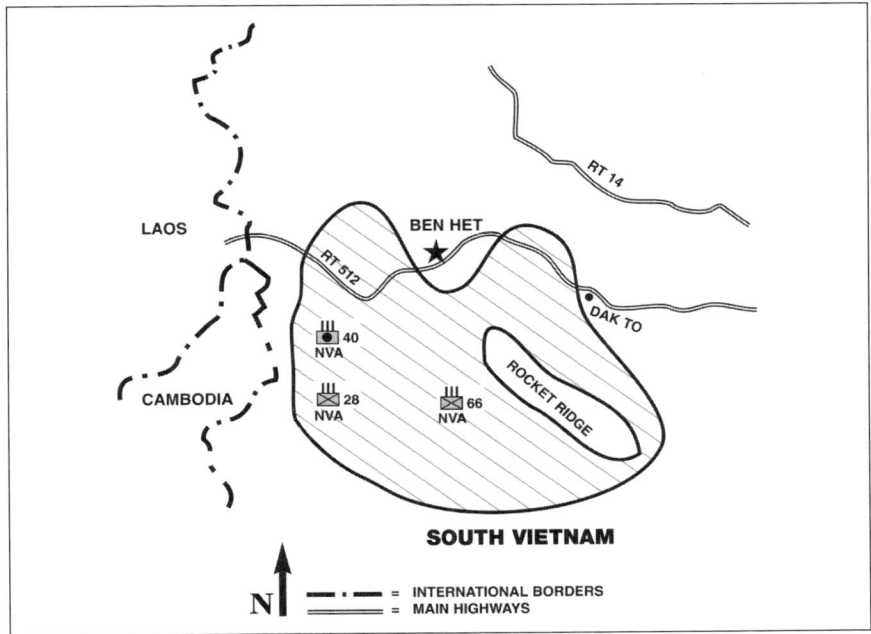

FIGURE 5-5 Deployment of NVA regiments.

Apparently, the enemy attack plan called for the shelling of Ben Het/Dak To from Rocket Ridge, followed by the interdiction of the road between the two camps. Thus, having insured that no Allied reinforcements could be brought to Ben Het from the east, along Highway 512, the VC/NVA planned to move in and seize the camp.

Ben Het itself was defended by about 440 CIDG personnel, 511 ARVN soldiers, 207 artillery troops, and 25 U.S. advisors.

> The above-mentioned defense force figures are only valid for the fighting during May 1969.
>
> To the west and south of Ben Het and Dak To [Figure 5-6], ARVN ground forces moved with widely dispersed screening actions and reconnaissance-in-force operations, hopefully to engage the enemy units and possibly gain a decisive victory, preempting an assault on the critical areas in the 24th STZ.[5]

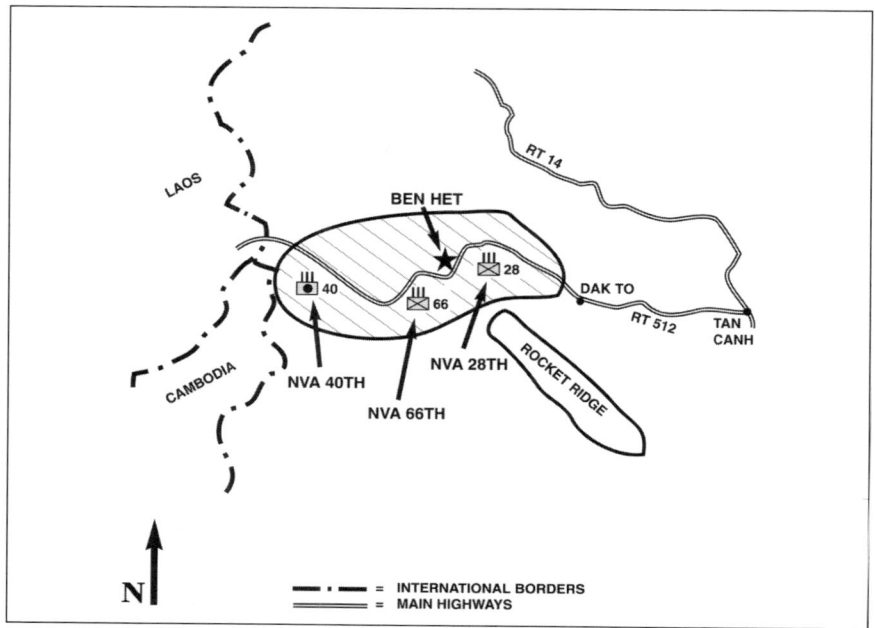

FIGURE 5-6 Movement of ground forces in June, 1969. October 1969

Meanwhile, a daily barrage of enemy 122mm rockets rained down on U.S. Army military installations in the Dak To/Ben Het area. The NVA rocket crews employed sophisticated launching equipment that enabled them to deliver their deadly fire with pinpoint accuracy. U.S. battle casualty figures took a sharp upturn.

As the battalion S-2, I had access to all intelligence information concerning the ongoing military offensive operation in the Ben Het/Dak To area. Of course, I was most interested in the situation at Ben Het because we had our own organic artillery firing battery collocated there with the 5th U.S. Special Forces A-Detachment. The request by the ARVNs for U.S. Artillery Forward Observation Party support was magnified to the point that it was nearly impossible to keep up with their requirements. One such team from 6/14 Artillery deployed with the 22d ARVN Ranger Battalion.

The 22nd Rangers soon clashed with the NVA and were engaged in mortal combat with elements of the 66th NVA Infantry Regiment. With these troops in contact (TIC), our organic FO Team attached to the rangers found themselves right in the thick of the battle since they moved with the forward elements of the elite rangers. I was kept well informed by our TOC RTOs (radio-telephone-operators) with up-to-the minute news from the battlefront. The 1/92 Artillery Battalion TOC, along with some of the firing battery elements, was located at Dak To. See Figure 5-7 on page 45.

The following casualty information was passed on to me: U.S. soldiers gathered near the flagpole for evening retreat at Dak To received incoming enemy fire in the form of a 122mm rocket. The enemy gunners obtained a direct hit on the flagpole base. One casualty I recall was the unit first sergeant. They identified one part of his remains by retrieving a combat boot with a human foot in it. The first sergeant had sewn his name and SSAN number in the boot, which was a standard U.S. Army requirement.

Next, a request for volunteers came down by way of a teletype message. The 1/92 Artillery needed ten men to replace 155mm-howitzer section's men who were all killed when the gun position received a 122mm rocket direct hit. As I recall, 30 to 40 men stepped forward as volunteers. American morale was high and we maintained a high degree of esprit de corps.

I next received some bad news that hit closer to home. The 6/14 FO Team that I had assigned to support the ARVN 22nd Ranger Battalion had all been WIA when the rangers were overrun. They had avoided capture by the enemy but all had to be medically evacuated by "dustoff" (U.S. Army medevac Huey slick air ambulances). As it turned out, two of the team members were brought to the hospital in Pleiku. The third man, E-4 Harris, the team RTO, was medevaced to Japan. Lieutenant Anthony Ditullio, the team FO, and Buck Sergeant Savage, the team Reconnaissance Sergeant, were the two at Pleiku hospital. I went over there to visit and debrief the team leader. Sergeant Savage had taken an AK-47 round in the neck that had exited through his mouth. He was barely able to talk. Ditullio had less severe wounds, but this had been his third such mission to date, and he had been WIA in each case.

E-4 Harris, who had begged me to allow him to go on the mission as a volunteer, had been "gut shot." The team had been required to walk, or crawl, nearly a mile prior to reaching a suitable LZ for helicopter extraction. Harris had exacerbated his condition by refusing any attempt to walk. Gangrene set in which made his wounds critical. They had no choice but to send him to Japan.

During my debriefing session with the two men at Pleiku hospital, I was able to determine how Ditullio received his wounds. When the chopper came in to make the extraction, they asked the team leader (Ditullio) to identify his position. Ditullio used an unauthorized signaling device to flash a signal to the chopper. The clear white flashes from his strobe light appeared as ground fire to the door gunners on the chopper and they expended on the target, wounding Ditullio in the process.

I never saw Specialist-4 Harris again. However, his father, a retired O-6, requested an investigation as to why his son had been sent on such a dangerous mission for which he apparently wasn't trained. When questioned later by LTC Bailey, I had a simple explanation. "He volunteered, Sir!" The case was closed.

A bit later, following my hospital visit and the quick recovery and return to duty by Lt. Ditullio, I received a request for FO Team support once more. Checking the team roster revealed Ditullio's name to lead the team again. I sent word to the team barracks that Ditullio was on alert to standby for a new mission. A short time later, Lt. Van "Something" (I cannot remember his full Dutch name) came storming into my S-2 shop at the Artillery Hill TOC. "Sergeant Lamerson!" He shouted, "What the hell do you mean assigning Ditullio, a three-time wounded man, back into the field of battle?" I answered, "I am sorry, but his name is the next one available for duty as an FO Team leader." Lt. Van said, "I don't care. You should be ashamed of yourself!" Well, I was following my orders to the best of my ability. LTC Bailey had been very explicit about fair assignment of FO duties. I explained all this to the lieutenant to no avail. So I said, "Lieutenant, if you can't live with my decision, I suggest you take it up with the Commander." He refused to consider that option, so I made a new appeal to him. "If you feel so strongly against Ditullio going out again, why don't you go in his place?" This pissed him off, but after a few moments of fuming and fussing, he agreed to do it. I briefed him on the mission and in turn called over to the FO Team barracks with instructions for Ditullio to return to his parent firing battery.

Once back at C Battery in Kontum, Lieutenant Ditullio was sent on an artillery mission. He led a "hip-shoot" to a forward firing position. (An artillery hip-shoot is when a gun or platoon [2 guns] of an artillery firing battery, are displaced and deployed to a temporary forward firing position, in order to add depth to the firing fan.) Ditullio, along with two enlisted cannoneers, were killed when their poorly constructed field-fortified three-man bunker took a direct hit from an enemy 122mm rocket. Shortly there-after, I got some more bad news.

The 22nd Ranger Battalion had been overrun. An undisclosed number of rangers and Lt. Van were MIA. However, their NVA, captors in an unprecedented move, decided to release several prisoners from the

Ranger Company that had been overrun. Ten days after their capture, the group of prisoners, including Lt. Van, emerged from the nearby jungles at a Dak To outpost.

Still back in Pleiku, I was attending to my normal duties when who but Lt. Van came storming in. He slammed his steel helmet down on the floor, and with a look of disgust, he turned his attention to me as he spoke. "Damn it, Sergeant, you son-of-a-bitch. You damn near got me killed." "Whoa, Lieutenant!" I motioned for him to back off. "You came in here, volunteered to take your buddy's place in order to keep him alive. Now he is dead, but you are still alive. What can I say?" The young officer finally settled down and we had our required debriefing session. One interesting thing I recall about Lt. Van's captivity was the way the ARVN Rangers protected him from his captors. The NVA knew that there was an American in the group and demanded that they turn him over, lest they themselves receive harsh punishment. They camouflaged his American features by using human urine to darken his skin and then they shuffled him from group to group. He was never found out. I was able to tell Lt. Van that a special intelligence team was on the way from IFFV G-2 to debrief him as well.

I received orders myself. I was to lead a five-man group (including myself) to An Khe in Dinh Binh Province for the purpose of being trained on a new piece of artillery fire control equipment. Following the training, we were each to sign a hand receipt for a unit of the equipment, which was classified with the "Confidential" grade of military classification. We were flown to An Khe aboard a C-123. The course of instruction was a couple of days long and was on the newly introduced "Medium Range Nightlighting Device" (a very large starlight scope). The scope with tripod was housed in a stainless steel box, which was slightly larger than a traditional army footlocker. After successfully getting certified on use and operation, maintenance, and so forth, we each signed a hand receipt for one each of the five units. Now we awaited air transportation authorization back to Pleiku.

The host unit first sergeant came to the barracks where we waited. "Sarge," he said, "Here are the plane tickets to go along with your travel orders. One catch though, you will have to go to Cam Rahn Bay, where you can arrange to go on from there." In near shock, I lashed out at him. "No damn such day First Sergeant! We are down here from Pleiku and I have no intention of striking off in the wrong goddamn direction. No sir! I refuse to accept these damn tickets." The first sergeant seemed stunned and he became quite irritated with me. I said,

"Tell you what, First Sergeant, just you hold tight while I see what I can do about this shit!" I stomped away, leaving the barracks.

Once outside, I briskly walked the distance over to a nearby helicopter aviation company's area. Entering their barracks area, I spotted a small PX store nearby. Heading toward the PX, I met up with two helicopter pilots, both captains. I hailed them. "Oh Captains, Sirs." They stopped to see what I wanted of them. I explained my dilemma and told them that I was traveling with some sophisticated classified equipment and could not, therefore, risk traveling to Pleiku over the infamous Mang Yang Pass by way of convoy. After haggling with them a bit, one of them asked me what I had to offer as trading material. "Hey" I said, "I'm TDY. I got nothing here with me." One of them asked, "Have you got any training films back there in Pleiku?"

Being quite naïve, I did not understand what the captain actually was asking. "No Sir," I answered. "We don't use training films. We only use actual equipment as training aids," I explained. They both acted overly surprised at my answer, which tipped me off to my ignorance. "Just kidding guys," I joked. "Sure, we have all kinds of smokers," and pulling a notepad and pen from my breast pocket, I stood poised to write. "What are the titles of the skin flicks you guys are looking for?" I queried the pair. They rattled off several titles, as I pretended to write. "It will take me a couple of days to round these up," I explained, "but we have someone coming down here every day or so. Is that OK?" I asked. Rather reluctantly they nodded their heads in agreement. "Do we have a deal?" I asked. "Go get your men and equipment and be at our airstrip in 15 minutes," I was instructed.

It was very late afternoon or early evening by the time we were loaded aboard a Huey Slick. I was asked to provide instruction as to our call sign and final destination once reaching Pleiku airspace, which I provided. By the time we got over Pleiku City, it had turned dark. The pilot contacted our battalion CP for permission to land at our battalion headquarter's landing pad, as per my request. As we made our final approach, the headlights from a pair of jeeps marked the pad. The pilot avoided making a hard landing and as we hovered several feet above the ground, I bailed out. I turned back so that I could catch my gear and equipment that was passed out to me by one of my men. Lowering the chopper, the pilot made it possible for the others to follow my lead. Once we were all off, the pilot lifted off and the chopper disappeared into the night sky.

As I turned to face one of the jeeps, I made visual contact with my battalion commander and his XO. "Sergeant Lamerson," LTC Bailey addressed me. "How the hell did you get a Huey Slick to fly you home? Hell, I'm a colonel and I can't even get a Huey. We thought you were a general coming in for a surprise visit!" We all had a good laugh. I never kept my end of the bargain, since I had no access to any damn smoker films. But somehow, I don't think those pilots took me seriously in the first place. If they had, they were guilty of being as naïve as me. During my absence, the fighting up north was raging on.

Notes

1 Samuel Zaffiri, *Westmoreland: A Biography of General William C. Westmoreland,* (New York: William Morrow and Company, Inc., 1994), 239.
2 Ibid., 239.
3 U.S. Air Force, *CHECO Report:* "Interview with Major William Yenke, Pleiku Sector ALO, II Corps," (13 July 1969), 1.
4 Ibid.
5 U.S. Air Force, CHECO Division, *The Siege of Ben Het,* prepared by Ernie S. Montagliani, (1 October 1969), 5.

FIGURE 5-7 "CHI-COM" RPG 2 Rocket Launcher with 40mm rocket ammunition

CHAPTER 6

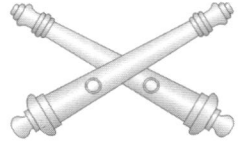

7th USAF TAC Air Support

Dan Quyan 38 A

The duty of a soldier in time of war is to fight and if need be to die.
T.R. Fehrenbach

The responsibility for providing most of the air support for the 24th STZ remained with Free World Military Assistance Forces (FWMAF) system under the direction of the Direct Air Support Center (DASC) Alpha. The Vietnamese Air Force (VNAF) had its own system for air support under II DASC at Pleiku, but its contribution was minimal.

DASC Alpha, collocated with headquarters I FIELD FORCE VIETNAM (FFV) at Nha Trang, was keeping a continuing watch on the traditional infiltration routes through the border areas in western Kontum Province. As early as February 1969, the 7th AF began a program to interdict these routes to vehicular traffic, making it more difficult for the enemy to move men and supplies into South Vietnam from Cambodia and Laos. The program, named the "Seventh Air Force Special Interdiction Program (SASI)," took in an area along the western border of South Vietnam from above the tri-border area and extended southward to a point west of Pleiku.

The northern portion of the program, called SASI ZULU (see Chapter 5, Figure 5-4), covered most of the routes in the tri-border vicinity, specifically those which directly menaced Ben Het/Dak To. The Commanding General (CG), I FFV, directed that targets in SASI ZULU receive priority during May as the situation in the 24th STZ was developing. Later, the Director of DASC Alpha, Lt. Colonel Thomas A. Crawford, stated, "We worked pretty hard on the interdiction effort, for in March they (the VC/NVA) had used tanks against Ben Het ... So we paid special attention to these roads... ."[1]

Cessna O1 Bird Dog

The Headquarters, 24th STZ, along with the Zone Tactical Air Control Party (TACP), was located at Kontum prior to the siege. As soon as the enemy's presence in force was recognized, Colonel Lien and his American advisors decided to move a Tactical Operation Center (TOC) to Dak To. In order for close contact to be maintained with the ground forces, an additional TACP was collocated with the TOC. Initially, the TACP, manned by an Air Liaison Officer (ALO) and radio operators, was forced to use radios that were mounted in a jeep outside the command bunker at Dak To. The radios were later moved inside under cover. On 9 May, the TACP inside was operational, but only during daylight hours due to difficult circumstances. Later, it was able to achieve a 24-hour capability.

In addition to the TACP at Dak To, the Tactical Air Control System (TACS) serving the 24th STZ was augmented by Forward Air Controllers (FACs) and ALOs brought in from quiet areas of II Corps and elsewhere. The FACs were evenly divided between Pleiku and Kontum cities to reduce the possibility that they might all be weathered in at one time. Lt. Col. Thomas, the 24th STZ ALO, was scheduled to leave shortly, as his tour was ending. The Pleiku sector ALO, Major William

F100 Super Sabre

Yenke, was sent to Dak To so that an experienced officer would be available to make a smooth transition from Colonel Thomas to his successor and to insure that no serious problems developed.

Major Yenke was stationed at Pleiku. He commuted, flying to the TACP at Dak To in the morning and returning home at night, during the time prior to the arrival of the new ALO and during the time of the first enemy attack. He had just taken off from Dak To to return to Pleiku when he observed one of the initial ABFs.

> ... "Well, I was just leaving—it was just before dark ... I took off and decided to fly patrol around the area until dark... ."
>
> He noted that the rockets had been launched from the hill about three kilometers to the southeast and gave the A-1 pilots directions to the targets.
>
> "Well, the lead rolled in and was releasing his CBU, and three more rockets came up directly in front of him. Also three 50-caliber machine guns and small arms opened up on him from the ridge line so they CBU and Naped the whole area. I got some F-4's right behind the Spads with 750-lb bombs and spread those all over the area ... and I left ... ."[2]

A Possible Enemy Diversion in I Corps

With Allied knowledge of a potential large scale enemy offensive operation looming on the horizon, it did not seem logical that the lightly defended 24th STZ in northwestern Kontum Province would not be reinforced by much larger ARVN infantry forces. Perhaps the reason for the decision to hold back from deploying such forces was influenced by the enemy's sudden renewed interest, as demonstrated in the vicinity of enemy Base Area 611, in the I Corps A Shau Valley.

At its extreme western edge, straddling the Laotian border, lay Base Area 611, the old objective of Operation Dewey Canyon where the 1/9 and 3/9 Marine Battalions conducted across-the-border operations during February 1969.

During the marine operations, it was confirmed that the enemy was deploying full tracked prime mover vehicles, armor, and large caliber artillery field pieces just across the Laotian border in the vicinity of Base Area 611. It was realized at that time that the NVA had the capability to move armor/mechanized artillery units down Route 922 from Laos into SVN where they could spearhead NVA infantry attacks against the coastal Provinces in I Corps.

Within days after the completion of that marine operation, intelligence sources reported the movement of three NVA regiments back into Base Area 611. Aerial reconnaissance reported intensive building activity on the roads leading from Laos into South Vietnam. Other intelligence gained from prisoners revealed that the 9th NVA Regiment was already on the move toward Hue. All signs showed a repetition of the behavior the enemy followed before attacking Hue in 1968. Rather than wait until the enemy struck in a populous coastal region, the 101st Airborne directed the 3d Brigade, augmented by a battalion from the 1st ARVN Division, to initiate Operation Apache Snow. The operation was conceived by XXIV Corps to block any further eastward movement by the enemy and began early on the morning of 10 May 1969.

On the afternoon of 11 May, Company B, 187th Infantry Battalion, following contact with a sizable but unidentified enemy force on the southeastern slope of Hill 937, was forced to withdraw. However, searching the area, the company found evidence of a sophisticated telephone network and documents that identified the enemy on Hill 937 as part of the 29th NVA Regiment.[3]

The 29th NVA Regiment was a major infantry maneuver element of the 325 C NVA Infantry Division. The 325 C was identified as one of the three NVA Infantry Divisions that surrounded Khe Sanh during the

A1E Sky Raider (SPAD)

1968 siege. At the same time that the 325 C Division was being deployed at Khe Sanh, the 29th NVA Regiment was discovered to be part of a three-NVA regimental-size force used as a blocking force to prevent the Allied forces from rushing to the rescue of Hue during the Tet of 1968 attacks. It is important to note that the 325 C Division was miles away and in another province while the 29th Regiment was just outside of Hue.

The ensuing battle that followed the B/187 discovery is recorded in the American annals of warfare as "The Battle of Hamburger Hill." There was nothing special about Hill 937. The Vietnamese called it Dong Ap Bia and, in the words of an army historian, it was "as a particular piece of terrain of no significance." However, significant USAF air firepower resources were siphoned off for the purpose of supporting the American operation. But not the B-52s. Comey, referring to the enemy force, explained, "If I backed away the distance necessary to launch a B-52 strike he would have disappeared in the dark of the night and attacked us somewhere else."[4]

Meanwhile the fighting in II Corps' northwestern Kontum Province around Dak To/Ben Het received no mention by the Western news

F2 C Phantom II

media. All of the press corps had converged on the A Shau Valley in I Corps to cover the American snafu at Hamburger Hill. This almost immediately became a source of controversy in the United States. The press widely reported Senator Edward Kennedy's comment that the battle was "senseless and irresponsible." Much of the criticism was directed at General Zais's (Commanding General, 101st Airborne Division) decision to take the hill at all cost.

Defending his decision, Zais responded that the enemy had suffered 630 KIAs, compared to 56 American deaths, better than a 10 to 1 ratio. Hamburger Hill was destined to become the last American battle in which victory would be determined by "body count."[5] Within a month following the Battle of Hamburger Hill, the Western newsmen were on their way into Ben Het.

There are some who may disagree with me, but I have come to recognize the enemy threat used to trigger the fight for Hamburger Hill as a thinly disguised enemy diversionary tactic. This tactic was designed to draw Allied troops and firepower to the remote area in the A Shau Valley so that the enemy's superior-sized forces, spearheaded by a newly formed mechanized infantry division, could move with unimpeded lightening-like speed and capture the control of Kontum and Pleiku Provinces. The enemy general staff saw this as an opportunity to be exploited for the purpose of a quick negotiated peace at Paris, France.

About the 15th of May 1969, while the battle for Hamburger Hill was still raging. ARVN Operation Dan Quyan 38 A took a sudden turn, which caused the operation to enter a critical second phase.

Notes

[1] U.S. Air Force, CHECO Division, *The Siege of Ben Het,* prepared by Ernie S. Montagliani, (1 October 1969), 2.
[2] U.S. Air Force, *CHECO Report:* "Interview with Major William Yenke, Pleiku Sector ALO, II Corps," (13 July 1969), 2-3.
[3] Edward Doyle, Samuel Lipsman, and the editors of Boston Publishing Company, *Fighting For Time,* a volume of *The Vietnam Experience,* (Boston: Boston Publishing Company, 1983), 16–17.
[4] Ibid., 19.
[5] Ibid., 22.

CHAPTER 7

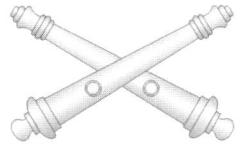

Dan Quyan 38 A

Phase II

To seize and control the highlands is to solve the whole problem of South Vietnam.
Vo Nguyen Giap, General, NVA

Since the intervention by U.S. ground combat troops in the war between North and South Vietnam during the spring of 1965, American military leaders feared that the NVA planned to cut South Vietnam in two. "General Giap intended to gain a spectacular victory—a Southern Dien Bien Phu with all the trimmings—by slicing South Vietnam in half on the line from Pleiku through An Khe to Qui Nhon. Between October 1965 and April 1966, he planned to commit three full divisions along that axis."[1]

Soon after he brought the colors of the 1st Cavalry Division (Airmobile) to Vietnam, Major General Harry O. Kinnard received a personal order from Army Chief of Staff Harold K. Johnson. "Harry, I want you and your division to stop the enemy from cutting South Vietnam in two."[2]

By the time of the 1969 planned enemy spring/summer offensive, Allied commanders had no indication that General Giap had abandoned his plans for obtaining a "spectacular victory" by attacking through the II Corps border provinces. So, when intelligence sources revealed the possible presence of four of Giap's veteran NVA infantry regiments reinforced by an NVA artillery regiment in northwestern Kontum Province, the Allies had to validate the information. ARVN Marine Colonel, Nguyen Ba Lien, dispatched elements of his ranger battalions into the hills southwest of Dak To and Ben Het to locate and identify the enemy force threatening the area. The enemy, it was reported, was planning to launch a large-scale offensive operation in the Kontum Province of South Vietnam. Creating a southern Dien Bien Phu was bragged about over NVA clandestine radio stations.

The Allied Command, however, was not prepared to tout Giap and Dung's real reasons for launching their spring/summer offensive in May of 1969. Rather, they found it more to their liking to tout the following:

> Specific enemy objectives were outlined in a notebook of unknown origin which was captured on 5 May (1969) in Pleiku Province, thirty kilometers southeast of Pleiku City. These objectives were:
>
> ♦ Destroy regimental and brigade level units and force the enemy to give up,
> ♦ Destroy the 42d ARVN Regiment and 1/3 of the PF,
> ♦ Control larger rural areas and skirt the cities,
> ♦ Destroy one U.S. brigade,
> ♦ Destroy allied artillery by separating their activity.[3]

The more probable goal was never discussed as a matter of public record, but I think that my own conclusion in reference to the enemy's goal is more accurate than those presented above. A realistic goal would be to seize and control Kontum and Pleiku Provinces along with both Provincial capital cities. Pleiku City was of the most strategic value to the enemy. Its loss would come as a huge blow to the Allies and would set the stage for a quick negotiated peace in Paris, France.

To add further to the importance of controlling these two border provinces is to recognize the fact that hard surfaced highways leading to the coastal province of Binh Dinh were in existence. In Binh Dinh Province, the NVA/VC would be most welcomed by the populace. As the record indicates, a year prior to the 1965 battle of the Ia Drang Valley, the CIA had declared Binh Dinh Province, with its 800,000 population, "just about lost" to the South Vietnamese Government. Binh Dinh Province was considered to be "the Communist Heartland of the South."[4]

When the northwestern portion of Kontum Province was turned over to ARVN control under the guise of "Vietnamization," which both North and South detested, the lone 42d ARVN Infantry Regiment left to protect the area seemed to be an insignificant obstacle to the NVA generals' plans. So, the spring/summer offensive was launched on schedule.

> On 15 May, earlier ARVN strategy changed markedly. Intelligence sources indicated there was a large build up west of Rocket Ridge, and the South Vietnamese reacted energetically. Instead of widely

> dispersed screening operations, which were carried out previously, a mix of eight battalions of government troops took command of key terrain south of Ben Het and aggressively sought out and engaged the VC/NVA.5

Lt. Col. Jack Cude Jr. arrived on 18 May to replace Colonel Thomas as the 24th STZ ALO. He spent the first days familiarizing himself with the situation at the TCAP at Dak To.

The fight for Hamburger Hill ended on 20 May 1969. In his own words, Colonel Cude explains the situation.

> When I got there, Ben Het and Dak To were getting ABFs, and air strikes were being flown throughout the area. Some of the first flights I made as an FAC were in support of friendly positions under fire … .

The new ALO noted the weather in May was "excellent" and targets were lucrative—facts pointed out by most of the people interviewed. (These interviews were given to support the preparation of the writing of the 7th AF Oct. 1969 CHECO Report, "Comprehensive Historical Evaluation of Combat Operations in Southeast Asia.") One of the people interviewed was the Director of DASC Alpha, Lt. Col. T.A. Crawford.

> During the first phase [May], we had troops in the field and consequently high priority targets. In other words, we knew where the enemy was … and we found out where the guns were firing from … and the weather was good.6

It is important to note that problems arose in reference to air support, during the May fighting. Some of those who were not trained to work with the system misunderstood how to use it to their best advantage. For example the ARVNs were not used to getting much air support, so when they did get some, they thought it was a lot. They had not yet learned to appreciate what air support could do for them. Therefore, they tended to lean toward the use of the more traditional firepower, which was the field artillery. The overuse of artillery by the ARVN, rather than the use of Tac Air, caused American artillery commanders to often neglect to notify the Air Force people of the fact that they were responding to support for fire request. The problem of artillery fire hazards was outlined in an official Air Force interview with Major William Yenke:

> … Let me say a word about the artillery up there. The artillery commander up there, Colonel Thompson, he said we have what are called "Contact Missions," and in cases like this, when they start getting fire, even though there are FACs and Spads flying over the target, they start firing artillery at it. And then, this is a quote, "When it is

convenient, we broadcast an artillery warning." Well, we are right in the next room and he could stick his head in and tell us so we could call our people flying around the target area ... but, as it was, we got shot at by American artillery so often that we didn't even pay attention to it anymore ... and we quit calling for advisory [warnings] and just figured that the odds were against us getting shot down. I've been as close to being shot down by our own artillery as I have by the enemy, I believe. You know when you'd go out and get a good target and the fighters were checked in—you'd roll in and mark; here would come American artillery, without prior coordination. So anyway, we got the artillery in and they did a good job on the area.7

The 7th U.S. Air Force people were anxious to get the ARVN to use more air assets as is pointed out by Lt. Col. Thomas L. Crawford. Jr. Director, DASC Alpha.

> ... We tried to encourage ... the Army to request sufficient air to protect forces that were employed. The ARVN system is not used to getting much air, therefore when they get some air, they thought it was a lot ... We were perhaps pushing it a little bit in trying to force more air on them ... We worked with G-3 air here—to go to the G-3 air at II Corps in an effort to get them to push it down through the Army system to get them to ask for more air. During the initial part of the battle, when the ARVN was deployed south of Ben Het-Dak To and to the west and northwest, I don't believe we used sufficient air—all the air we could have put in.8

One U.S. Air Force Support Squadron supporting the May action was located at Pleiku AFB, Pleiku City. Perhaps the least known Skyraider outfit [A1 E], because of it's short life, was the 6th Special Operations Squadron at Pleiku, in existence only from mid 1968 to late 1969. Lt. Colonel Alexander E. Corey commanded the squadron. The squadron's call sign was Spad (to add to history's litany of Hobo's, Zorros and Fireflies). The Spad pilots, most of who were veterans of both WWII and/or the Korean War, were branded as "Mavericks" by the more traditional USAF, because they were flying these old obsolete aircraft, hold-overs from WWII. They were considered to be unruly and undisciplined while building a prestigious name for themselves. Therefore, they were a tight-knit group who drank together at a hootch called "the Spad Bar."9 These guys were tough, and they were proud to be members of the 6th SOS. As you may recall, I mentioned Colonel Corey as being the flight leader during the February 69 action south of Ben Het that resulted in the destruction of a 100mm enemy field gun.

The A1E Skyraiders had the ability to stay aloft for up to 12 hours, to fly low and slow, and to carry so much ordnance they were nicknamed "flying dump trucks." These piston-engine airplanes, fighting a jet-age war with their big four-bladed props, were deemed to be the right weapon at the right time.[10] I speak for myself when I say, "I owe my life to those wonderful guys that piloted the Spads during the upcoming Siege of Ben Het."

In May the weather was good. There were good targets available; however, what was lacking was BDA (Bomb Damage Assessment). This was pointed out in the following reference to an ABF against Firebase #5 near Dak To. Following are some remarks from Major Yenke's interview of 13 July 1969:

> The Spads broke that first attack with just 20mm fire—God knows how many they killed—because there was no ground follow up. That was the problem—ARVN liked to stay in defensive positions and let the idiots come to them. Well that's all right, but you don't get KBAs like that. All this time we were killing people all over the area but nobody knew it. We were forbidden to call it from the air—if we saw a guy lying there with no head that was an "estimated KBA." I think they since changed that. We killed over 1,000 people in my opinion.[11]

Another important point is brought out in Major Yenke's interview as he makes reference to the following action:

> Well the enemy didn't take Rocket Ridge. The VC/NVA must be very inflexible, because they continued with the overall plan and up came the bridge-blowers and the road interdictors. But, we had bypasses around the bridges. So they got 500 VC/NVA out ambushing convoys. Well they ambushed the ARVN Rangers, and that was a mistake. The ARVN killed 16 of them before they got orders to continue to Dak To. You know, when you shoot at the Allies, all of these airplanes suddenly appear overhead ... [W]ell, an FAC, Captain Marx, was flying at this time and he saw the enemy running around down there. He had F-4s on station and he called me in the TOC and said, "Here are all these dinks, 150 or so running around in this field down here, and I got a set of Phantoms with 750lb bombs—get me clearance—I can't get clearance. We didn't know where the Armored Cav. was, so we called around and found out that the ARVN wasn't there yet. We got Captain Marx a clearance and he salvoes the bombs. —We didn't get BDA because all of the bombs blew hell out of the enemy—some were in pieces.
>
> The Armored Cavalry went in and they were chasing the enemy troops around in the bushes. Captain Marx is on the radio describing what's going on down there. Then he got some fighter with napalm, and expended them, and the Armored Cavalry continued to flush the enemy out of the bushes.
>
> This was a couple of days later. After all the strafe on Rocket Ridge failed, the enemy tried to initiate phase two—bridge blowing and ambushes. So they got annihilated.

> The ARVN is bad when it comes to fighting. They'll do anything to get out of fighting.
> Well, most of the enemy plan had failed—they didn't get Rocket Ridge, they blew bridges but the ARVN drove right around them. But, they were after the tanks. They (the ARVN) lost 9 out of 17 tanks ... I think (an armor advisor told me).
> A note of significant importance here: The fact that the ARVN tanks were targeted as a prime target by the enemy indicates that they wanted to eliminate the ARVN anti-tank capability.
> If they would have had the sense to blow this one bridge between Dak To and Ben Het, none of the tanks could have gotten through, but they didn't.
> There were intelligence reports that the enemy had either 10 or 26 tanks over in Cambodia. Well they [the enemy] were picking out the tanks and command APCs with all the antennas on them.[12]

Note: The one bridge alluded to was the Dak Mot Bridge that spanned the Dak Poko River where it intersected Route 512. My take here is that the NVA lured the ARVN tanks and APCs into vulnerable positions where they were marked for destruction. They did not destroy the Dak Mot Bridge because they had plans to use it for their own armored crossing later on in the fight.

It is clear to me that Major Yenke had no clear understanding of enemy ground tactics. As an old armored soldier myself, I can pretty well interpret the enemy's intentions here. They intended to, and did, destroy the ARVN's ability to respond to an enemy armor threat. Without the 3rd Armored Cavalry to brunt an enemy armored assault, the ARVN-protected Ben Het/Dak To area was vulnerable to such an attack. The NVA were successful in setting the stage for opening the route east to Tan Canh. Tan Canh was headquarters for the ARVN 42d Infantry Regiment. Highway 14, which ran south to Kontum, ran through Tan Canh. To advance, the enemy had to take Ben Het/Dak To, as well as Tan Canh. Highways 512 and 14 were hard surfaced roads, very suitable for use by enemy armored columns. To achieve any significant depth to the battlefield, the enemy would have to introduce mechanized forces. General Dung, working under General Giap, was ready to test his newest addition to the NVA war machine. That is to say, it was likely that the 325 C NVA Infantry Division had been converted to a mechanized division that was reinforced by the 202d Armor/Artillery NVA Regiment. The truth of the matter is that the ARVN 3d Cavalry element attached to the ARVN lost all of their tanks but two during Dan Quyen 38A.

It was during the latter part of May that I first became personally involved in the action up there in the vicinity of Dak To/Ben Het. While still stationed at Pleiku's Artillery Hill, I was alerted about an upcoming aerial observation mission. I was ordered to report to Camp Holloway for the mission briefing. While there, I would also be assigned a pilot and an aircraft for the mission. I had been instructed to report to the Air Operations building that belonged to the 219 Aviation Company's "Head Hunters." Prior to leaving Artillery Hill, I checked out all of my survival gear and insured that I had all of the seven extra water canteens filled with fresh, potable water. When my transportation arrived, I instructed the driver to transport me to Camp Holloway. I was expected to be there NLT 0730 hours in the morning on the day of my mission.

As for weapons, I carried an Army issue, 45-caliber, semi-automatic pistol strapped to my hip and an old, U.S. Army, 30-caliber carbine. I had two 30-round magazines for the carbine, which were reversed from each other and taped together so that they could be reversed during action, allowing me to use 60 rounds without having to reload any magazines. I always covered the aircraft seat with my flak vest. We did not wear parachutes aboard the Cessna L-19s (AKA 01 Birddog). An Army issue waterproof ammo bag contained a sizable amount of extra ammunition. I had already made up my mind that if I survived being shot down, I would fight to the death to avoid capture. If I failed to die at the hands of the enemy while trying to evade capture, I would continue to fight.

At Holloway, the pilot and I were briefed on the mission. First, we were to fly to Dak To, where we would get an update on the situation and top off our fuel supply. I was fortunate to draw an experienced pilot. Once airborne, he placed us on a northern heading. We soon flew over Kontum City and continued north. A couple of miles out of Tan Canh, my pilot suddenly changed the course and brought the little observation aircraft on a heading that lined us up on some apparently abandoned bunkers/fox holes below. Without a word of warning as to his intentions, the pilot expended one of the four white phosphorous marking rockets carried beneath the wings. Blam! I got a quick adrenaline rush from thinking that we had been hit by enemy ground fire. I waited until later to complain to the pilot. Next, he put us on a westerly heading and we flew on to Dak To, where we landed.

Once on the ground and dismounted, I kindly asked the pilot to inform me in the future when he planned to expend rockets. On the ground, the people replaced the expended rocket and topped off our fuel tanks. We were updated on the situation, but no radical changes were required. We were instructed to VR (visual reconnaissance) south and west of Ben Het. I was informed that there was an 8-inch howitzer standing by at Ben Het (from B Battery 6/14) to render fire support as needed. Soon, we were back in the air and doing our thing. I liked the fact that the pilot was experienced, because he was not hung up on flying by the book. Policy forbade routine flying below a 1200-foot altitude when performing VRs. We maintained a much lower altitude of five or six hundred feet. I did not complain. Hell, you can't see much down below in those triple canopy jungles if you're up at 1200 feet.

I had plotted the gun battery position on my map and, thereafter, tried to keep Ben Het within sight. If necessary to fire, I would be required to make my adjustments along the gun target line. As we flew southwest of Ben Het, I navigated on my map. Suddenly I discovered that we had strayed across the Cambodian border. Before I could speak to the pilot, we received ground fire from an enemy antiaircraft battery below. As the pilot took immediate evasive action, I spotted the enemy gun position. I identified it as a 37mm antiaircraft gun. Within moments, we were safely out of range and back on the SVN side of the border. Of course we had no reason to report the incident, so we continued to fly VR.

My pilot was the silent type. He stuck to the business of flying and I, in turn, stuck to the business of observing. We were a few miles southwest of Ben Het when something below caught my eye. I tapped the pilot on the shoulder and motioned for him to take her down low and circle. I confirmed the presence of a huge new bunker complex on the top of a hill, a regimental headquarters, I suspected. I was euphoric as I prepared to issue a Destruction Fire Mission order or request to the gun battery. After passing a few anxious moments, my euphoria came to a sudden end. "Your request to take that particular target under fire is denied," the voice on the other end of the radio informed me. I was one pissed-off little sergeant. But I knew that it would do no good to question the gun battery. So we continued on with our VR mission and I could not help but wonder why. After only about 15 or 20 minutes, we received notification of a TIC (Troops In Contact) nearby. We arrived over the contact area within minutes. I had prepared most of the elements of a request for fire prior to our arrival. I spotted an estimated squad of enemy soldiers running across an open area below and sent my mission to the firing battery. Troops in the open meant that I would receive a High Explosive Shell (HE) with a Variable time fuze (VT).

Note: In the military the spelling for fuse is "FUZE" for military ordnance and "FUSE" for Engineer Demolitions.

In any case, the Firing Battery alerted me to the fact that the first round was on the way. Out of the corner of my left eye, I caught the flash and smoke from the exploding 8-inch artillery shell. It was to the left at 10 to 11 o'clock and too close for comfort. As the last two or three enemy soldiers disappeared into the wood-line, I radioed an EOM (end of mission). Results: Enemy dispersed.

By this time, it was almost noon. Feeling lucky that we had not been hit by our own artillery, we returned to Dak To. On the ground, I hurriedly walked to the Air Operations Hootch. "What the hell is going on?" I inquired, asking about my mission that was canceled earlier. "The ARVNs have a mission ongoing in that area," I was told. "If your fire mission had gone forth, it might have jeopardized their mission." I did not appreciate the answer, but could do no more. I was asked if I would accept another four-hour mission for the afternoon. I accepted before being released to go to noon chow. For lunch, they had fresh cucumbers soaked in vinegar and oil, one of my favorites, and I overindulged a bit.

Following my after-meal Camel cigarette, I returned to the Air Operations hootch where I was introduced to my pilot for the upcoming mission. The pilot, a young first lieutenant, was new in-country. This would be one of his early missions. Once airborne, I realized that he was inexperienced and was bent on flying by the book. The pilot leveled us out at 1200 feet and flew in straight lines while dipping the wings from side to side. Flip-flop, flip-flop, back and forth, back and forth. Well, after a couple of hours of that crap, I got airsick. The cucumbers had caught up with me. I motioned for the pilot to bank steeply to the right as I attempted to puke through the open window. That was a mistake and the puke blew back in, hitting me in the face and splattering all over the back area of airplane. Due to the heat, the smell was overwhelming. My pilot radioed for permission to abort the remainder of the mission. His request was accepted and we returned to Pleiku. During Air Observer School at the headhunters, we were told that if we puked in the airplane we'd have to clean it. I was relieved to find out that this was untrue.

I returned to Artillery Hill, where I resumed my normal duties. I did not know it then, but I was destined to face, in combat, that very enemy regiment whose headquarters I had ordered fire on, but was denied.

Near the end of Operation Dan Quyen 38 A, the following interview was taking place.

> Colonel Lien [the 24th STZ Commander] had been told to hold casualties down—an advisor told me this during a meeting we had in which we discussed CSS (Combat Sky Spot) and everything—and I said you've got all your people out of the field and you can't get air support, if you don't have good targets. The problem is we don't have good targets—and you say the problem is that you're not getting air support. The 7th AF saying—"give them CAS-schedule 40 sorties per day or 60 sorties per day"—well, Christ, if you don't have targets the air strikes are useless and he said that DASC Alpha kept telling him that if he had targets he could get all of the air on immediate basis, in II Corps—yes, and all the air in the whole damn country. If they had targets—troops in the open and that sort of thing. But, he said that Colonel Lien had been ordered to pull all of the people back to reduce casualties. So before, they had all of these battalions—Rangers, Mike Strike, Army, Armored Cavalry, 42d Regiment, out in the area—and they were in constant contact, attacking. God, the rangers killed 960 themselves in our location, and the Mike Forces killed 70 in one night—this was when they had arms and legs blown into the perimeter. The friendlies took heavy casualties but the rate was from 8 to 15 to 1, I think. So, then, even though they were taking heavy casualties, they were killing a hell of a lot of VC/NVA. Well, either because it was Phase III of the plan or ARVN came in out of the field (I don't know which), they started moving these two Regiments in [66th and 28th], and then I got out of direct touch, because I was putting in air strikes and checking new people out. I was no longer in the TOC where I knew exactly what was happening.13

The ARVN Forces appeared to have won the battle when intelligence reports indicated an NVA withdrawal from the area around Ben Het/Dak To.

> During the latter part of May and early June, it appeared the South Vietnamese had won the battle. The VC/NVA forces were seemingly withdrawing westward toward the Cambodian border. The ARVN units began to return to their camps, having fought aggressively the preceding month, and having inflicted severe casualties upon the enemy—the comparative figures were 156 friendly Killed In Action (KIA) against 1,162 enemy dead.14

Note: Due to misinformation, disinformation, withheld information, lies, and deceit, coupled with miscommunication, etc., I find the above figures suspect; e.g., the ARVN losses were greater than were admitted to. This is partly due to WIA count.

The transition into Phase III began during a heavy concentration of ARC Light strikes on 3 June in the area where previous, heavy ground contacts had occurred during Phase II. A three-battalion size force conducted BDA operations on 4–5 June during which there were no major contacts.... [See Figure 7-1.]

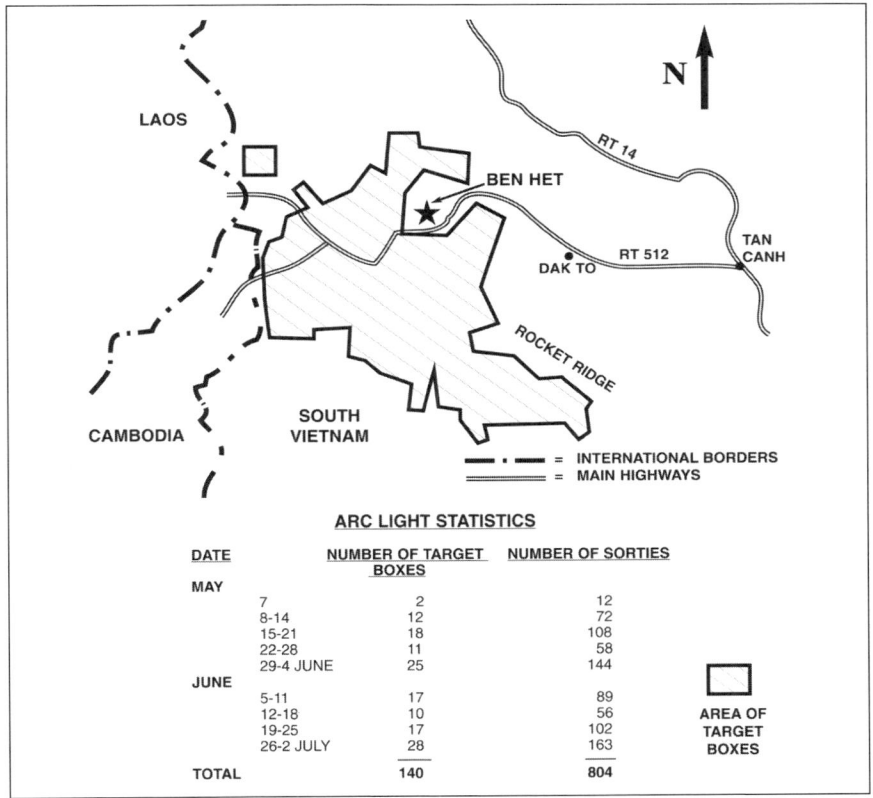

FIGURE 7-1   ARC Light Strikes around Ben Het.

Therefore, the ARVN and MSF forces withdrew into nearby population centers. However, the NVA forces again moved in around Ben Het. The South Vietnamese did not move into the field to establish contact. The Siege of Ben Het tightened.[15]

Note: ARVN Operation Dan Quyen 38 A (Will Win) ended here.

Notes

[1] Harry G. Summers Jr., *On Strategy: A Critical Analysis of the Vietnam War,* (New York: Dell Publishing Co., 1982), 182.

2 Terrence Maitland, Peter McInerney, and the editors of Boston Publishing Company, *A Contagion Of War,* a volume of *The Vietnam Experience,* (Boston: Boston Publishing Company, 1983), 32.
3 U.S. Air Force. Air War College, *Tactical Air Support and the Battle of Ben Het: A Professional Study,* by Thomas M. Crawford, Jr., No. 4029 (Air University: 1970), 7.
4 Terrence Maitland, Peter McInerney, and the editors of Boston Publishing Company, *A Contagion Of War,* a volume of *The Vietnam Experience,* (Boston: Boston Publishing Company, 1983), 35.
5 U.S. Air Force, CHECO Division, *The Siege of Ben Het,* prepared by Ernie S. Montagliani, (1 October 1969), 8.
6 Ibid., 7–8.
7 U.S. Air Force, *CHECO Report:* "Interview with Major William Yenke, Pleiku Sector ALO, II Corps," (13 July 1969), 3.
8 U.S. Air Force, *CHECO Report:* "Interview with Lt. Col. Thomas M. Crawford, Jr," (10 July 1969), 2.
9 Robert F. Dorr, *Skyraider,* a volume of *The Illustrated History of the Vietnam War, (New York: Bantam Books, 1988), 139.*
10 Ibid., 140.
11 U.S. Air Force, *CHECO Report:* "Interview with Major William Yenke, Pleiku Sector ALO, II Corps," (13 July 1969), 6.
12 Ibid., 7–8.
13 Ibid., 8–9.
14 U.S. Air Force, CHECO Division, *The Siege of Ben Het,* prepared by Ernie S. Montagliani, (1 October 1969), 10.
15 U.S. Air Force. Air War College, *Tactical Air Support and the Battle of Ben Het: A Professional Study,* by Thomas M. Crawford, Jr., No. 4029 (Air University: 1970), 10.

CHAPTER 8

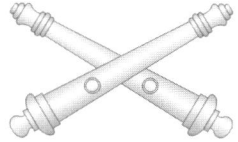

The Siege of Ben Het

... little bitty pieces of bodies lying all around and pieces of shredded clothing hanging in the trees... .
BDA team report, 1969

PART I

The Phantom Gunnery Team

Except for nuclear weapons, the most fearsome weapon in the U.S. military arsenal is the USA's B-52 bomber, nicknamed the "Whispering Death."[1] The B-52 bomber was used during the Vietnam War to make horrific "Arc–Light" bomb strikes against the enemy ground forces. As a U.S. Army "Red Leg" artilleryman, I had a deep appreciation for firepower. I was highly trained in the use of both conventional warfare munitions, and tactical nuclear weapons. As my date with destiny loomed on the horizon, little did I know that I was about to embark on a mission that would change my life forever. As a key member of an U.S. Army Field Artillery "Phantom Gunnery Team" that was destined to be inserted into a beleaguered and remote U.S. 5th Special Forces outpost, I would experience the employment of the full spectrum of U.S. conventional ordnance against a determined and tenacious NVA force, bent on overrunning this strategic little outpost located in the triple canopied mountainous terrain in one of South Vietnam's Central Highland border provinces. It was at a place we Red Legs simply referred to as "Ben Het."

When the war transcended into the month of June 1969, intelligence sources revealed that the NVA forces still posed a serious threat to the Ben Het/Dak To area. The NVA 40th Artillery Regiment kept up the daily bombardment of the U.S. Ben Het Camp. Very little patrol

B-52D

activity took place because the patrols were ambushed immediately outside the camp.

There were no ARVN Infantry units left deployed in the field around Ben Het. The IFFORCEV (US Army) Command in Nha Trang took the following action based on the belief that the ARVN would move back to the field, where they would launch a counteroffensive against the NVA. Based on lessons learned during the May fighting, U.S. Field Commanders wanted to establish improved command and control of U.S. Fire Support Assets as they were deployed in support of the expected "new" ARVN offensive operation. This was especially true in reference to the deployment of U.S. Army Field Artillery assets. Using available assets contained within the 52d Artillery Group, IFFV created a provisional-type unit called a "Battalion Group." Command and control was established at Dak To and at Ben Het.

Command of the newly formed battalion group was given to Lt. Colonel Nelson Thompson, the present battalion commander of 1/92d Artillery. LTC Thompson would wear two hats, so to speak. His battalion would continue to operate the artillery Forward TOC at Dak To, which would also continue to house the TACP (Tactical Air Control Party) for DASC Alpha of the 7th Air Force. Command of U.S. Artillery forces physically located at Ben Het was assigned to LTC Kenneth R. Bailey, present commander of 6/14. LTC Bailey was also assigned the responsibility of coordinating all fires for the defense of Ben Het. In addition, LTC Bailey was ordered to close out his battalion's forward TOC at LZ Mary Lou in Kontum City and to relocate it at Ben Het.

(See Figure 8-1.) He was also given the requirement to establish a targeting section. Following receipt of the orders as outlined above, LTC Bailey took the following action.

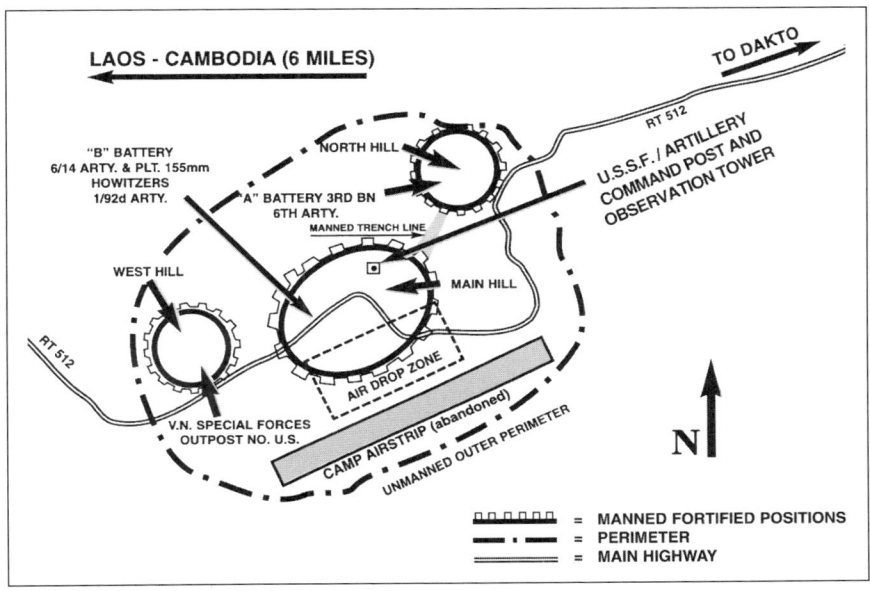

FIGURE 8-1   United States 5th Special Forces Camp Ben Het during the siege of June, 1969.

I was called to the battalion headquarters, where I was briefed on the full details of the situation that had just developed. LTC Bailey apologized to me for having to include me in the initial plans, as I had already been incountry for seven months and I was scheduled to go to Sydney, Australia, on R&R (rest and recuperation)[2] within just a few days. Colonel Bailey was a stickler for following the USARV regulation when it came to the R&R program. "Sergeant Lamerson," he explained, "I know that you are scheduled for R&R. However, I have no choice other than to take you to Ben Het with me. Your assigned task is to set up a targeting section. Once it is set up and running properly, you can return to Pleiku in time to fulfill your R&R reservation commitment." (If you were guilty of missing the reservations without the proper excuse, there was the possibility of forfeiting your entitlement.)

I was then directed to pack up the S-2's two and one-half ton van with all of the appropriate equipment, including a sufficient supply of new map sheets of the designated area. "Be prepared to depart Artillery Hill first thing tomorrow morning," Colonel Bailey instructed me.

The first thing I did was to notify the Headquarters Battery first sergeant of my new duty requirement. I was required to forfeit my assigned quarters. However, the first sergeant volunteered to look after my personal items, which I would have to leave behind. I had a collection of captured enemy weapons and enemy artillery shrapnel that I used for instructional purposes, and there were a few other small items for personal comfort, as well. I then returned to the TOC, briefed my Specialist 5 S-2 clerk, who would be staying behind and, with his help, we loaded out the S-2 van. Included on the van was a small refrigerator to which I owned the majority of the ownership rights. I then returned to my quarters and wrote a nice long letter to my wife and children. It went something like this:

Dear Mavis and girls,

This may be the last time that you will hear from me for awhile. I have been ordered to the boonies. I'm going to a place called Ben Het. It's no big deal, so don't worry, OK!

All my Love,
John D.

I had no reason to think otherwise. Sure, I was aware of the danger of moving to a "hot spot," but all of South Vietnam was a dangerous place to be. So, I just blew off this upcoming operation as routine.

When the 0800 hours convoy left the convoy checkpoint just outside our perimeter wire the next morning, I was driving the two and one-half ton S-2 van, as we made our way north up Highway QL 14 toward Kontum City. Colonel Bailey had given our people at LZ Mary Lou their instructions. We would be there to help them close out and load up the Forward TOC for movement to Ben Het.

The trip was moving without incident until we got about halfway to Kontum. The brakes on the truck froze up, so I pulled it over to the shoulder of the road. Within just moments, the rest of the convoy disappeared out of sight. After a couple more minutes, an MP jeep bringing up the rear pulled up. An MP sergeant jumped out and asked me what was wrong. "Breaks froze up," I exclaimed. "Have you got your OVM side-cutters handy?" he asked me. I had my tool bag laying right on the seat beside me, so I pulled out the side-cutters and handed them to him. He crawled beneath the vehicle, cut the brake line, crawled out, and handing the tool back to me. He exclaimed, "Get the hell out of here fast! This spot is zeroed in by enemy mortar crews!" He did not have to tell me more. I gunned the hell out of the engine as I raced to catch up with the convoy. Incidentally, that proved to be the only convoy that I was required to travel with during my entire tour of duty. I caught up with the convoy just as it entered the outskirts of Kontum City. Following Lt. Colonel Bailey's jeep as it peeled off towards LZ Mary Lou, I finally became concerned about my ability to stop the truck when the need arose. Nothing happened until I was required to turn off onto a small dirt road leading into C Battery, 6/14 Artillery at LZ Mary Lou.

I saw the 175mm gun tube sticking out across the road but I was unable to prevent the collision of the van box against the gun tube. Thud! Wham! Bumpity-bang! Thud! "Oh crap!" I muttered. "Now I'll have to fill out a damn accident report, as if I don't already have enough to do!" I grumbled to myself. When I caught up with the Colonel, I explained the accident to him. "Wait until we get to Ben Het to fill out the report," he instructed me.

It was now midafternoon. I got with the assistant operations sergeant at LZ Mary Lou, Staff Sergeant Pate, to determine help he needed from me in reference to packing up the TOC equipment. As we worked, Pate asked me, "You like steak, Sarge?" "Hell yes!" I answered. "Well," Pate continued, "The 2d of the 4th ID Brigade Headquarters ration breakdown is right next door. They couldn't deliver all of their rations to a couple of hot spots, so I was able to scrounge the makings of a steak and tossed green salad dinner for tonight!" Pate pointed to a homemade horizontal half of a 55-gallon drum charcoal grill that was setting just outside the TOC. "I'll get us each a couple of beers to go along with our meal," he said. (At the fire bases, the daily ration of beer per man was two. Hard liquor was prohibited at artillery fire base outposts). We enjoyed our fine meal prior to retiring for the night. We were scheduled to marry up with the convoy from Pleiku by early afternoon the following day.

Following morning chow, Staff Sergeant Pate invited me to take a little trip with him. I climbed aboard the jeep that he was driving and he drove us to downtown Kontum. Hell, it was only about 0900 hours. After driving around for a bit, Pate stopped the jeep in front of a small building. "Come on, Sarge," he said, getting out of the jeep. I got out. I followed Pate as we both passed through an open doorway. Once inside, I realized that we were in a waiting area. After a few moments, an old Vietnamese "Mama San" came into the little room. Pate greeted her and she, in turn, called out something in Vietnamese. A young Vietnamese girl, about 18 to 20 years old, appeared. Pate ordered two beers and the girl led us into an adjoining room where she directed us to a small, low oriental table. There were pillows for seating, so we sat down. The girl disappeared, but a few minutes later she returned with our beer.

Pate got up, told me to stay put, and stepped back out of the room. I could hear him as he talked with the old "Mama San." I figured he was bartering with her because I heard the mention of two or three cartons of cigarettes. (At Pleiku, things were far more restricted. We were not authorized to go ramming around on our own. Perhaps I was naïve, but I don't think such goings on were as prevalent as in Kontum.) In any case, within a couple of minutes, a young Vietnamese maiden (I use the term loosely) entered the room and quickly approached my table. As I took a slug of beer from the bottle, the girl's robe fell to the floor. Standing there in the dimly lit room, she appeared to be quite beautiful. I was astounded. Hell, I did not dare, even had I wanted to, take a chance on catching a venereal disease. I extracted my wallet from my hip pocket and flipped a flap in the wallet open, which exposed a picture of my four small daughters. I put my finger to my mouth as I signaled for her to "shush." She nodded in understanding about my refusal to engage in intercourse. She re-robed, sat for a few minutes, and then left. A bit later, Pate returned and asked me, " What did you think of that, huh?" I just smiled, but said nothing.

We climbed aboard the jeep and Pate drove us back to LZ Mary Lou. One of the assistant S-3 lieutenants was awaiting our return. We were not late for the convoy but in our absence, all hell had broken loose. "Where have you sergeants been?" The lieutenant demanded to know. Pate gave some lame excuse that seemed to satisfy the young officer, who, in turn, explained the change in the situation.

"The enemy has cut the roads from Kontum City to Ben Het. Convoy travel has been curtailed until further notice. We have been able to snag a Huey Slick for the purpose of inserting our people into Ben Het. The Colonel and Major Waukahiro (the S-3) have already left. Sergeant Lamerson, you will be flown in on the next sortie. You are ordered to take two of our RTOs in with you. Furthermore, except for two map boards and a supply of maps, you are not to take anything else aboard the chopper other than your toilet articles, shaving cream, and your individual TOE equipment (weapons, gas mask, etc.). The chopper is already on its way back. Grab your gear and stand by."

Wump! Wump! Wump! I heard the distinctive sound of the Huey Slick's engine as the pilot brought the aircraft to a low hover a few feet away. Once our equipment was pushed aboard, all three of us climbed aboard as well. A door gunner shouted into my ear. "The pilot is going to take some special evasive flight action once we get as far as Dak To. When we land, treat this as a combat assault. That is to say, take up a covering position to protect the aircraft once you're on the ground. As soon as your men get your equipment unloaded, they, too, will take up defensive positions."

I replied in the affirmative; I understood. As we passed over Dak To, the pilot took the helicopter down to an altitude of only several feet above the water of the fast flowing Dak Poko River. We were flying westerly and following the path of the river; the vegetation above us on the riverbanks whizzed by. The enemy would have to really be on the ball to get a shot at us. A sudden rise in altitude allowed the pilot to maneuver the aircraft over the Dak Mot Bridge where it spanned Highway 512 a few "clicks" (kilometers) out of Ben Het. He then dropped the ship back down near the surface of the water. Suddenly our pilot maneuvered us out of the river path and we descended into Ben Het's Main Hill compound. The pilot put the Huey into a low hover over the 5th U.S. Special Force A-Detachment's helipad.

Following instructions, clutching my M-14 Rifle, I jumped out and hit the ground running while in a low crouch. I ran for several paces to the north before I stopped, whirled, and took up a stationary, crouched position from where I could observe the Huey Slick as it remained in a low hover. Looking toward the south in the direction of the camp perimeter wire, I watched my two RTOs as they reached into the chopper in an attempt to retrieve the map boards and maps. In an instant with no warning, the first 60mm mortar shell impacted just meters south of the chopper. At almost the same instant, I witnessed as my two RTOs were thrown clear as the Huey Slick lifted off and away to safety. I called to my two men to follow me. There was an unmanned ARVN tank setting nearby. The three of us took refuge behind that tank as we waited for the mortar ABF to cease. (I say behind the tank, on the north side, because the perimeter was to the south. I considered the enemy mortar to be firing from the south.) Once the all clear was sounded, I received verbal instructions from the top of the hill. I was directed to a hole in the wire where a path leading up to the SF complex was available.

Once again, I commanded my two RTOs to follow and all three of us ran at a crouch with our weapons at port arms. Married and the father of four children, I was proud to have been able to get to the top of the hill well ahead of the other two. I was 37, and they were in their teens or early twenties. When we got to the top of the hill and had reached the safety of the heavily fortified bunker complex of the A-Detachment, Lt. Colonel Bailey was there to greet us. He then called me aside for a quick briefing on the immediate changes affecting our mission. "First off, we are attached to the 5th Special Forces A-Detachment for rations and quarters. However, they do not have room for our whole group of people." He then explained that we would have to seek a place to "bunk out" wherever there was room.

Meanwhile, the helipad at the Main Hill was closed to further traffic into Ben Het. The other team members would have to come by convoy at a later date. Ben Het Camp occupied a total of three hills. Main Hill, North Hill, and West Hill made up the complete camp. There was little I could do immediately because I had none of the equipment that I needed to establish the targeting section. Now, I even lacked the maps that I had brought with me to Ben Het. They were still on the chopper when it took evasive action during that mortar attack. I was introduced to the key members of the A-Detachment. The top noncoms were Master Sergeant Trout and a SFC Thomas (I think that was his last name), who was the A-Team Intelligence Sergeant. "I have been ordered to make room for you to establish your targeting section in my portion of the TOC," he grumbled. Still, he dutifully showed me to the area. It was a small room, maybe 8′ × 12′. Since I could not find space in the TOC for me to bunk down, I spent the rest of the day familiarizing myself with my new surroundings. I visited B Battery, 6/14. I could bunk out down there, but I was reluctant to do so. Ben Het, as I have already stated, had been bombarded by enemy artillery since early February. They had taken uninterrupted fire on a daily basis for over the past month. Therefore, walking around on the Main Hill compound, especially during darkness, was almost as dangerous as walking through a minefield.

Army engineers had not been able to send an EOD team into the camp, which was seeded quite liberally with "dud" enemy ammunition. These dud shells were very unstable and sensitive to being bumped or kicked. With such danger in mind, I decided to try the SF TOC. Since the SF personnel had their quarters at the opposite end of the bunker complex, I knew that there was no reason why I could not sleep in my designated working space. There was a small aisleway where I had to stand in order to post my map and briefing board. I had brought a medical stretcher aboard the truck, but it was back at LZ Mary Lou in Kontum. The first night I slept on the dirt floor of the mostly earth and log bunker. The TOC end of the SF bunker complex boasted over three feet of reinforced concrete as part of the overall 15 feet of overhead cover. There was a large fan in the middle of the small room, which I was thankful for as it kept the malaria-carrying mosquitoes off while I slept. Rats were still a hazard that I would have to face. If you were bitten, you automatically qualified for receiving a series of painful rabies shots. In those days, the rabies shot was administered through the stomach (so I was always told). In any case, no one wanted to be bitten by a rat. Of course, there were many other natural dangers, like poisonous snakes, banana spiders, and many more.

My first full day at Ben Het during the June fighting commenced with a trip to the SF latrine at the Main Hill compound. I had always envied the resourcefulness of the Special Forces troops. Here at Ben Het was this elaborate latrine, fitted out with porcelain sinks and commodes with running water. They even had showers. Well, that was before the enemy shelling. Now, all that remained was a shrapnel-riddled mess of broken sinks and commodes. To make matters worse, some of the ARVN soldiers and CIDG still tried to use the facility. By the time I first entered it, it was a stinking cesspool of human waste and urine. Hell, it was bad enough to gag a maggot. I was forced to hold out until the following evening, after dark. There was no slit trench latrine, so one had to do one's best to dig a hole and cover it. Of course, you knew that the next exploding enemy shell was apt to uncover and scatter the contents of these deposits of human waste.

Potable water was in very short supply. However, the monsoons were starting up in northwestern Kontum Province. One of the SF team members rotated out and left me his canvas cot. Except for the fact that I would have to fold it up each morning and stow it away for the day, I appreciated having the luxury of being able to sleep off the ground. Of course, my duty day was suddenly changed from 18 to 20 hours. Later, some of my days were 22 to 24 hours long.

I ate my next breakfast in the A-Detachment mess. Following breakfast, accompanied by a young buck sergeant who had been assigned the task of being my assistant, I toured the complete three-hill camp. My primary purpose was to take a close look at the perimeter defenses and to check out all available firepower that was physically at Ben Het:

- 6, 105mm, self-propelled howitzers
- 2, 155mm, towed howitzers
- 4, 175mm, self-propelled guns
- 1, M-106 jeep, mounted recoilless rifle (5th SF, but assigned to the CIDG over on west hill)
- 2, M-41 tanks, (3d ARVN Cavalry)
- 1, 81mm, mortar tube (5th SF)

Following this inventory of all available firepower, I made some special recommendations in reference to my observations:

- ♦ Change one of the 175mm guns back over to an 8-inch howitzer
- ♦ Take into account that the platoon of 155mm howitzers had a very limited field of fire, which for safety reasons, could not be helped
- ♦ Tie the two ARVN tanks (platoon) into the camp perimeter defenses, and finally
- ♦ Establish an artillery OP (observation post)

The following described action was taken on the above recommendations.

LTC Bailey and I discussed the fact that the monsoon weather prohibited the 7th U.S. Air Force from rendering TAC air support for the camp defense during periods of early morning fog, which blanketed the area and seldom cleared before noon. To counter this lack of air support, we had to insure that an artillery fire plan was in place that would provide 24-hour protection for Ben Het's defense. The enemy guns firing from their concealed cave positions over in Laos and Cambodia would have to be attacked by artillery counter-battery fire. The only weapon available to us that had the necessary range and accuracy was the 8-inch howitzer. So, that issue was settled and Bailey ordered the conversion of one of the 175mm guns of B/6/14 to an 8-inch howitzer. Next, we again considered the restricted field of fire for the 155mm platoon of howitzers of the 1/92nd Artillery Battalion. The original purpose for their presence at Ben Het was to cover the enemy-held abandoned U.S. 4th ID Firebase 29, where the 40th NVA Artillery Regiment had some of their elements entrenched and threatening Ben Het. The 155mm howitzer emplacements were well fortified and it would have been suicide to attempt to change these positions.

The ARVN Tank Platoon was not under the SF A-Team's jurisdiction or ours. All we could do was ask the tank platoon commander to support our perimeter defense plan. Without explanation, he refused to do so. I assumed that he was holding back in case our position was overrun by the enemy forces. He would then have a means of breaking out and running down Highway 512 to the east. This caused a mild rift for the moment. LTC Bailey and I concurred on the fact that the Special Forces Observation Tower that stood next to the southwest corner of the TOC would serve our purpose well for the establishment of an artillery OP. The next step was for Bailey to order one of his battalion survey parties into Ben Het on the next available (transportation) for the purpose of supplying us with modified or field-type survey data for pinpointing the tower's exact map location. This was important, because the copies (translated into English) of maps of the area were old error-riddled French maps. Sergeant First Class Stanley's survey team was picked for the job and soon arrived in Ben Het on the first convoy, since ours has been canceled a couple of days or so before.

During those first two days, I spent a lot of time just getting my bearings and checking out the area. I spent time in the tower. I had my artillery binoculars and M-2 compass with me and used them to assist me in pinpointing some reference points on my map of the area. These were then recorded for my future use. The convoy was finally able to break through to Ben Het, and my two and one-half ton truck pulling the water trailer (full of 250 gallons of potable water) was with it. SFC Stanley and the survey team also made it in with that convoy. They set to work immediately and by nightfall we had our survey data to the tower. The convoy people had spent the night, so Stanley and his crew were able to return to Pleiku with them. Aboard my truck was my full supply of maps, the BC Scope (Battery Commanders Scope—a special periscope-type instrument with telescopic lens used to observe the battlefield, without exposing one's head), and my newly acquired Night Lighting Device (big starlight scope). These were taken up into the tower. The tower would become my second daylight home for awhile. I was now prepared to assume the duties of the camp's only artillery forward observer. I was assigned an RTO to work with me as necessary. We had a choice of radios. We could use the PRC-25 or the PRC-77 (the 77 was secure). Most of the time we chose to use the PRC-25 (Prick), because it was lighter and did not require the use of codes to operate it.

The tower was to become a dangerous place to be, although the ground was very unsafe as well. I found out right off that the driveway between hills was extremely dangerous as well, because the enemy soldiers could come in real close in those two locations. Therefore, we avoided travel between compounds as much as possible. A bit earlier, the SF engineers had dug some large entrenchments into the sides of the hill. These cuts provided a protected area to move our vehicles into for safety against enemy artillery. Within 48 hours after my truck with the attached water trailer was parked in one of those trenches, they were both destroyed by enemy fire. Our precious potable water was gone. The only good thing that came of that disaster was I didn't have to make out an accident report. My map board was set up in the TOC on the first day because I was able to borrow some maps and the board from the A-Team. I took time to cover the maps with acetate. With a black grease pencil, I drew a series of large circles on the map of the whole area surrounding Ben Het. The center of the smallest circle represented the observation tower—and the maximum range of the enemy 60mm mortars. The second circle represented the 82mm mortar; the third and fourth circles, the 57mm and 75mm recoilless rifles, respectively; the fifth circle, the 120mm mortar, and the sixth and final of the series of circles represented the 85mm Russian field gun. Now, any time one of those types of enemy weapons fired, I could perform crater analysis or actual sightings to locate the enemy weapon's position. Counterbattery fire could then be called against these enemy weapons with a great degree of accuracy due to the firing data.

I was at a point that would allow me to depart for R&R transportation connections out of Pleiku. That proved not to be on my agenda any longer.

The Situation: Unknown to the Defenders of Ben Het

Personnel at Ben Het was now comprised of the following forces:

- The three-man KB Team on temporary duty at Ben Het (SF)
- The 12-man SF A-Team
- 180 U.S. Army Artillerymen
- 400 CIDG
- The ARVN LLDB (SF counterpart to U.S. SF)
- The ARVN tank platoon personnel

The total force numbered under seven hundred fighting men. The Allied conservative estimates for the enemy, which were totally misleading, ranged from 1,000 to 2,000 NVA Infantrymen.

Note: An average strength for an NVA Infantry Regiment was from 2,000 to 2500 men. By my simple arithmetic, the 28th and 66th NVA Infantry Regiments alone could number up to a 5,000-man fighting force.

Not shared with us was a 7th U.S. Air Force CHECO Report, dated March 1969, in reference to the use of U.S. Air Assets. Also unknown to us from the onset was Colonel Nguyen Ba Lien's philosophy on the enemy situation and how he planned to solve the problems it posed to his command. Lien had his own intelligence sources, in which he (not the Americans) placed full trust. Knowing that he had suffered severe combat losses during the May fighting, which had been heavily downplayed by Allied officials out of Nha Trang and Saigon, he relied on his own intelligence reports. The reports indicated the presence of a much more powerful enemy force in the area than was being supplied by the Allied command.

Based on such intelligence information, Lien made the following decision: He determined that his forces were too small to cope with the superiority of the enemy numbers. Therefore, he would adhere to the standard practice used by U.S. Allied commanders. American generals such as Westmoreland, Abrams, and Rosson, among others, used the tactic of creating giant killing fields. These fields were where the enemy would be drawn to mass, so that the superior U.S. artillery and air assets could be used to destroy them. The killing fields were used to create a trap by using Allied troops as bait. It must be noted that author Samuel Zaffiri in his book, *Westmoreland,* explains the above noted tactic:

> Westmoreland failed to mention two other reasons why he wanted to keep the base at Khe Sanh, which was to serve as bait to draw Giap into a showdown and later hopefully as a staging area for an assault on the Ho Chi Minh Trail.[3]

What he always wanted, they felt, was to set up a giant killing field at Khe Sanh and then, using the Marines as bait, to entice the North Vietnamese Army into entering it. When they did, he would turn loose his artillery, jet fighter-bombers, and B-52s and pulverize them; thereby producing the big World War II-type victory that he so badly wanted. Being used as bait did not set well with the Marines.[4]

We, at Ben Het, were not informed as to why the ARVN had not re-deployed to the field. According to the USAF CHECO Report of 1 October 1969:

> ... The South Vietnamese did not counterattack and the siege tightened. In previous situations such as this, American troops had rushed to the relief of the beleaguered installations, but at Ben Het they did not, because it lay in an Area of Operation (AO) recently turned over to ARVN. The U.S. commanders did not want to give credence to the view that South Vietnamese could not or would not cope with the VC/NVA. Further, the tactic of using airpower to defend an isolated camp was a standard one that reduced friendly casualties by using ordnance instead of troops to destroy a massed enemy.5

It had been nearly a week since our "Phantom Gunnery Team" had been inserted into Ben Het. The reason I refer to it as a Phantom Gunnery Team is because our arrival was kept at a low profile; as the situation developed our presence and mission were never officially recognized. Within the next 48 hours, I, along with other key personnel, would come to realize the true gravity of our perilous position. I came to the conclusion that this was no ordinary operation when, on 11 June 1969, I witnessed the following incident. I later wrote up a recommendation for an Award of Valor containing, in part, the following information:

> While performing duties of observation from the SF Tower at Ben Het on 11 June 1969, I was in a position to watch a water supply detail leave the compound. A security force accompanied the water truck.
> Approximately two thirds of the way to the water point, the truck received a B-40 rocket round by the enemy. The truck continued on for a short distance, where the wounded were taken off. The security force was trying to withdraw to the perimeter with their wounded; the camp came under intense enemy artillery fire.
> I observed Sfc. Thomas J. Scoppa, RA 20-320-487, of the special forces KB team, rush to a ¼-ton vehicle, and without regard to his personal protection or well being, proceeded out of the camp and all the way out to the security force area of contact and recover the wounded. It was necessary for him to make a return trip to get all of the wounded in.

It was at that very point in time, that I made a critical decision. Realizing that the enemy had Ben Het surrounded, the water point now cut off, and the roads into Ben Het interdicted, I knew that I was needed at Ben Het if we were ever to get out of that place alive. So I marched right out of the tower and looked up my commanding officer, LTC Bailey. Addressing the colonel, I began to speak. "Sir, I've made a decision to ask for your permission to cancel my R&R plans to Sydney." I continued, "Sir, you need me here. This is what I came to Vietnam to do. Fight. Besides, it's as dangerous trying to catch a chopper out of here as it is to stay." As previously stated, the Main Hill chopper pad was closed for the duration following my arrival. Now the only pad open at Ben Het was on the North Hill compound. Colonel Bailey spoke. "Well, if that's what you want, OK." He did not need to say another word, because I could tell that he was happy and relieved about to my decision to stay.

The very next day I was in the Special Forces Tactical Operations Center. The team house above took a direct hit. The incident gave me the rest of the "ammunition" I needed to justify the write-up of Sfc. Scoppa for a Valor Award. My recommendation quoted in part above is continued here:

> The next day, while everyone else was running for cover, Sfc Scoppa was proceeding top side to check out the team house for wounded personnel. Such unselfish actions on the part of Sfc. Scoppa bring great credit upon himself and the United States Army. I therefore, recommend Sfc. Scoppa be awarded the Silver Star for Valor.

I received a copy of my signed statement along with a note dated 11 July 1969, from the CO of the 31st Engineers and was signed: G. E. Dooley, Cpt. Inf., Adj. B–24 (detachment).

Following the 11 June water point detail ambush that had in effect cut off our fresh water supply, it was realized that we could not survive long in the jungle heat without water. We turned to the U.S. Air Force for relief. An aerial re-supply mission was requested.

Note: No one explained to the Air Force people that the air strip at Ben Het had been abandoned as untenable and the perimeter pulled in to the north of it.

Notes

1 Tim Page and John Pimlott, eds., *Nam: The Vietnam Experience, 1965–75,* (New York, Barnes & Noble, Inc., 1995), 330.

2 Linda Reinberg, *In the Field: The Language of the Vietnam War,* (New York: Facts on File, Inc., 1991), 183.

3 Samuel Zaffiri, *Westmoreland: A Biography of General William C. Westmoreland,* (New York: William Morrow and Company, Inc., 1994), 273.

4 Ibid., 270–76.

5 U.S. Air Force, CHECO Division, *The Siege of Ben Het,* prepared by Ernie S. Montagliani, (1 October 1969), xi–xii.

CHAPTER 9

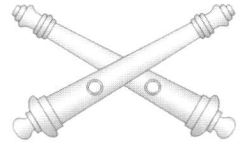

The Siege of Ben Het

*They've got us surrounded again,
the poor bastards.*
Lieutenant Colonel Creighton Abrams during
the Battle of the Bulge, 1944

PART II

Airlift and TAC Air Support

Convoys attempting to keep Ben Het resupplied by way of Highway 512 were destroyed, disabled, or driven off. The enemy completely controlled the ground environment in the area because the ARVN refused to mount an offensive counteraction against them.

Except for a small number of Mobile Strike Force (MSF) patrols and those forces manning Fire Support Bases (FSBs), the area did not contain any friendly troops seeking the enemy. Thus, the responsibility for the defense of Ben Het in June fell squarely on the shoulders of American artillery and the U.S. 7th Air Force. The ARVN contribution of artillery and air assets was minimal. U.S. air assets were called upon to protect the perimeter along with U.S. artillery. The U.S. Tactical Airlift Wing stationed at Pleiku received the mission of keeping Ben Het resupplied by airdrop delivery systems. The TAC Air support organizations were required to continue with their massive air support program throughout the 24th STZ.

I find it necessary to discuss the limitations of overall air support of Ben Het. During June, the weather had changed. The monsoon settled over the western highlands, blanketing the 24th STZ with fog in the morning and thunder showers in the afternoon. The FACs could operate in the periods of acceptable weather, but when it became marginal CSS (Combat Sky Spot) was needed as a backup. If an attack were to be successfully launched, it would have to come through a curtain of fire either ringed around the camp from the air or laid down by U.S. and ARVN artillery units, which were located at surrounding area fire support bases. One thing remains very clear; neither air, nor artillery alone could get the job done. Neither could provide enough fire support.

DASC Alpha planned to use the CSS program extensively to compliment the FAC-directed strikes around the camp. "Bongo," an MSQ-77 radar site located at Pleiku was the only radar station installation near enough to be effective in placing ordnance accurately in the Ben Het area, and there was no alternative site. This fact posed a question: What would happen if the site were knocked out or failed for some reason? In an attempt to answer the question, low key discussions were conducted at the Operations Division, Headquarters, 7th Air Force. Colonel E.W. Rosencrans, spokesman for the Operations Division, explained. He indicated that we could have moved another site from somewhere else in SEA (South East Asia), or we could have one shipped over from CONUS (Continental United States). "We discussed other possibilities, using a Marine TPQ-10, for one. U.S. Marine personnel here indicated that a TPQ site could be airlifted in four C-130s, and could be operational in from 12 to 30 hours after arriving ... . We also considered the use of the A-6/Beacon system and Commando Nail. (Airborne Radar Bombing) ... ."[1]

LTC T.A. Crawford of DASC Alpha also noted that Bongo had no backup: "This would have been a situation for the A-6/Beacon system. We could have used an additional capability of some type. To give us not only a backup, but also an alternate so we could be working in close to Ben Het and on interdiction at the same time. Luckily, all of II Corps was quiet at this time ... We discussed with TACC, informally, the use of a TPQ-10 Site ... ."[2]

The fact that Bongo was also directing the many Arc Light (B-52) sorties in the area had an effect on its ability to handle CSS, as Colonel Crawford pointed out: If we had Arc Light going in, we couldn't put in Sky Spot at the same time. Bongo is set up so they have a sterile period before Arc Light ... The strike would take 20 to 30 minutes to get off, so for each Arc Light that went in, we lost an hour and a half.[3]

"The use of CSS was widespread around Ben Het, especially during bad weather conditions and at night. In early June, targets were hit about 1,100 to 2,000 meters away from the camp, and later the CSS strikes were flown as close as 500 meters. The missions directed as close as 500 meters required special procedures. In these cases, DASC Alpha would call TACP at Dak To, who would then call the ground Commander in Ben Het. The DASC would explain the limitations of CSS, and then ask him if he would accept the responsibility. The ground commander answered in the affirmative in each case."[4]

The above information must be used as a guide in following the rest of the story on the siege.

It became quite obvious to me that the higher-ups did not truly appreciate the gravity of our situation on the ground at Ben Het. Hell, there was no way we would have been able to win without Bongo. As far as CSS is concerned, I was personally involved in the close-in use of it. In one case, we were able to use a single B-52 bomber in a close-in CSS role. Too, we used one close-in LZ clearing system, known as Daisy Cutter, to wipe out a nasty nest of enemy snipers.

During fog and bad weather, as well as at night, we used artillery fire to suppress enemy activity. The main point that I must make clear is that when an isolated and lightly manned camp like Ben Het is faced with the perils that we were, unorthodox methods of defense must be employed. When all of the defense assets are being deployed, the whole battlefield scene becomes "surreal." We employed the full spectrum of our available assets. Airlift, TAC Air, Strategic Air and Artillery Support all came together in one grand effort for defense of the besieged SF Camp.

In my role as the artillery S-2, targeting section OIC, and as an FO, I was in a unique position that allowed me to observe the whole scene from a perspective different from that of any one other individual serving on the ground at Ben Het.

While conducting artillery forward observation duties out of the observation tower, I often became involved in the coordination of tactical air support missions. I had the choice of calling in the artillery or requesting that the mission be supported by air delivered firepower. I first had to assess the situation and determine the best course of action open to me. However, if there were aircraft on station overhead and a FAC was available, it was usually advantageous and speedier to use air assets. In most cases, I worked hand in hand with the FAC (via radio) to coordinate fire on SELs or known enemy locations.

I recall one such FAC-controlled mission. The camp was receiving murderous fire from a well-camouflaged 75mm recoilless rifle position just south of the camp. I was in the tower. We had a pair of "fast movers" overhead with no ongoing air strike. I called up a FAC, who responded to my request for support. He was over the target area within seconds. I was talking to him in the clear. I directed his attention to where I had determined the enemy weapon to be firing. He responded. " I see them!" He then marked the target with a WP (white phosphorous) rocket. "Hell," I muttered. "He is two hundred meters off the target." The jets came in and the pilots pickled their bombs, hitting right on the marked target. I complained to the FAC. "Hey, you were 200 meters off the coordinates I gave you!" He came back with, "Well, when I looked at the point on the ground you gave me, I saw three dinks running across an open area. Two of them were holding on to a long black pole-looking thing and the other one was carrying what looked like a tripod. What do we get credit for?" I answered him, "End of mission, recoilless rifle silenced, estimate 3 enemy KBA (killed by air). Thanks, out." A lot of our Tactical Air assets were fragged to support the many C-7 Caribou TOTs (Time On Target) airlift missions that were required to keep Ben Het resupplied. See Figure 9-1.

FIGURE 9-1 C-7 Caribou, the main cargo transport during the early days of the Vietnam War.

Airlift played a critical role in the defense of Ben Het. One feature of the enemy's plan was to isolate the camp on the ground and deny it logistical support. Because the small airstrip at Ben Het had been determined to be untenable, it was abandoned and lay outside the camp's outer perimeter wire. Actually, Highway 512 ran along its axis just north of the strip. The Main Hill compound entrance was located on the north side of 512 as well.

Resupply by C-7 (Caribou) airdrop countered this portion of the enemy's plan. They brought everything from fresh water to ammunition and food, and once started, continued until the siege was lifted. As I recall, the first airdrop was scheduled for 12 June 1969. The water detail, ambushed on 11 June, triggered the first request by the senior advisor and ground commander who was the A-Detachment Team Leader. The 250-gallon water trailer that we hauled in behind my two and one-half ton truck had already been destroyed by enemy artillery fire, so the A-Team commander had requested an immediate resupply by airdrop.

The initial resupply flight was led into Ben Het air space by a U.S. Air Force Forward Air Controller. The flight was made without any tactical air support being used for escort duty. This caused a problem in the area of security as explained earlier. ALO, Lt. Col. Jack Cude Jr., who was flying as the FAC, also noted that there was a problem with the first drop missing the desired drop zone.

"In the airlift situation, the FACs were the number one coordinator. The area was small. The first drop I directed and the Caribou dropped the load right on the ramp. I thought that he was right on the ball. But, the strip was outside the perimeter, and the man on the ground said that they would get someone killed trying to go out and get that stuff. That was strange, the strip being outside the camp, but that's how it was."[5] I am sure that it was me who told the colonel that the supplies were partially unrecoverable. Colonel Cude, who had arrived at Dak To on 18 May, had no knowledge of the abandonment of the Ben Het airstrip. I find this lack of communication upsetting. But that is the type of thing that causes operation foul-ups.

I remember well my day of duty on 12 June 1969. My workday started at dawn each morning. At Ben Het, I slept fully clothed. At dawn I would get up, move topside, where I would make my way out of the TOC and enter a small revetment at the base of the observation tower. There was a "piss tube" (field expedient urinal) located there. The PSP (pierced steel planking) walls of the revetment stood no more than four and one-half feet high. I had acquired a dangerous habit in the time that I'd been at Ben Het. I would always observe the area to the south while relieving myself each morning at dawn. On 12 June, I followed that same routine. I was hunched down to lessen the exposure of my helmeted head. However, my eyes were level with the top of the parapet wall of the revetment. I had just unbuttoned my fly and was still in the process of relieving myself, while, at the same time, training my eyes on the jungle growth just south of the airstrip. "Zing!" The enemy sniper bullet, which passed a "millimeter" from my left ear, sounded like the buzz that mad hornets make just before they attack. "Damn," I muttered as I realized just how close I'd just come to buying the farm. I could do no more at the moment but finish my business.

I once more observed the area to the south and speculated about the location of the enemy sniper. I reckoned his nest to be located in the camp garbage dump, which was on the south side of the abandoned airstrip. It was in line with the center of the strip.

My next priority was morning chow. I went to the A-Detachment mess hall and ate breakfast before retrieving my field gear from the TOC. My field gear included my 45-caliber automatic pistol, binoculars, and M-2 compass. Of course, I always carried my special arrangement of field maps.

I mounted the ladder to the observation tower and made the climb to the floor hatch (trapdoor). I entered the tower platform, organized my equipment, and then prepared an artillery fire mission. The selected target was the garbage dump. I requested high explosive (HE) shells armed with delayed time fuzes. These would burrow deeply and detonate below the surface of the ground. The FDC (Fire Direction Center) alerted a 155mm-howitzer battery for the fire mission. Once I adjusted the center platoon of the battery guns onto the target, I called for Fire for Effect! I then had the battery move their settings so as to enable repeat FFEs to work the whole target area over with the deadly accurate and usually effective artillery fire. I recall that we had an unusually high percentage of "duds" that day. In any case I finally called for End of Mission! Area harassment mission successful. I then continued to perform routine FO duties. We had already been told that we were to receive our requested airdrop by 1230 hours. Word was next received that in conjunction with the airdrop, a convoy was on the road. The convoy would attempt to run the enemy roadblocks so that they would arrive at Ben Het during the airdrop. This tactic was designed to confuse the enemy, who we hoped would lose their concentration as they focused their fires on the C-7 Caribous.

To carry out this extensive resupply operation would require a high degree of professional coordination. LTC Bailey had our people in the TOC notify me that he was on his way to the tower to supervise the upcoming resupply operation. Present with me in the tower at that moment was my RTO. LTC Bailey was accompanied by two of his assistant S-3s, a captain and a lieutenant. The tower space was very limited, so it was now overcrowded. We had been eating cold C-rations for a couple of days, due to a shortage of rations caused by the present enemy situation. Each man, prior to mounting the tower, had been issued his lunch rations for 12 June. Since we were expecting a 1230 hours airdrop, we decided to eat a bit before noon. LTC Bailey, a West Point graduate, was not one to play the role as "one of the boys." This is not to say that he lacked a sense of humor, but he closely followed the code of military bearing. So, I was mildly surprised when he made the following, joking remark as we were eating our meager rations of cold Cs. "You can't beat this, hey Lambo? All the comforts of home." (Lambo was one of two nicknames given to me by the battalion sergeant major back in Pleiku; the second nickname was "Point Man".) Before I could reply, Colonel Bailey removed his steel helmet momentarily to scratch his head. Within another split second, my sixth sense kicked in and I instinctively ducked down. Whump! The enemy mortar round exploded near the tower base. When I looked up following the explosion of the enemy incoming fire, I saw Colonel Bailey clutching at the back of his head. I pulled his hand away so that I could examine his wound. Shrapnel wounds often appear to be worse than they are, however, head wounds must never be taken lightly. I could not tell the extent of Colonel Bailey's head wound. I decided that he would have to be helped out of the tower and taken to the TOC for medical attention. I asked Captain Eno, the assistant S-3, to have everyone help me get him out of the tower. I had some rope in the tower that was used for pulling up items, such as ammunition boxes. We tied one end of the rope to Colonel Bailey's waist and lowered him from the tower. I exited the tower first in order to lead Bailey down the ladder to the ground below. Our luck held and no more mortar rounds hit close enough to harm us during the evacuation. I helped the Colonel to the TOC where a medic was available to take over. I returned to my duty station in the tower.

My duty position as the Battalion S-2 placed me in command of the scheduled ground control of the resupply operation. As soon as I returned to the tower, I discovered that all of the others had received minor shrapnel wounds as well. Captain Eno, the assistant S-3, even though wearing his steel helmet, received wounds to his neck just behind his ear. My RTO had received his second wound to date, and the other officer also received small shrapnel wounds. I directed all three men to leave the tower in order to get checked over by a medic, as well as to get credit for their WIA status. Keep in mind that our ground commander at Ben Het was the A-Detachment Commander, 5th U.S. Special Forces. He was busy with other high priority duties, such as dropping smoke for the FAC to guide in the C-7s. My job was to observe for enemy action during the drop, as well as to watch the road to the east in case the convoy came under attack. I would then direct suppressive artillery fire against enemy antiaircraft firing positions or convoy ambush sites.

Alone in the tower now, I focused my attention on the road (Highway 512) to the east. Within a very short period of time, I heard the explosions of command detonated mines as an enemy force executed an ambush against our approaching convoy. I next heard the eruption of withering small arms and automatic weapons fire. At that same moment, I spotted an L-19 "Headhunter" Army observation plane that was flying cover for the convoy. The aerial observer radioed the map coordinates of the ambush site and took over the adjustment of artillery fire while the pilot continued to fly the aircraft. At the appropriate time, the A-team captain popped the smoke grenades used to mark the Ben Het DZ (Drop Zone). A moment later, the C-7s came into view. As they made their approach from the east, camouflage-colored parachutes unfurled.

I could see the supply-laden pallets that were attached to the parachutes. The pallets weighed up to 1200 pounds apiece, so we had to make sure that our troops were not out where they could be hit by the air-dropped cargo. On this first run, the enemy opened fire on the C-7s with an array of small arms and automatic weapons including heavy machine guns. Several of the aircraft were hit. As I recall, the flight consisted of three aircraft with a FAC in trail flying an O-1 Birddog (a small fixed-wing Cessna observation airplane). The drop was faulty in that much of the cargo missed the drop zone. We notified the people at DASC Alpha in Dak To. They were told that we would get our people killed trying to recover the cargo, since some was out on the airstrip, while more was in our outer perimeter wire. The enemy had these areas zeroed in with mortars and heavy machine guns. We knew then that the enemy, too, had been resupplied at our expense.

At the same time that the airdrop was executing their TOT (Time Over Target), the convoy approached Ben Het from the east down Highway 512. About two miles out, they were ambushed by a well-planned and well-executed NVA operation. The ambush site was heavily fortified. The enemy had a double line of these fortified positions that were all connected by a series of trenches so that the enemy soldiers could move freely from one position to another. Other trenches trailed off into the jungles, providing escape routes for the bushwhackers once they decided to break off contact and withdraw. The FAC leading the airdrop now focused his attention on the convoy as he called in air strikes on the enemy ambush positions. There were U.S. Spads overhead and the FAC used them to help the artillery drive the enemy away from the ambush site. This is one case when artillery fire and air strikes were being delivered without prior coordination between USAF/US Army firepower delivery systems.

The army engineer captain designated as the convoy commander came on the radio following the initial ambush action by the enemy. "We are getting slaughtered out here, order the convoy to turn around!" "Well," I said to myself, "That's not the proper action." The convoy vehicles (heavy ammunition-laden five-ton cargo trucks) were in the "ambush killing zone." Any attempt to turn them back now would be disastrous. Therefore, I refused to even consider such a move.

A couple of minutes passed before I spotted the convoy commander's jeep breaking out of the jungle-covered highway as it sped toward the compound front gate a mile ahead. A two and one-half ton truck trailed the jeep. The two vehicles came speeding into the main compound; they were headed for the TOC location. I had already told the convoy commander that I refused to announce an order to turn around to the convoy vehicles. Confused by all of the radio chatter, one of the convoy personnel had directed one of the ammunition truck drivers to turn around. Well, that was a bad decision because enemy RPG rocket fire had blasted the vehicle. It was now turned into a burning, potentially explosive, roadblock. The convoy commander jumped out of the jeep, turning his eyes upward as he called to me in the tower. "For God's sake, turn the convoy around," he pleaded. I quickly explained the present situation and stood firm on my decision to break off radio contact with the convoy until order was restored. The young Army engineer captain was reduced to tears, but it did nothing to change my position on the subject. He climbed aboard the jeep once more. The two vehicles turned back and left the compound, turning back to the east when they reached the main road. When the convoy commander got back to his convoy, he organized a proper withdrawal. The enemy broke contact long before he arrived back at the ambush site. After retrieving the dead and wounded, the convoy commander led his people and the moveable vehicles back to Dak To.

We did not receive enough food, water, and ammunition to sustain us for very long, so the process of resupply had to be repeated ASAP. Meanwhile, the Air Force FAC came up on the radio. "The Spads have ordnance left, where do you want them to put it?" I radioed back the following instructions: "Work over the whole area south of the airstrip with whatever is available." Within minutes, napalm canisters were dropped and the area was strafed with 20mm cannons. The Spads were a beautiful sight for sore eyes. I also knew that the sniper nest in the garbage dump received a good hit. With this latest ambush of our supply convoy, we came to understand that heavy-laden ammunition trucks were just too vulnerable during an ambush to risk them running a "gauntlet of death" like the one that day provided. We understood that more firepower would have to escort future convoys into Ben Het.

Due to the results of the airdrop, some changes had to be forthcoming. Water was lost due to breakage of containers, as well as to misplacement on the DZ. Rations provided for the CIDGs were not acceptable to them. They refused to eat rice that was not grown in Vietnam (they knew the difference). These Montagnard tribesmen required fresh meat (water buffalo or pork), and the animals had to be delivered alive so that they could be slaughtered in accordance to tribal ritual. Now this may sound strange to westerners, but to the Montagnards, their tribal laws had to be followed to the letter. Fresh pumpkin is an example of food that we had to bring in. Their wounded and dead had to be evacuated back to their tribal homes, too. This posed another problem. All of this was reported to the rear echelon people, who vowed to do the best job they could in the future. We were scheduled to receive another airdrop.

Friday, 13 June 1969 arrived and we still had no Allied infantry troops to support us in the defense of Ben Het. Those of us who were in positions of responsibility felt a sense of betrayal. We felt that it would take nothing less than a miracle to save the beleaguered camp. We then knew that at least two NVA Infantry Regiments, the 28th and the 66th, reinforced by the 40th Artillery Regiment, sapper and engineer battalions had us under siege; we were cut off and surrounded. I personally estimated the enemy force to be from six to seven thousand, plus bearers. Our own defense force amounted to no more than seven hundred on that Friday, the thirteenth.

The early morning monsoon fogs would not hamper enemy operations should they decide to launch a predawn attack against Ben Het. It was foreseeable that the enemy in a predawn attack could take Ben Het, mop up the battlefield, and re-entrench in fortified positions before an Allied counter attack that included air strikes could even be organized and executed. This is why we thought that the enemy planned on using some type of armor support, which they had the capability of doing. The 13 June dawn arrived and the surrounding hills and jungles lay under a thick blanket of fog. I spent time updating my targeting data, which included a large number of "target concentration numbers." Any enemy movement at those target locations received immediate artillery fire. All the FDC had to receive was the target concentration number. They would simply order the firing battery to fire the particular target concentration that had previously been fired, and the target data was refined for accuracy. We received word that another airdrop was scheduled for approximately 1230 hours.

Based on a complaint from the USAF airlift people in Pleiku, who claimed that we were losing too many parachutes (to theft by the CIDG Montagnards, who loved to use the material and parachute cord for their personal use), LTC Bailey asked me to make a special effort to insure that the cargo chutes were recovered and returned to the proper people. When the airdrop arrived over the DZ, among the many pallets and crates dropped was a live water buffalo. He had been fitted with a special harness that allowed him to be directly attached to the parachute shroud lines. Of course, the enemy opened fire with a barrage of mortar and recoilless rifle shells delivered onto the DZ. When that wild-eyed water buffalo hit the ground a-running, I was right on his tail. I caught up with him and cut the parachute harness free. I retrieved the chute and the Montagnards got their live animal. I was told that hogs did not make such drops successfully. Satisfying the needs of our Montagnard population was only one of our many problems at Ben Het.

The CIDG soldiers of the local tribe had their families in the camp with them, so our total population numbered nine hundred. The Montagnards would not eat meat unless it was killed fresh in accordance with tribal rituals. A host of tribal laws interfered with the way we handled their needs (we would be hosting the CIDG Company from Plei Djereng a bit later during the siege). Special handling of their dead required that the bodies be returned immediately to their tribal village for burial. However, the Vietnamese refused to touch the dead, which complicated matters. Our medical evacuation resources were limited as it was.

Later, because of our isolation due to being cut off by the enemy, the payroll for the Plei Dejereng CIDG Company failed to arrive on time. The company mutinied by marching out of the compound and heading east to Dak To. Their U.S. advisor was able to talk them into returning, but I could never trust them after that. In any case, the accuracy of the airdrop improved somewhat.

During the enemy ABF, the CIDG manned Special Forces 81mm mortar pit took a direct hit, killing the crew. They were immediately replaced; however, the enemy mortar still posed an immediate threat. One of the Special Forces NCOs jumped my ass about it. "It's your job to get out there and make a crater analysis," he stated in an accusing manner. Hell, he didn't have to tell me my job. He was simply out of line. The surrounding ground was churned up so badly it looked like a farmer's plowed field. I had to wait for the instant of impact of the next round, mark the spot in my mind, charge out into the open area, throw myself upon the ground, and crawl to the spot where I would then perform a crater analysis. All of this action would be achieved while under enemy fire. To make a successful crater analysis, a series of steps must be followed:

1. Momentarily study the crater in order to determine the approximate direction that the projectile was traveling prior to impact.
2. Probe for the fuze tunnel.
3. Stake out and mark the long axis of the crater.
4. Shoot a back azimuth or direction with the M-2 compass.
5. Measure the angle of fall by using the M-2 compass.

These steps are completed at the crater site. Once back to a safe area, other steps are taken to determine where the SEL is located on the map. This information is passed to the Artillery Fire Direction Center. Terrain analysis is made. This information is applied to the artilleryman's knowledge of the enemy weapon characteristics, i.e., a mortar is usually fired from defilade, so you follow the line of fire back to the SEL and look for a likely firing position. A high level of training is required to achieve proficiency. See Figure 9-2.

On 13 June, I performed two crater analyses of newly created enemy mortar craters. The information I provided to the FDC was used to execute a firing mission by an artillery firing battery. The results were two secondary explosions and the enemy mortar tube was silenced. For my actions, I received an Award for Valor. I shall use that award, not as a tribute to myself, but as documentation for this part of my story.

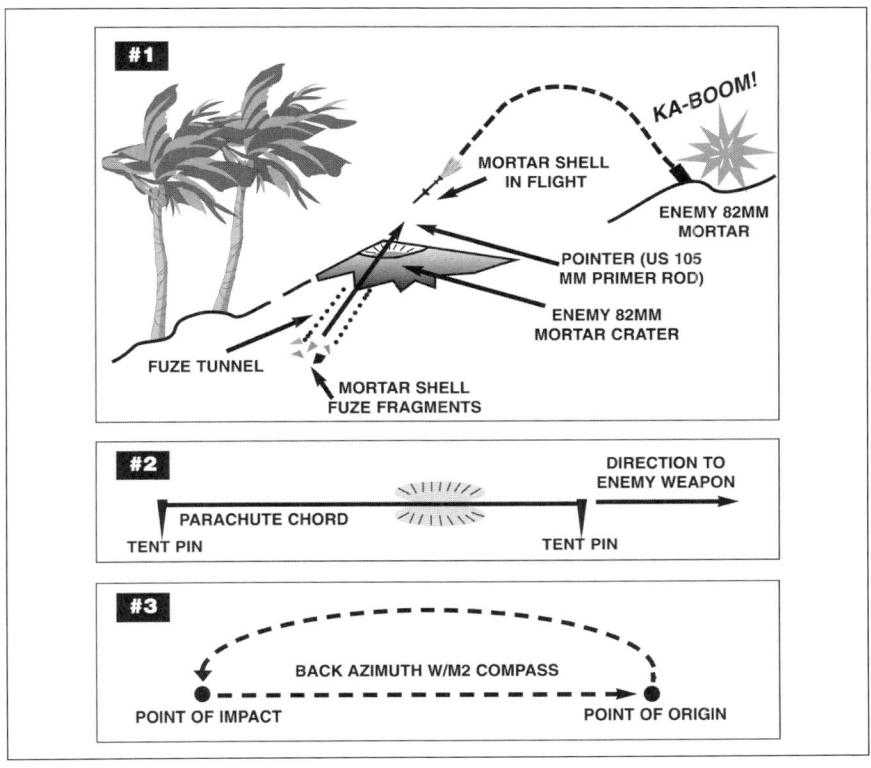

FIGURE 9-2 Artillery crater analysis.

GENERAL ORDER NUMBER 9065 September 1969
AWARD OF THE BRONZE STAR MEDAL
WITH "V" DEVICE

1. TG 320. The following AWARD is announced.

LAMERSON, JOHN 365-32-5646 SERGEANT FIRST CLASS, United States Army, 6th Battalion, 14th Artillery,
APO San Francisco 96318

Awarded Bronze Star Medal with "V" Device

Date action: 12 June 1969 to 13 June 1969

Theater: Republic of Vietnam

Reason: Heroism: Sergeant First Class John Lamerson distinguished himself by exceptional heroism in the Republic of Vietnam on 12 and 13 June 1969, while serving as Intelligence Sergeant at the Ben Het Special Forces Camp with the 6th Battalion, 14th Artillery. On 12 June, Sergeant Lamerson was in the observation tower performing the duties of a forward observer. Enemy mortar rounds were exploding all around the base of the observation tower and the Battalion Commander was slightly wounded. Without regard for his personal safety, he left the tower and assisted in taking the Battalion Commander to a bunker for medical attention. On 13 June, during a heavy volley of enemy mortar fire, Sergeant Lamerson again exposed himself to perform crater analysis to determine the direction of fire from which the enemy mortar rounds were fired. He performed two crater analyses while mortar rounds exploded all around his position and immediately plotted the results of the analysis and submitted a grid to the operations center. The grid was fired upon by artillery, two secondary explosions were observed and the mortar fire ceased ...

The individual who wrote up the above quoted award did not know that I was in fact assigned the duties of the Battalion S-2, not Intelligence Sergeant. I will provide proof of my assigned duty position near the end of my story.

During the next few days, our situation became more perilous than ever. I am now going to relate several anecdotes and events that happened in the third week of June 1969. They do not appear in any particular chronological order.

When I first arrived at Ben Het, I was introduced to the A-Detachment mascot, a little yellow mongrel dog named "Whore." "Watch Whore. When she runs for cover, you had damn well better follow her lead." Whore could always hear the incoming enemy artillery fire before the troops could. By the start of my second week at Ben Het, I had developed my sixth sense allowing me to know in advance that incoming enemy fire was on the way. The troops were starting to watch my actions, rather than Whore's.

We had our 6/14 Artillery Battalion M-10 radar section deployed at Ben Het. It had not been very useful. Its primary mission had been to spot those large enemy weapons over in Laos and Cambodia that had been plaguing Ben Het. The enemy's deployment of long-range field guns was done with the use of a tactic that precluded detection by our M-10, line-of-sight radar equipment. They placed the flat trajectory guns behind a "mask" of hills to their front. They then located "V" cuts in the terrain and laid the axis of the gun tubes along a line-of-sight that would allow the gun to be fired just barely high enough to miss the trees or ground located in the "V" cut. An observer on the other end would have to be looking at the "V" cut at the exact instant of firing in order to spot the flash of the gunfire. That same thing held true for our line-of-sight radar. So, the enemy was able to thwart any attempts by ground radar to locate his big gun positions. Too, the guns were placed in well-camouflaged caves with heavy iron doors. The doors would only be opened for firing. Once the enemy was through firing, they would close the doors. Again, aerial observers would have to be lucky enough to catch the flash just as the guns were fired in order to plot their positions. The M-10 radar section continued to monitor the areas toward the borders of Laos and Cambodia.

We knew, based on the NVA armor attack on Ben Het on 3 March, that the enemy had PT-76 tanks (Figure 9-3). We had heard rumors that they also had Russian T-34 tanks. We had just received 85mm gunfire onto the Main Hill compound. The radar section sent me the SEL based on radar data. When I plotted the coordinates on the map, I was shocked to see that they plotted only about three or four kilometers out, on Highway 512. Because of the angle of fall and the assumed range, I had to suspect T-34 tank fire. That was the only enemy tank that mounted an 85mm gun tube. I asked for a FAC mission to check the area out. The FAC reported that there was something down in that area, but he could not confirm tanks. I was then asked if I wanted to have an air strike put in. I answered in the affirmative. When the air strike hit the area, a large cluster of enemy bunkers and other field fortifications was uncovered. The target turned out to be very lucrative, but it was also a lucky find. I knew that "Charlie" must have been scratching his head as he tried to figure out how we had found his

FIGURE 9-3   PT-76 Russian-built tank.

position. Later, the radar section admitted to me that they had sent erroneous information. We never did learn whether the enemy possessed T-34 tanks or not. It is possible that they had some T-54s besides the PT-76s. As it would turn out, they were unable to use tanks against Ben Het during the May–June Siege of 1969.

Even with the addition of receiving resupply convoys on occasion, airdrops could not keep us adequately supplied. Rations and water were always scarce. The troops were becoming a bit testy. Tempers flared. Following the departure of one of the small convoys that had punched its way into Ben Het, we discovered that a small mongrel puppy dog had been left behind. The troops named him "Shithead."

One particular evening, chicken was served for chow. The little pup was begging for some of the chicken bones. Well, one of the SF sergeants resented this. He thought that the team mascot, Whore, should get all the bones. When I saw him give that little defenseless and hungry pup a swift kick, I lost my temper, and we had a few serious words about the incident.

I was seldom comfortable while eating in the SF mess because the enemy knew our mess schedules and most every mealtime the camp mess hall would come under intense ABFs. It was during the noon meal that I suddenly got a very uncomfortable feeling. So I forfeited my after meal cigarette and left the mess hall. Just as I reached the safety of the TOC entrance, the SF mess took a direct hit from an enemy 75mm recoilless rifle. The corridor leading into the mess hall had plywood lined walls. Behind the plywood were sandbags. I found a hole that had been made by the fuze just prior to the enemy shell exploding. I dug the fuze out of the wall and identified it as a 75mm shell. The enemy had discovered a unique way of employing the recoilless rifle so that the craters appeared to have been made by mortar rounds. This tactic was used to fool us into looking for the enemy weapon in the wrong location.

We were becoming more concerned each day about the fact that we had been abandoned on the battlefield without any infantry support troops to launch a counterattack against the enemy who were slowly inching their way into our outer perimeter wire. Our question was not *if* they were going to attack, it was "When?" (I allude to a massive ground attack.) Special Forces led patrols outside of the outer perimeter and were curtailed to a great extent. Every patrol was jumped on immediately after leaving the security of the compound. Nevertheless, we needed the intelligence information that these patrols generated.

The airlift people back in Pleiku were becoming very concerned about the safety of the C-7s and their crews. By 21 June, there had been 42 Caribou airdrops. Eight aircraft had been hit, and three USAF crewmen had been wounded. Thomas Crawford offers the following analysis:

> The protection of the aerial resupply missions had not been effective. The missions were not properly coordinated with the TACS prior to their arrival in the area. Times-on-target (TOT) was not precise due to weather and operational problems. Changes in the TOT were not passed to the TACS by the C-7A control center in Pleiku. Thus, when the C-7A arrived, the airborne FACs were often committed to air strikes in progress, there was not sufficient time to scramble a FAC from Kontum, and proper tactical fighter-bomber support was not available. Airdrops were made without prior, protective air strikes—only fire-for-fire support while the airdrop was in progress. Also, the C-7As procedure of staggering subsequent drops by individual aircraft at five-or-ten-minute intervals greatly compounded the protection requirements.
> At the request of the 483rd Tactical Airlift Wing (parent unit of the C-7As flying support for Ben Het), a meeting was held at DASC.[6]

On Saturday, 21 June 1969, the western news media discovered the fighting at Ben Het. According to some observers on the Allied side, everything went to hell. That is debatable. However, the news media did not do enough to help our cause, since they reported the information with the slant or spin that the officials supplied to them. A program of misinformation, disinformation, and withholding of information guided the official slant. Word had also gotten around that President Nixon, our commander in chief, had officially announced (at a meeting held at Midway Island in the Pacific on 8 June 1969 between Nixon and South Vietnam President Thieu) the first 25,000-man troop withdrawal by the United States. On the surface at least, Nixon's announcement had no impact on the enemy's determination to turn Ben Het into a "Southern Dien Bien Phu."

During that third week of June, they stepped up their ABFs, introduced their own form of aerial resupply, and executed a sophisticated psychological warfare program. The enemy released three ARVN prisoners who arrived at Ben Het carrying notes. These notes explained the enemy position. They said that the NVA did not want to hurt or kill the dependent wives and children of the Montagnard CIDG, nor did they want Vietnamese killing Vietnamese to help the American criminals to advance their war by initiating the "Vietnamization" program.

Many of the ARVN soldiers and officers alike detested the term, "Vietnamization." The enemy next targeted the Americans at Ben Het with their psychological warfare attempts. Clandestine radio broadcast forewarned of a "Southern Dien Bien Phu," and predicted the imminent fall of the camp.

Late on the evening of 20 June, the enemy hung loudspeakers on the front gate of Ben Het and warned us that unless we surrendered immediately, we were all going to die. We knew that there were spies amongst our ranks, however, this did not affect the gallant stand we were making at the muddy little hellhole that was represented by no more than a pinprick on the map of SVN. On Saturday, 21 June 1969, a critical period in the fighting loomed just around the corner, and it was just in time for the press to discover Ben Het.

Notes

1 U.S. Air Force, CHECO Division, *The Siege of Ben Het*, prepared by Ernie S. Montagliani, (1 October 1969), 14.
2 Ibid., 14.
3 Ibid.
4 Ibid., 14–15.
5 U.S. Air Force, *CHECO Report:* "Interview with Lt. Col. Jack G. Cude, Jr., ALO 24 STZ," (13 July 1969), 9.
6 U.S. Air Force, Air War College, *Tactical Air Support and the Battle of Ben Het: A Professional Study,* by Thomas M. Crawford, Jr., No. 4029 (Air University: 1970), 37.

CHAPTER 10

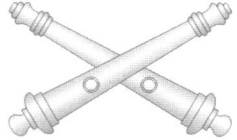

The Siege of Ben Het

Battles are won by the infantry, the armor, and artillery and air teams, by soldiers living in the rain and huddling in the snow.
General Omar Nelson Bradley

PART III

The News Media

The first story by the news media, based on a statement to the press on 20 June, did not appear in the papers until Saturday, 21 June 1969. Very little was mentioned about the fighting. All that was said was that the fighting in and around Ben Het represented a "First Test" of ARVN Forces.[1] This was in reference to their ability to take on the fighting, once the Americans were withdrawn. On 19 June, NVA sniper fire felled one of the 3/6 Artillery cannoneers. We determined that there was a nest of several snipers held up in a thick growth of jungle located on the northwest side of North Hill and close to their outer perimeter wire. I got wind of a special weapon that the U.S. Air Force had in their arsenal. It was identified as a tool used by the Air Force for "jungle covered DZ clearing operations." The way it was explained to me was that a C-130 deliverable piece of ordnance was in stock and available for use. The verbal picture that was painted caused me to conjure up a mental picture of a big round ball-type bomb with a piece of demolition time fuse sticking out. The fuse would be lit just prior to rolling this thing out of the ass-end of the C-130, like in the old comic strips.

That was not the correct picture at all. The weapon described turned out to be what the Air Force referred to as a "Daisy Cutter." It consisted of two 10,000-pound bombs, held over from the days of the B-36 bomber, skid loaded onto a special pallet. It was rigged with a mechanical time fuse that was set to go off at the appropriate time once it reached the target area. This ordnance was loaded aboard a C-130 cargo plane. The plane would make a low-level drop over the target zone and then climb like hell to a safe altitude prior to the bombs detonating. The one dropped at my request cleared about five acres of heavy jungle growth. That took care of the sniper problem. This Daisy Cutter mission was dropped on the night of 19–20 June to the best of my calculations.

When the morning fog of 20 June lifted, I looked out of the observation tower to see a battalion of Mike Strikes, bivouacked in the newly cleared DZ. They had made a night occupation of the position. Led by Australian advisors, the force moved out to the northwest. Following a fierce firefight in which they took an undisclosed number of casualties, the force withdrew.

On Saturday, 21 June, a newspaper article in reference to the action stated that the enemy suffered only 26 NVA soldiers killed, while the American-led South Vietnamese irregular's losses were 18 killed and 54 wounded. The clash was only two miles northwest of Ben Het. It is interesting to note that the newspaper headline read: "Renewed Fighting Breaks Out In Viet Central Area."[2] Our question was, "What the hell are they talking about?" The overall fighting had already entered its third straight month.

Back in Pleiku, The DASC was holding a special meeting on that 21 June Saturday. A portion of the report of that meeting is as follows:

> 1. Colonel L.J. Greenwood, DCO, 483d TAW, stated the purpose of the conference, that being to improve the escort procedures and suppressive fires in support of Caribou drops in the Ben Het area. He stated that his pilots are taking too many hits, are flying without parachutes, and, in case of fire aboard, have approximately $1\frac{1}{2}$ minutes in which to set the aircraft down on the ground. He stated that unless the situation improves with respect to ground fire being received, he would not permit his pilots to fly the Ben Het run.
> 2. [In any case the] discussion that followed centered upon present techniques of [S]pad aircraft escorts firing when fired upon, a defensive posture. Col. Greenwood stated that this was inadequate and that he required coordinated suppression of ground fire, in an offensive posture, prior to, and during the drop. It was agreed to by all present that this would be a more effective tactic.
> 3. The point was made that Army artillery fire in the area should also be employed in coordination with the air support in the suppression of ground fire and the undersigned was asked to initiate the necessary action.
> 4. After discussion of various courses of action, the following concepts were adopted:

a. Caribou drop TOT will be scheduled during realistic good weather periods (1230–1530) with automatic built-in slippages of one hour in case of weather.
    b. All suppressive fire will be built around the Caribou TOT.
    c. Seventh Air Force will frag 4 F-4 acft with 11x800 LB cans of Napalm, each in coordination with Caribou TOT and 2 Spad acft with smoke and CBU munitions.
    d. Caribou delivery aircraft will close their drop time intervals from 30 seconds to one minute apart.
    e. The FAC will be the fire and drop coordinator.
    f. The tentative time schedule for the suppressive fires and drops, as a function of the Caribou TOT is as follows: (1) TOT-20 minutes. F-4's with napalm will strike north and east of Ben Het. Artillery can begin suppressive fires South of the road.[3]

Note: The G-3 Air IFFORCEV, Lieutenant Colonel J. J. Trankovich, USA was among those attending the conference. I wonder what words in our defense he rendered, since we were surrounded, without food and water, and short on ammunition. How could an O-6 stand there and make such a callous statement?

The system operated as follows: 7th AF would frag four jet fighters (F-4s or F-100s with napalm and two A-1s [Spads] with smoke and CBU munitions) to arrive at Ben Het prior to the C-7 TOT. About 20 minutes before the scheduled drop, the jets would strike north and east of the camp's perimeter, while artillery pounded the area to the south. At TOT minus three minutes, the jet fighters were to be off target. Next, the Spads were to drop the smoke and CBUs on both sides of the Caribou run in heading, forming a corridor, and were to fire their 20mm and 7.62mm guns on return passes.

Then the Caribous would begin their run-in, escorted by A-1s off the wing tips and a FAC in trail. If any ground fire was noted, the FAC was to mark and the Spads were to fire on the target without delay. The system was inaugurated on 22 June and was immediately successful. Lt. Col. Jack Cude, Jr. described one of his experiences while FACing for Caribous and Spads:

> …I was in trail position and I noticed small arms fire coming up at us from a location a short distance away. I dropped a wing and marked—and told the Spad to hit the smoke. He did and the fire from there stopped. I guess the whole thing took 15 seconds… .
>
> …After awhile, Charlie got the idea that we were serious and he quit firing at the formations. The system was successful… .

The success was also demonstrated in statistics relating to the airdrops from 21 June to 3 July. During this period, 57 Caribou Sorties were flown, with no aircraft hit and no crewmen wounded. There were 70 TAC air sorties used to furnish the suppression in support of these C-7s.[4]

With the introduction of the news media to the area and with airlift operations modified, the enemy also pressed his operations against Ben Het. He stepped up his artillery bombardments; he pressed his attempts to build trenches and to dig tunnels on the three hill compound perimeters. The latter is especially true in reference to the North Hill compound. The NVA was bent on destroying the 105mm-howitzer battery, because the 105s were mounted on full track, armor-clad vehicles that each mounted a 50-caliber machine gun. The 105s were armed with antitank, armor-piercing ammunition-plus (Beehive and HE). Undoubtedly the enemy planned to use armor to spearhead his main assault. The 105 battery was capable of breaking up such an assault. The enemy sapper and combat engineer battalions worked feverishly to breech the North Hill perimeter defenses, where they planned to spike the American guns and blow them up in an operation reminiscent of Dien Bien Phu against the French.

As a point to ponder, consider the fact that a strong pocket of NVA infantrymen were discovered two miles northwest of Ben Het during the action mentioned early in this chapter. Contact was broken before any determination as to their unit identification could be made. Based on the whole enemy scenario that was being played out at the time, I believe that enemy force was from the 18th NVA Infantry Regiment. Most likely they were on a Reconnaissance in Force mission. We were not used to receiving much action to the northwest except for the real close-in stuff. I did get an order from LTC Bailey to report to North Hill to examine some suspected enemy heavy-gun-fired shell craters that had hit directly in the center of A/3/6's battery position. We feared that the enemy was introducing larger caliber guns. If this threat proved to be true, we had a real problem.

I traveled the short distance by jeep, (the only one left on the Main Hill), because it was too dangerous to walk between the hills. As I arrived on North Hill, Army Captain John Horalek of Fort Collins, Colorado, met me. He was the 3rd of the 6th A Battery commander. He led me to a cluster of shell craters right smack in the middle of the small cleared area that represented the battery hub. I removed my hunting knife from its sheath, knelt down, and with my left hand felt around for the mouth of the fuze tunnel. When I found it, I was careful to probe with my knife. (I had learned early during my tour not to probe with my bare hands; deadly banana spiders seeking warmth from the cold morning air were quick to move into the warm shell craters.) I was positive that the first fuze fragments I recovered were American, so to be sure I did some more probing until I was able to recover some shell shrapnel fragments. I positively identified them as U.S. 155mm. I made a two-crater analysis, which provided a direction to the point of origin of fire. I reported the total results of my findings to Captain Horalek. "Damn ARVNS," he hissed. "They came from Firebase 3. The damn ARVNS have a bad habit sending a close-in fire as a signal to wake up their FOs." I agreed that it was not only a bad habit, but also a dangerous one. Cold artillery gun tubes do not deliver accurate fire. This incident was the only friendly fire accident that I witnessed during the fighting at Ben Het. Captain Horalek seemed impressed by the speed and proficiency of my work.

I returned to the Main Hill where I took up my duties in the observation tower as the artillery FO. The enemy was waiting for me.

The first round of the day, screaming out of Cambodia, slammed into the base of the tower. It was fearsome to hear the 85mm incoming enemy gunfire; it made the sound of a shrieking Banshee. I found the sound alone to be unearthly. My RTO, who had already been wounded twice during the fighting, was badly shaken by the enemy fire. I gave him permission to "un-ass" the tower, which he did. During the next few salvos of enemy gun fire, the enemy gunners got a series of "overs" and "shorts," "lefts" and "rights," which means that they had bracketed their target. Their target was me!

I figured that I was about to buy the farm, but I had been able to see a muzzle flash and had made a quick terrain analysis. I pretty well knew where the enemy gun was in relation to a map location. Unfortunately for me, I would never get the chance to send a fire mission to the guns. I knew the score—there was not enough time left, so I called the TOC on my radio. "Request permission to quit my post!" I was questioned. "Why?" I quickly answered. "I have been bracketed!" "Permission granted," came back the terse reply. I did not have to be told twice. I jerked open the floor hatch, exited the platform, and almost let myself free-fall to the ground below. My hands hitting the ladder rungs on the way down were all that broke my fall. Once on the ground, I ran as fast as I could while in a crouch and was able to make it to the TOC before the next enemy round exploded right beneath the tower platform. As I entered the TOC, still shaken from my close call, Colonel Bailey met me. "Where are they coming from?" He queried me. Hell, I was shaking so bad that when I pointed to the spot on the wall map; I could not hold my finger still enough for anyone to tell where I was pointing.

Everyone had a good laugh at my expense. After I was able to calm myself down, we got a hold of an USAF FAC, whom we vectored to the vicinity of the enemy gun location. The FAC was able to spot the enemy gun as it fired. We had our 8-inch howitzer from B/6/14 fire on the target. The first round entered the mouth of the cave where the enemy gun was located. We got no more gunfire from that enemy gun. However, the NVA began using 120mm mortars against the Main Hill compound. I recognized the shells as being from a siege weapon, because of the way they were fuzed. They employed fuze delay. The 120mm could penetrate to a depth of ten feet. This was sufficient to enable the enemy to destroy most of our fortified positions.

I reported my concerns to IFFV Artillery Headquarters in Nha Trang. Some "armchair commando" back there in Nha Trang blew me off. "We have no intelligence information to substantiate your concerns. We do not have anything to confirm 120mm mortar fire." I became highly "pissed off" and decided to obtain the proof that we were, in fact, receiving 120mm mortar fire. I went out and staked out a suspected 120mm-shell crater. After it was good and dark, I went to the spot with a shovel. It took me several hours of digging down far enough to find and recover fuze fragments. I returned to my S-2 room in the TOC. I had been able to procure a case of captured 120mm mortar shell fuzes from the A-Team intelligence sergeant. When I ran a comparison test, the captured fuze was an exact match to the fragments that I had recovered. Exhausted to the maximum from my hours of digging, I flung myself onto my canvas cot and was soon fast asleep.

The predawn hours of Sunday, 22 June, found me up and at 'em. I hurriedly ate my breakfast and returned to my duty station in the TOC. I sent word for the Colonel to come see me ASAP. When he arrived on the scene, I was prepared to brief him. I had a small shelf in my S-2 area, where I had arranged a display of the recovered fuze fragments, along with one of the captured ChiCom 120mm fuzes. Also located on the shelf was a Styrofoam cup containing some cordite-flavored rainwater that I had managed to save for a tooth brushing session. (I broke my partial plate just prior to shipping over to Vietnam. I was told, "Don't worry. They have dentists over there.") Well, not where I was at, so I was trying to keep my natural teeth cleaned, as well as possible. I was just in the process of telling Colonel Bailey about those "bastards" in Nha Trang who had doubted my word about the enemy using 120mm mortars. "Well, I wonder what them sons-of-bitches are going to have to say now...?" Ka-wump!

The lights went out. I could feel my body being slammed against the bunker wall. I then felt myself sliding down the wall and hitting the bunker floor. The dust was so thick I could almost eat it like a mouthful of dirt. I felt around my chest area as I tried to find the flashlight that should have been hanging there on my web harness. The flashlight was missing; however, I felt a big wet spot on my chest. I felt around on the bunker floor, where I found and recovered my flashlight. The dust was so thick that my light did very little to help my vision in the now pitch-black darkness of the TOC. I finally made out the form of Colonel Bailey, who was now sitting all crumpled up in the corner of the little bunker room. As I shown the light in Bailey's face, I detected a look of astonishment on his face. I made sure he was all right before I looked for my buck sergeant assistant. He was no longer in the room with Bailey and me. He had, I discovered, been blown out through the narrow doorway and lay in the corridor leading to the S-3 section. He, too, appeared to be OK, so I checked to see that the wet spot on my chest was not blood. It appeared to be water. I heard moans and coughing coming from the direction of our S-3 section, so I made my way back there to check on our people. None appeared to have injuries. Now stark fear began to set in as we wondered what the hell had just hit us. The TOC was more than twenty-five feet below ground and had three feet of reinforced concrete added to the more than twelve feet of logs, earth, and sandbags. "How did the enemy shells penetrate so deep?" Lying in pitch-black darkness and without electrical power (our generator had also been knocked out), we had lost all communication with the outside world.

As the Special Forces people worked on repairing the TOC generator, Colonel Bailey ordered our 6/14 Communications Team to re-install our 292 (two-niner-two) radio antennas that had been blown over. Meanwhile, the Special Forces A-Team Lieutenant came looking for me. When he found me he said, "Sergeant Lamerson, you have got to see this," as he motioned for me to follow him to the back entrance to the TOC. We had to crawl over a few tons of log and dirt debris before reaching what had been the rear entrance steps leading out of the TOC. I suddenly realized that both the Colonel's and the Major's quarters had been totally destroyed. Had either one been in there, it is likely that he would have been severely injured or dead. I clawed my way through the rubble until I was able to break through to the outside. As I worked, the Lieutenant was explaining to me that "the biggest shell crater that you have ever seen is out there." As I poked my head through the small opening, I gained an immediate appreciation for what the lieutenant had told me. The crater was about twenty feet deep and thirty feet across. I crawled through to the rim of the crater and down into its base. I took out my hunting knife and started to probe for shell fragments or bomb fragments since I had no idea what could have caused such a crater. I immediately hit pay dirt. I located large chunks of an explosive composition containing double-aught buckshot. "Claymore mine fragments," I deduced. Next, I recovered a primer rod from an M-106 recoilless rifle shell casing. Then I recovered some 50-caliber machine gun slugs. They had no land and groove markings on them so I knew that they had not been fired through a machine gun barrel. I'd seen enough. I called to the lieutenant, "Hey, did you guys have an ammo bunker or magazine in this spot?" I queried him. "Oh," he said, "that's right. We did have a conex container full of demolitions and ammo sandbagged into the bank by the back entrance to the TOC." I was stunned at hearing his reply and could not resist telling him, "I'd think you guys would know better." I let it off at that and climbed out of the big crater.

Now I looked around for some newly formed mortar craters, which I discovered between the tower base and the crater at the rear entrance to the TOC. There were two craters about twenty feet apart. As I made crater analysis on both of them, I was able to recover the mortar shell bases. I identified them as 120mm. Again, I complained to the colonel about those SOBs in Nha Trang.

It was determined that the wet spot on my chest noticed earlier must had been made when the cup of water previously mentioned was dashed against my chest during the initial explosion. With communications and power restored, we were able to resume normal operations within a couple of hours. Colonel Bailey briefed me on the latest enemy situation report received. "Enemy attack is imminent for the night of 22–23 June." Bailey gave me my instructions. "Prepare an extensive firing program" for that night's H&Is, (Harassment and Interdiction Fire). I worked the remainder of the day on the program and had it in the hands of Major Wakahiro, the S-3, by nightfall. That night was a dark one and we fired all night long, creating a curtain of artillery fire all around the Ben Het camp's perimeter and to a depth of three kilometers outward. It worked. The night passed without the expected mass attack being launched by the enemy.

Unknown to me, on the 22nd the Special Forces led patrol on North Hill's perimeter and discovered enemy trenches outside the wire. They discovered a cache of enemy wire-breaching demolitions stored in the five-foot deep trenches. During the early evening hours of darkness on the 22nd of June, a team of enemy sappers carrying satchel charges entered the inner perimeter defenses through a tunnel dug under North Hill. Before the two-man team could move toward the batteries' guns, they were discovered. Captain Horalek, while being accompanied by the Army Chaplain at Ben Het, pulled out his holstered 45-caliber automatic pistol and shot the lead sapper through the head from point blank range. The other sapper escaped back down the tunnel.

The next morning, 23 June, a captured NVA prisoner revealed that the enemy was prevented from launching their long-expected massed ground assault against Ben Het due to the intensity of the Allied artillery fire. The incident was described in a newspaper report as follows:

> This massive display of U.S. Firepower is what American Officials say is the only thing that has kept the camp from being overran ... one North Vietnamese, who surrendered, supported that view this week when he said heavy U.S. Artillery fire kept the NVA from making a massive ground attack the night of June 23.[5]

To further support the claim that the NVA planned to attack during the night of 22–23 June, I present the following:

> In the upper portion [of SASI Zulu] Route 512, leading past Ben Het was interdicted in 24 places between the border and Ben Het. The next one down, Bravo Road showed 5 interdictions and was unusable. McElroy Road (see Figure 10-1) the next one had 3 points which were impassable.
> ...On each road we noticed foot traffic. One specifically, on 20 June, the road was struck with 2 sorties. They cratered the road and blew down trees. The next day [Saturday June 21], a reconnaissance mission was flown and it was found that they had repaired the craters and covered them with bamboo. The next day [22 June], we launched four aircraft with 2,000-pound bombs and destroyed the repairs. Charlie Road the next one down, showed 4 interdictions and was not usable.[6]

Note: The 7th Air Force people thought that the interdiction of the above-mentioned roads was ninety percent successful, which precluded the possibility of use by not only truck traffic, but also enemy armor. I think that the Air Force people were dead wrong. The fact that the enemy displayed determination in their attempts to keep Bravo Road open is very significant. Coupled with the fact that the enemy made no earlier attempt to blow the bridge at Dak Mot four miles to the east of Ben Het, this ties in closely with my point of view about the enemy's overall plan of action. Even though the enemy did not employ armor during the 58-day battle (May–June), does in no way prove that the intent was not there.

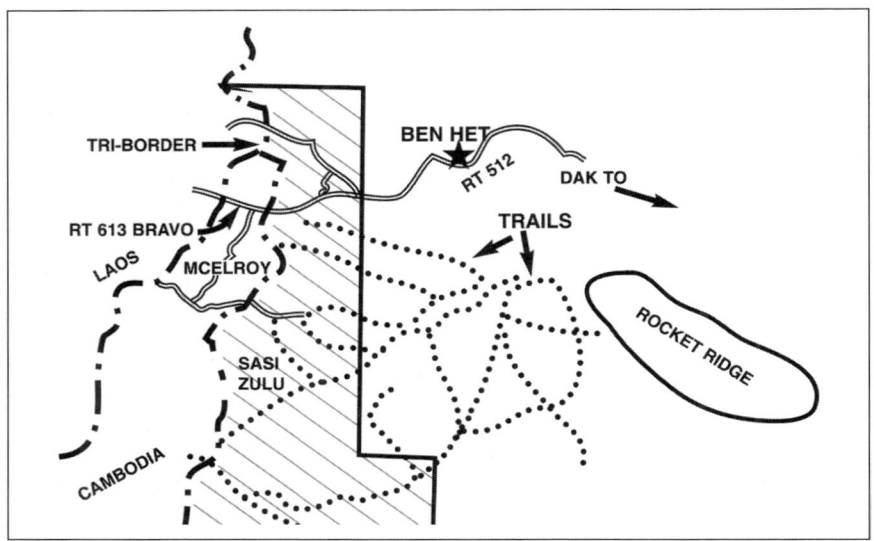

FIGURE 10-1   Ben Het and the surrounding targeted area.

In his interview for the CHECO Report, Lt. Devilbliss said:

> We think that the enemy was going to try and take Ben Het on 23rd of June with sapper action. The FSBs in the south were attacked on the 23rd, and that same day an action took place on the perimeter of Ben Het, but somebody (NVA) stopped it in a hurry. This shows a great deal of command flexibility on their part.[7]

I do not agree that sapper action alone would have been used by the NVA in an attempt to take Ben Het. However, it would have been used to initiate the overall attack. As I have concluded, the capture or destruction of the artillery battery at North Hill was a primary target for the NVA. This is reinforced by the following information, gleaned from a news release out of Saigon (AP), dated 28 June, 1969:

> Earlier today, a security patrol discovered two enemy tunnels under the barbed wire perimeter of a U.S. artillery base at Ben Het, military spokesmen said. Spokesmen said the trenches led to a series of trenches inside the camp indicating the enemy wanted to reach the heart of the base and blow it up, a tactic the Viet Minh used in 1954 against the French in the decisive battle for Dien Bien Phu.[8]

An extract from a news story written by AP News Correspondent Peter Arnett, (a Pulitzer Prize recipient) and published in the *Daily Intelligencer Journal,* Lancaster, PA, on 27 June 1969, read:

One night eight sappers penetrated our perimeter, sapped No. 2 gun with a satchel charge killing one of seven gunners and wounding five. We have killed two sappers in each of the past two nights. They all got in our wire.

It seems very unlikely that the enemy would attack North Hill with sapper action without following up the attack with their main assault on the rest of the Ben Het camp. It is also unlikely that they planned to take Ben Het and then stop there. No, it is probable that the capture of Ben Het was to be only the first step of their overall battle plan, which I believe was to take Dak To, Tan Canh, Kontum City, and finally, Pleiku City. If successful, their plan would place them in a very strong bargaining position at the Paris Peace talks.

My Proposed "Likely Scenario" for the Enemy's Plan of Attack

As the sapper action against North Hill signaled success in destroying the 105mm battery, the main assault on the other two compounds would be initiated. The Main Hill would be attacked with a two-infantry regiment frontal assault from the southeast and southwest. The 28th, massed to the southeast of the abandoned airstrip, would lead the assault. The 66th, advancing along the axis of Highway 512 from the west, would advance until they were at the southwest corner of the airstrip. Here, they would hold up until a battalion from the 24th Infantry Regiment, advancing along behind them, peeled off and attacked the poorly manned west hill. This of course would cause a diversion in conjunction with the sapper attack going on over on North Hill. The 66th would now cut across the airstrip and attack the southwest end of the Main Hill. On the heels of the sapper/engineer attack against the North Hill would follow the 18th NVA Infantry Regiment. The 18th would insure that the North Hill had been neutralized before signaling the rest of the 325 C Division to advance. As all attack forces achieved their objectives, a quick mop-up operation would follow. By the time the 325 C Division, led by the tank companies of the 202 Armor/Artillery Regiment minus the 18th Infantry Regiment, passed south of Ben Het's Main Hill (followed by artillery elements of the 202 Armor/Artillery Regiment), vehicles would move up and pick up the 18th 's troops. Except for a rear guard action, all enemy ground forces would now move east down Highway 512 in order to launch an early morning "Armored Spearhead" attack against Dak To.

The enemy would use the early morning fog to cover their initial advance. They would use the heavy guns of the 202d to provide depth to the battlefield. The enemy expected Dak To to fall into their hands before the first American TAC Air could respond. B-52s could not reach the battleground for hours. By that time, the enemy expected to be entrenched in fortified positions on the outskirts of Tan Canh. They planned a repeat of a predawn attack on Tan Canh, and following its fall, they would advance on Kontum under the cover of fog. The same scenario would be played out to advance on and capture Pleiku City. Even with moderate success, the enemy was sure that a clear message would reach the "peace negotiators" in Paris.

The coinciding action by the remainder of the 24th NVA Infantry Regiment (minus the one battalion) that was involved in the Ben Het attack, was to move to capture and secure the Dak Mot Bridge, four miles to the east of Ben Het. Meanwhile, the 1st NVA Division, minus the 24th Infantry Regiment, would act as a blocking force to prevent reinforcements from traveling by way of Highway 14 from the south or by Highway 19 from the east.

Of course the above scenario could never be put into action, because of the enemy's failure to launch the 22–23 June predawn attack. The battle continued.

By now the news media had become fully aware of the bad situation that faced the small Ben Het defenses force. By anybody's standards, Ben Het's immediate future looked bleak. We needed a miracle.

Notes

[1] "Renewed Fighting Breaks Out in Viet Central Area," *Stars and Stripes*, 21 June 1969, Pacific edition.

[2] Ibid.

[3] U.S. Air Force, Air War College, *Tactical Air Support and the Battle of Ben Het: A Professional Study*, by Thomas M. Crawford, Jr., No. 4029 (Air University: 1970), Appendix C, 60-61: Department of the Army memorandum, dated 21 June 1969; "Suppressive Fire Support for Caribou Aircraft on Ben Het Resupply Missions."

[4] U.S. Air Force, CHECO Division, *The Siege of Ben Het*, prepared by Ernie S. Montagliani, (1 October 1969), 18.

[5] Spec. 4 Bob Hodierne, "Rain Of Fire Continues to Slam Ben Het," *Stars and Stripes*, June 1969, Pacific edition.

6 U.S. Air Force, *CHECO Report:* "Interview with Lt. Col. Jack G. Cude, Jr., ALO 24 STZ," (13 July 1969), 3.
7 U.S. Air Force, *CHECO Report:* "Interview with Lt. D.A. Devilbliss, Assistant Highland Desk Officer, G-2, Hq. IFFV," (8 July 1969), 3.
8 Associated Press Reporter, "Fresh South Vietnam Troops Hit Ben Het," *Independent Times,* vol. 42 no. 52, 28 June 1969.

CHAPTER 11

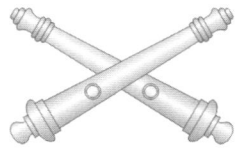

The Siege of Ben Het

*Yea, though I walk through the Valley of the
Shadow of Death, I shall fear no evil, because I'm
the meanest son-of-a-bitch in the Valley.*
Author Unknown

AN UNPREDICTABLE CONCLUSION

Ben Het, South Vietnam
Monday morning, 23 June, 1969

We were relieved to wake up to find the camp shrouded in fog once more and to realize that we made it through one more perilous night. I awoke thirsting for a drink of water, which was not available at Ben Het. We had been out of potable drinking water for five days now. However, there was cold beer available at 50 cents per can. I hated the beer that was available, because it tasted like a generic-type brand. The reason we were charged for the beer was that our benefactor, the Special Forces A-Team, used the money for a slush fund, which in turn was used for the betterment of all. So, after checking this system out, I found no quarrel with it. I was dying from thirst, so I capitulated and bought my first drink of the day. (I had no use for the small refrigerator that I had brought to Ben Het, so I gave it to the B Battery, 6/14 first sergeant. They needed it for the troops).

We received word that a convoy was on the way, in addition to airdrops already scheduled for a midday arrival over Ben Het. The Special Forces people had led an early morning patrol outside of the camp to check out the perimeter. When they returned, they brought in a prisoner. He claimed that he had not eaten in three days. Of course, that information led us to believe that the enemy was in trouble. He revealed that they had been prepared to launch their massive ground assault the night before; however, intense Allied artillery fire prohibited them from doing so. We also learned that the convoy was beefed up with extra security and that the CIDG Company from Plei Djereng was going to insert by way of the incoming convoy—they would be used to strengthen our perimeter defenses. I guess the enemy held off hitting this particular convoy due to its added firepower and the size of its infantry security force.

The convoy arrived on schedule and would not return east until the following day. I was happy to have the "Duster" (full truck vehicle-mounted twin 40mm cannons), and "Quad Fifties" (truck-mounted gun carriage with four 50-caliber machine guns) aboard for the night. We used them to beef up our southern perimeter. I still had an ongoing beef with the ARVN Tank Platoon Commander. He had already lost one stockpile of ammunition, which was destroyed by enemy fire due to his carelessness in securing it. Now, the convoy had brought him some more ammunition, and I found it stacked unprotected out in the open once more. I complained to Colonel Bailey, who in turn asked the ARVN to secure the ammunition. It did no good, so Bailey finally, in desperation, threatened to destroy the unprotected pile of tank ammo by friendly fire. At least this way we could control the time and place of the explosion, thereby protecting our own troops. That threat worked and the ARVNs got off their dead asses and secured their ammo. The airdrops also made it in on schedule.

We had become inundated by the visits of the news media. I got word that a "big name" Pulitzer prize-winning reporter by the name of Peter Arnett was over on North Hill. Some of us thought that he would ferret out the truth about our dilemma and tell the entire world, but that was wishful thinking. Arnett decided that there was too much danger in coming to the Main Hill, so following his interview with people of A/3/6's firing battery, Arnett boarded the next Huey medevac chopper and returned to the rear area. (In actuality, he wasn't permitted to come over to the Main Hill because of the danger.) We would not get to read his story for several more days.

Reporters were safe from challenge, due to the fact that we would not receive the newspapers until too late to successfully protest against biased and false reporting. The news about Ben Het was getting out to the world despite of the faults in the reporting. Back in the United States, military families with loved ones at Ben Het were holding their breaths. The national newspapers all featured daily "Banner Headline" stories about the perils facing the Ben Het defenders. These sensationalized reports were destined to run through the first week of July 1969.

My wife, Mavis, was among those most worried. She had no one to lean on for support during the time she knew I was one of the "trapped" and "doomed" at Ben Het. Being left alone to raise four little girls was her big concern. Meanwhile, I, too, remembered the image of them all standing there on that tarmac in Lawton, Oklahoma, on the day of my departure. That sight always haunted my memories while I was in Vietnam, and now my own worst fears seemed to be looming on the horizon. "Would I make it out alive? Would any of us make it out, or were we all destined to die in one last gallant stand?" From a vantage point in the observation tower, I observed the on-going airdrop.

Immediately following the airdrops, I was informed that the pair of Spads that had flown a suppression mission for the TAC people still had ordnance available. I requested a strike on the Ben Het "garbage dump." I was still after that little S-O-B that had sniped at me. Well, the Spads made their approach and released napalm as they strafed along the south side of the airstrip. As they were completing their pass, I could hear the rat-a-tat-tat of an AK-47; it was either one brave or one stupid "Dink" who opened up on that pair of heavily armed Spads. The Spads circled and flew right back around and this time the pilots pickled their bomb loads. As the bombs hit their target and exploded, I saw human bodies and individual weapons flying through the air. I chuckled to myself. "It cost a million dollars to get that one sniper, but what the hell," I rationalized, "I'm worth it." We now had a fulltime FO, Lieutenant Goodwin (I think his name was). I still filled in when I could.

As darkness fell on the 23d, I was prepared to mount the tower for the purpose of night observation duties. I had earlier taken the new Medium Range Night-Lighting Device (scope) up into the tower. With a range of 3 kilometers, I could use this new piece of equipment to observe for any ground movement around our Main Hill perimeter. Things were pretty quiet until about 8 or 9 P.M. All of a sudden, and without any prior warning, a fusillade of friendly gunfire erupted on the southwest corner of the Main Hill perimeter. The twin 40mm guns of the Duster,[1] as well as those of the Quad Fifty, joined in the gunfire. I decided that I should give fire support for whatever they were targeting, so I opened fire with the tower's 50-caliber machine gun. I got an immediate field telephone message from Colonel Bailey. "What the hell is happening?" he asked. "Hell, I don't know," I answered. "All I know is that everyone opened fire, so I did too." "Well stop!" Colonel Bailey ordered. We did and everything quieted down once more. An hour or two later, as I was peering through the night scope, I detected movement in our southeastern perimeter wire. I called a fire mission. A/3/6 responded to the movement, which stopped following one six-gun volley of fire being expended against the target. It was quiet for the remainder of the night, except for "Spooky" and "Shadow" flights over the area. They remained on guard all through the night. Artillery illumination fire also was fired at specified intervals. Together they kept the area pretty well lit up all night. Dawn on 24 June came and Ben Het had survived one more long night. A number of dead NVA were spotted in the perimeter wire where the volley of A/3/6 hit, per my called-in fire mission the previous evening.

On the 50th day of the "Siege," the battle took on a whole new meaning. It acquired the desperate, but magnificent character of all gallant and heroic struggles against hopeless odds. Even in the words of our enemy, our situation was desperate. Ben Het appeared to be "doomed."

A bit later on that morning, I got word to come to the S-3. When I walked in to the S-3, I was greeted by a couple of the Special Forces NCOs. They had an enemy soldier standing there waiting with them. "Sergeant Lamerson, we think you might be interested in talking with this man. However, he is not a POW, he is a *Chieu Hoi*."[2] The SF people turned the soldier over to my charge. I sent for an interpreter. Through the use of the interpreter, I asked a series of questions:

> *Question:* "Why did you turn yourself in?"
>
> *Answer:* "No want to die. When we attack, many will die. No want to die!"

My analysis: Soldier was telling the truth.

> *Question:* "What is your unit and where is it?"
>
> *Answer:* "I was with the Headquarters Element of the 28th Regiment." (NVA)

My analysis: Undecided at this point.

> *Question:* "What is your unit's mission?"
>
> *Answer:* "Command and control of the planned attack."

My analysis: The answer had merit. (Seemed believable.)

> *Question:* "Where is your unit located?"
>
> *Answer:* " Southeast end of the airstrip. Your soldiers abandoned a bunker complex; we moved into them. We are preparing to attack. I no want to die!"

My analysis: I required verification in reference to the abandoned bunker complex.

I broke off the interrogation session and sent for the SF senior man available. I asked if it was true that they had abandoned a bunker complex down there and was shocked at the answer, which was in the affirmative. I released the Chieu Hoi for evacuation to the rear. I believed the Chieu Hoi's story, and therefore knew that we had a major problem to deal with. I now studied my options.

1. Plan and execute a U.S. Field Artillery TOT on this "high priority" target of opportunity.
2. Plan a well-executed air strike against the important target.
3. Discuss my air strike options before executing a plan of attack. The latter would require me to converse directly with the 7th AF ALO stationed in Dak To.

I wrestled with the problem for a short time. As I gave attention to the artillery option, I decided that it could not provide enough concentrated firepower in order to guarantee complete destruction of the target. We did not have the time to be taking such a gamble. I chose to contact the ALO and seek his guidance, based on what was available in the nature of air support. I was leaning toward a B-52 option if available, or fell within safety guidelines. "Put me in touch with the ALO in Dak To," I instructed the RTO on duty at the 6/14 S-3.

My initial contact with the ALO was completed. I told him that I had a very important high priority target that I thought he might be able to help me take under attack. I followed through by asking him, "How close-in can you bring B-52s?" I guess he took my question to be a joke. "Right on top of you, but I wouldn't recommend it." He chuckled over the radio. I realized that he did not know my duty position, nor was I interested in trying to explain it. I composed myself better as I explained my problem more in detail. That got the ALO's attention, and we began to discuss the options that were open to us. We could not bring Arc Light in that close, so we scratched that option. A tactical aircraft CSS (Combat Sky Spot) was out, too. What the ALO offered as a viable option was the possibility of a modified CSS using a single B-52 instead of a tactical aircraft to deliver the hard ordnance on the target. This last option appeared to fit the ticket. I told the ALO to set it up. His immediate response took a bit of wind out of my sails. "I cannot do that," he informed me. "I have to obtain permission from the Ben Het ground commander first." "I can get his permission," I explained, " but

I need to know what we're asking for." The ALO explained the mission proposal to me. "We can use a single B-52 loaded with 750-pound bombs." I interrupted him. "Can we make that 500-pound bombs?" I asked. "No, they are not available," he told me. "We will frag a bomber en route and divert it to Ben Het. We will bring it in at a greatly reduced altitude, which will increase the safety factor. We can have it on target NLT 0300 hours in the morning (June 25)." I asked the ALO to stand by while I discussed the mission request with my superiors.

I first discussed my request with Colonel Bailey. Colonel Bailey's first concern was necessity. I explained my feelings. If either one of us wanted to be around for breakfast come morning, we had damn well better act now. Bailey's second consideration was the safety of the troops. Again, I made it clear that we had no other viable alternative. We jointly decided to seek Captain Noble's permission. As the Senior Special Forces Advisor at Ben Het, he wore the title of ground commander, since the real estate belonged to the SF. Captain Noble expressed the same concerns as did Bailey. He received identical answers to his questions. Understanding our true peril, Captain Noble put his stamp of approval on the plan. He contacted the ALO, who explained the limitations of CSS, and then asked if Captain Noble would accept full responsibility for putting in the requested strike. Captain Noble's answer was in the affirmative.

Colonel Bailey, Captain Noble, and I decided to keep the mission request classified SECRET until 0250 hours, at which time a warning to the Ben Het defense force would go out over landline field telephones. We would warn all troops to hunker down into bunkers. The reason for the secrecy was that we knew there were spies in our midst. I decided to take up a position in the dugout area of the TOC entrance. The area had basically the same overhead cover as did the main TOC. I elected not to sleep. The night was coal-black dark and the time ticked by slowly until TOT minus 10 minutes. The warning to the troops was released. Almost every man at Ben Het was deep in sleep and would not hear or feel a thing. At precisely 0300 hours, the earth trembled and there was a long low rumble as the bombs exploded in unison. Ka-thunk. I heard the impact of what I knew to be bomb shrapnel hitting and resting in a sandbag just above my head. As all fell into dead silence, once more I reached up, probed, and located the still warm "half-fist size" chunk of bomb shrapnel. I tucked it away in my pocket and awaited the break of dawn.

As the cold damp dawn arrived, I was relieved to know that our besieged camp had survived another night. I looked out toward the airstrip. Through the mist of the foggy monsoon morning, I could barely make out the surface of the runway. I placed my binoculars to my eyes in an attempt to get a closer look. I could see what I believed to be a couple of bomb craters, which I attributed to the early morning B-52 strike.

I stepped across the way, where I entered the SF mess hall and had breakfast. Following breakfast, I went to the S-3 section in the TOC. No special news was available. So I was just hanging around while I waited for something to break, when a Special Forces sergeant came in. He was looking for me. "Come on Sarge. I have something I want to show you." He motioned for me to follow him. He led the way over to the LLDB bunker (LLDB was the ARVN counterpart to our own Special Forces advisory team). We entered the LLDB bunker and descended the earthen stairs.

At the bottom, we stepped through into the main chamber of the bunker. Daylight was pouring through from a gaping hole in the bunker roof. I discovered that I was standing ankle deep in paper leaflets. (The Air Force dropped psychological warfare leaflets, urging the enemy to come over to our side.) As I looked around I saw the remains of an inert bomb casing lying in the middle of the leaflet-laced debris. "Wow!" I commented. "Did anyone get killed or injured?" I asked the A-Team Sergeant. "Just one man." He pointed to two of the upright posts that reinforced the bunker roof. "He had his hammock tied between the posts. The leaflet bomb just missed him, but the shock of impact rolled him out of his hammock and his leg was broken." "Whew!" I said. "I sure am thankful for that." Several other people visited the LLDB bunker following my visit. I heard no more on the subject. The way I figure it is this: When they fragged (I am unsure of terminology here, it may be that the mission was changed in flight, and the one plane diverted) the B-52 was already in flight. No one thought about the time setting of the leaflet bomb. Since the normal altitude of the bomb run was reduced by one-third, the bomb hit the ground before the time fuze could activate. The oversight also led to the leaflet bomb traveling a different trajectory from the normal bombs. In any case, the live bombs were dead on target. However, there would be no BDA because there was no one available to make one. There was no way to assess the damage done to enemy forces. No one else seemed to take any further interest in the strike. I was just too busy with other pressing combat problems to dwell on the subject. We had more convoy airdrop activity scheduled. The news media was very active, but we were running far behind, hardly to keeping abreast of the news. A/3/6 had a small TV that they watched. They would share the latest news reports with us; however, the TV got knocked out, too. Now we could only wait until we got newspapers from the rear.

Wednesday, 25 June, enemy artillery bombardments were increased. A record 445 enemy rounds fell on the camp that day. Hindsight reveals that the enemy was most likely covering a partial withdrawal of some of its siege force. However, this was unknown to us. For all we knew, it was business as usual. The NVA ambush forces were still active along Highway 512 between Dak To and Ben Het. Even though our convoys were far better protected than earlier on, it did not deter the enemy efforts to stop them. Two men were lost on the 25th convoy, one of whom belonged to 6/14 Arty. One hell of a firefight broke out between convoy escort people and the enemy ambush force. As I recall, an estimated 150 enemy dead were reported in the clash. A total of 17 Allied troops, including the two Americans, were lost. The airdrop planes were experiencing no antiaircraft fire since the 7th Air Force people had changed their tactics. Shortages of water and hot food were worsening more each day.

During the ambush that day, I witnessed the following incident from my tower vantage point: I saw a Huey Cobra gunship making a run against the enemy bushwhackers. I heard one of the two-man crew say, "Hey did you see that Dink shoot at us with an AK?" "Yup," said the other "Stupid asshole!" At that very instant, the Cobra gunship trailing black smoke nosed into the jungle, crashed, and exploded on impact. Of course no one could move to the crash site. That same afternoon, a patrol was forming up. I had just met a news reporter from the *San Francisco Chronicle*. He was a longhaired hippie-type, whom I seldom had time for, but this one I found to be different. He asked the Special Forces Patrol Leader, "Hey man. Where you all going?" "On patrol," the patrol leader answered. "Just a minute," said the hippie reporter. "I'll see if I can borrow a gun and I'll go with you guys." The patrol leader handed him a CAR-15 and off they went. (I recognized the fact that the longhaired hippie's report would be factual. I respected the man for his professionalism and true grit.)

Following the patrol's return to camp later, I was handed an Army issue waterproof bag by the patrol leader. "Here's a present for you Sarge," said the patrol leader. I took the bag and untied the opening. The fumes that escaped from the bag as I opened it caused me to gag. I think there is no smell as putrid as that of a decomposing human body. I tagged the enemy documents and an NVA gas mask following my own examination. I was required to send them back to higher headquarters.

They would have to be delivered to North Hill to go out with our next mail pickup. It must be pointed out here that the enemy did resort to using CS (tear) gas against us during the fighting.

Following this episode with the waterproof bag, I went to chow. We had round steak and canned corn. It was great. But, after a few bites, I detected the smell of the rotting human flesh still clinging to my unwashed hands, as we had no water in which to wash up. I had not had a shower since leaving Pleiku some four weeks earlier. I have a strong stomach, but the stench from the rotting corpses lying out there in our perimeter wire permeated our living space. Just the thought of what was causing the odor ruined my meal. I could not force myself to take another bite. Later that night, I was in the S-3 section of the TOC. Colonel Bailey was there. He was writing to the mother of the boy who had been killed during the convoy ambush. It was very late, and I was making my daily Enemy Situation Report (SITREP) by radio to Nha Trang. The Colonel interrupted me. He handed me a Zippo cigarette lighter and indicated for me to read the inscription on it. He said, "How can I send this to the soldier's mother?" The inscription read, "Yea though I walk through the Valley of the Shadow of Death, I shall fear no evil, because I'm the meanest Son-of-a-Bitch in the Valley!" I didn't hand the lighter back to Colonel Bailey. Instead, I carried it in my hand as I went topside, where I threw it as far into the black night as I could throw it. I simply told the Colonel, "It's not your problem anymore."

A patrol, led by Special Forces, got hit hard the next morning as they checked out the southeast end of the runway again. Captain Eric Noble, the Senior Advisor and A-Team leader, was wounded during the ensuing firefight. The team medic was able to get close enough to the enemy fortified position, an underground bunker-like fortification, to lob a hand grenade inside. Following the explosion of the concussion grenade, he entered the enemy's lair. There was one lone survivor of a 12-man NVA Combat Assault Team inside who tried to kill the SF medic, but failed. The SF medic shot the NVA soldier through the groin area. The enemy's wound sent him into an unconscious state. The team medic tossed the wounded enemy soldier out of the bunker. He and two KIA CIDG soldiers were loaded into the back of the team jeep (a commo type, with tailgate) that returned to the Main Hill compound. The jeep driver stopped the jeep at the compound aid station. Someone sent word to me. "Come to the aid station and bring along your interpreter."

When I was a few yards away someone called to me and said, "You're too late. The prisoner just died." Curious, I looked at the three bodies lying there in the back of the jeep. A moment later, I spotted movement in the NVA soldier's big toe. (He was barefoot.) I then directed the men standing nearby to get him inside to the 6/14 Battalion surgeon. I asked the surgeon, who was an Army captain (I can no longer recall his name), to see what he could do to revive the man. I made it plain to the doctor that I needed very much to interrogate this POW. The medics and doctor pumped the prisoner full of morphine. The surgeon then turned the man over in order to examine the bullet exit area of the wound. A hole just above the buttocks was discovered. It was the size of a saucer. A bullet fired from an M-16 rifle makes a very small hole going in, but as the bullet tumbles after making impact, it leaves a very large exit hole. Surprisingly, the prisoner suddenly regained consciousness and appeared very alert. From my experience and training I knew that this was the very best time to do the initial interrogation. As it turned out, I got some pretty accurate information from the prisoner. He was a warrant officer and his mission had been to make preparations for an assault on the Main Hill complex. I suspected that they were an engineer demolition team. We called in a "Dust-off," and had the prisoner transported to the rear area where higher intelligence people wanted to interrogate him further. As it turned out, I was the only one who got any useful information from him. He died somewhere in a rear area aid station while on the operating table.

Later that afternoon, I was in the observation tower. During the previous evening, I had used up most of the 50-caliber machine gun ammunition so I decided to restock it. I asked the Special Forces to send me four cans of 50-caliber machine gun belted ammo, along with a man to assist me in pulling it up into the tower by rope. An SF E-4 showed up with the ammo cans, and I could tell that he was very irritated. He demonstrated hostility towards me. It was obvious to me that he resented helping a "Leg" do such a menial task. ("Leg" refers to a non-airborne-type soldier.) In any case, I had a knotted rope available (knotted at 18-inch intervals to prevent slippage while pulling), and we tied the four ammo cans together and then hooked them to the end of the rope. We both then climbed up into the tower platform.

We had to leave the trapdoor open while we pulled the ammo up. The trapdoor was heavily sandbagged and had a counter balance system attached to help in opening, holding open, and closing it. To increase our leverage, we locked knees. Just as we were giving a final pull on the rope, a mortar round exploded directly below. The Special Forces soldier fell backward. He screamed as he lay writhing in pain. I jumped to his aid. Examining his knee wound, I discovered a big chunk of his kneecap had been blown off. As I prepared to dress his wound, he reared up. Cussing at me he said, "Don't touch me, you son-of-a-bitch!" and with that he exited the tower. I rang the TOC on the tower field telephone and alerted them to have someone rush out to help him to the aid station. It was decided to "Dust" him off. In the meantime, I was able to locate the bloody piece of mortar shrapnel that had caused his wound. I got someone to run it over to North Hill and offer the souvenir to him as he was about to be dusted off.

That evening we received a rare visit from a senior officer. I was in the S-2 working on some targeting information. The Special Forces intelligence sergeant was in the room talking with me. Colonel Andrew Marquis, the senior Green Beret officer in the area, who was commander of the B24 Detachment at Kontum, walked in. He "dressed down" the E-7 Intelligence NCO. "I want to hear no more about you harassing the ARVN tank commander (he was referring to the ARVN 3d Armored Cavalry). He is fearful of losing any more of his tanks." (They had lost all but two during the May fighting.) "Just lay off!" Well, the ARVN tank commander was a sore point with me. I knew the real reason why he refused to employ his tanks for perimeter defense purposes. He was protecting his two remaining tanks, keeping them as a "Hold Card." If the enemy threatened to over run our position, he planned to use the two tanks as a means of breaking out, in order to save his ass. I did not approve of his reasoning. So, not having anything to fear from Colonel Marquis who was not over me as per se, I spoke up. "Well, I'd like to see that son-of-a-bitch risk a couple of more" (of his tanks). Colonel Marquis gave me an icy stare. I felt that if looks could kill, I'd surely be dead. The Colonel stomped out. I would read a newspaper article later, based on an interview he did while back in Kontum that night. You can bet your ass he didn't want to spend the night with us there at Ben Het. No one, not even news reporters, ever elected to spend the night at Ben Het.

The next couple of days just sort of run together in my memory. I was suffering from shear combat exhaustion. We were getting the backlog of newspapers from the rear. Of course, we only received the *"Stars and Stripes."* Many of the articles were written by Staff Corespondent SP 4 Bob Hodiern, who did the best job he could to bring out the truth. However, official Allied spokesmen, who executed a program designed to mislead, misled the news reporters. Touting the fighting as a test for

Vietnamization by ARVN forces, they could ill afford for the truth to get out. Despite their efforts, Ben Het was receiving some very bad press. The daily headlines "screamed out" a message of "gloom and doom."

SURROUNDED CUT OFF BY ENEMY
Reds Heavily Attack U. S. Special Forces Camp
June 23, 1969[3]

105 North Viet Troops Killed
Bloody Battle Rages Near Ben Het Camp
24 June 1969[4]

Allies Fly In Reinforcements
New Enemy Attacks Hit Ben Het Camp
25 June 1969[5]

Supply convoy arrives
B52s Saturate Ben Het Jungles
26 June 1969[6]

Allied Camp Defenders 'Desperate,' Reds Claim
27 June 1969[7]

Ben Het: Sitting on a Bombarded Pinpoint
28 June 1969[8]

Headlines carried stories that were not intended to provide entertainment. Rather, they told of misuse of U.S. soldiers who were overused, exhausted, and short on infantry support to relieve them from the grips of a besieging enemy force.

I got my hands on a newspaper that featured an article quoting Colonel Marquis. The arrticle read… "Who said today the North Vietnamese have two *full strength* infantry regiments around Ben Het—The 28th and 66th—plus the 40th Artillery Regiment and a sapper battalion. We figure there are 3,000 men up there, plus bearers." He [Marquis] said, 'If they wanted to send those two regiments straight up the hills, they could probably take Ben Het. But we would make it so costly to them in human life I doubt if they will try.' … [D]id you take note of the estimated enemy strength? Two full strength regiments of NVA infantry only totaled 3,000?"

Note: Isn't it easy to sit back on your ass in the rear, and make such cocksure statements?

The top U.S. brass became upset about all the bad press. To top it off, a story was about to be released in reference to a U.S. Senatorial investigation being conducted by Senators Edmond Muskie and Margaret Chase Smith of Maine, and both had asked for full reports on the Ben Het situation.

Lieutenant Colonel Nelson Thompson had written a private letter to his father, who was a doctor. His father used the information contained in Colonel Thompson's letter to file a complaint asking for a Senatorial probe. Thompson, the artillery commander at Dak To, did not know of his father's actions and did not intend to have his private correspondence made public.

On Saturday morning 28 June 1969, three general officers followed by a large entourage descended on Ben Het. I looked up from the S-3 desk in the TOC to recognize Lt. Colonel Bailey escorting a high-ranking general officer into the room. Col. Bailey introduced me to the general. "General Rosson, this is Sergeant Lamerson. Sergeant Lamerson is my S-2." The general made no comment, only nodding his head as a form of recognition. They both left the room as fast as they had entered. I was proud that the colonel had introduced me the way he did, but I was disturbed by General Rosson's apparent disinterest in talking to me. General William B. Rosson, and General Creighton Abrams were recognized in military circles as the top military tacticians in the U.S. Army. General Rosson had spent his first tour in Vietnam from 1954 to 1955. During the primary years of the U.S. involvement in the war, he served as Chief of Staff, MACV; Commanding General, Task Force Oregon (later the Americal Division); Commanding General, I Field Force; Commanding General, Provisional Corps, Vietnam (later XXIV Corps); Acting Commander, III Marine Amphibious Force; and he was currently Deputy Commander, USMACV.[9]

I have never learned for sure who the second ranking general officer was who accompanied General Rosson on this visit to Ben Het was, however, the third ranking officer was Brigadier General Winant Sidle, Commanding General, I Field Force Vietnam, Artillery. According to General Rosson,

> ... in 1965 and again in 1966, Giap described his strategy for South Vietnam as being one of "strategic mobility." Also in 1966, [Giap] spoke of an "offensive-defensive" version of strategic mobility wherein major NVA and VC forces were positioned in South Vietnam near border sanctuaries. These forces would attempt to attract friendly forces into previously prepared killing zones.[10]

Giap's strategy, as outlined by Rosson, fit the scenario that was played out by Giap's forces during the 1967 Battle of Dak To. However, by early 1969, there are strong indications that support my hypothesis, which is that the NVA under NVA Generals Giap and Dung, had gained a "Mechanized Warfare" capability that included the use of armor/track drawn mobile artillery and mobile infantry forces. These forces were combined to form a "fully mechanized, Armored Spearhead Infantry Division." To support such divisions, large fuel pipelines would have had to exist.

Part of my hypothesis states that such a fuel pipeline did exist as early as the spring of 1969. I do not believe that it stretched all the way to Loc Ninh yet, as was the case by the time SVN fell to the North in 1975.[11] However, with all the armor/track vehicle movement that had been detected from inside Laos near the A Shau Valley and Ben Het by the spring of 1969, it is certain that the large amounts of fuel being used had to come from such a source.

The U.S. Army had been careful not to admit that Ben Het was under an enemy siege. MACV found themselves in an embarrassing situation at Ben Het. As General Abrams had been sent by General Westmoreland during the Battle of Dak To,[12] so, too, had General Rosson been dispatched to Ben Het to defuse a potentially "explosive" political situation. Meanwhile, General Abrams had another very important situation with possible political repercussions to deal with. His problems stemmed from the alleged Special Forces disposal of a double agent, Thai Khac Chuyen, whose turncoat activities during Project Gamma threatened several hundred lives. That action received widespread attention when MACV Commander Creighton Abrams insisted on arresting and charging 5th Special Forces Group personnel with "premeditated execution of a Vietnamese national. Unable to produce any evidence, Army Secretary Stanley Resor ordered all charges dropped."[13]

Still smarting from the above-stated decision, General Abrams certainly did not want to heap any praise on the 5th U. S. Force's people and their CIDG program. As a matter of fact, he was setting the stage for having the 5th U.S. Special Forces discontinue the entire Civilian Irregular Defense Group program and "stand down." This he would do by early 1970.[14] There was a high-level conference held in Saigon during July 1969. The conference was attended by Joint Chiefs of Staff Chairman Earle Wheeler, MACV Commander General Abrams, and Pacific Command Admiral John S. McCain. They were all conventional line officers who opposed the CIDG concept and sought to remove the

5th Special Forces Group from Vietnam, because they failed to comprehend the guerrilla nature of the war.[15] Speaking in General Abrams' defense, however, the Vietnam War was moving toward becoming a strictly conventional war, with the introduction of NVA Mechanized Infantry Divisions that would be doing the lion's share of the offensive fighting.

The pacification program had failed. With the newly announced troop withdrawal on the drawing board there was no need to keep the Special Forces in Vietnam. General Rosson, being Abrams' Deputy Commander, had little choice but to carry out his wishes. General Rosson was not at Ben Het on this Saturday in June to "give praise and award medals." He was there to "still the waters" and to bring some silence to the "bad press," and nothing more. The American military command in South Vietnam was charged with the mission of putting the newly acclaimed Vietnamization program into effect, and that was their main focus. "To hell with the unparalleled heroics of a handful of America's fighting best. The show must go on."

In any case, I looked up again following only a few minutes delay after Colonel Bailey and General Rosson had departed from my presence, to see General Rosson reappear followed by most of the commissioned officers and perhaps a senior 5th Special Forces NCO or two. I did not see Colonel Bailey, however, I am sure he was off briefing General Sidle. Someone from the group was making a feeble attempt at briefing General Rosson. Several others in the group were guilty of interrupting the man. I could see that the General's patience was waning. At that precise moment, "Ker-wumpf!" a 120-mortar shell exploded near the TOC and just above us. "Eighty-Two's," someone blurted out. "No Sir!" I said. "Those are One-Twenties," as the second mortar shell exploded. "And that is the problem, General." As I finished my sentence, the General's hand went up in a signal for silence. Everything stopped. You could have heard a pin drop. "What do you mean, Sergeant?" asked the General. "All of the wrong people are doing all the talking, Sir," I answered him. Once again the General signaled for silence, which was broken only when the General spoke. He said, "Let's listen to the Sergeant, he seems to know what's going on. Sergeant, is there some place that we can go to talk in private?" asked General Rosson. "Yes Sir!" I said, as I beckoned him to follow me.

I led the way back toward the front of the TOC where my S-2 briefing room was located. Since there was not a solid door, the General's aide and the I Field Force Artillery Command sergeant major stood guard outside of the doorway. I was expecting to receive my "comeuppance," but it was not so. The old (about 52 years old) General turned to me and said, "All right, Sergeant, what's the skinny?" I am not going to attempt to go into all of the details, but I can say that I was able to give the General a more than satisfactory "one-on-one" briefing. As our talk was about to reach conclusion, I told the General that I, along with many of the others at Ben Het, thought that we had been placed on the proverbial "sacrificial block." Looking the General square in the eyes, I asked him bluntly, "General, are we going to be sacrificed?" The General seemed taken aback by my bluntness; however, he was very composed as he answered me honestly and up-front. "Certainly not Sergeant! You men have done a magnificent job here; no one is going to be sacrificed. As a matter of fact, the consensus is that the enemy is making a full withdrawal." With that, the General turned to leave. I followed, and as we reached the doorway, he placed his hand on my shoulder and guided me ahead of him through the doorway. He spoke again so that his aide and the command sergeant major could understand his every word. "If you need anything in the future Sergeant, anything at all, you just ask, OK?" Both his aide, an Army captain, and the command sergeant major were busy taking notes as they clung to his every word. As the General walked back toward the S-3 section, both men hung back as they smiled and patted me on the back. I said, "This battle (The Siege of Ben Het) is bound to go down in the history books as one of the most significant of this war." The captain was off to catch up with General Rosson, but the command sergeant major stopped to take the time to ask me, "Sergeant Lamerson, is there anything that I can send to you that you really need?" I thought for a moment and replied, "Yes there is. We desperately need a portable commode, one small enough to be placed here inside the TOC, but also with the capability of being emptied on a daily basis." "OK," he said. "You've got it." For all practical purposes, the siege was over.

What none of us knew at Ben Het was that History was about to be misrepresented, and we were to be robbed of our well-earned gallant and heroic victory.

Notes

1 The nickname of an M-42 tracked vehicle with two 40mm antiaircraft guns, used mainly as ground support in Vietnam. See: Linda Reinberg, *In The Field: The language of the Vietnam War*, (New York: Facts On File, Inc., 1991), 69.

2. The open arms program promising fair treatment to enemy soldiers who voluntarily stopped fighting. (*In The Field,* 41)
3. Associated Press Reporter, "Reds Heavily Attack U.S. Special Forces Camp," *Independent Times,* 23 June 1969.
4. Associated Press Reporter, "Bloody Battle Rages Near Ben Het Camp," *Independent Times,* 24 June 1969.
5. Associated Press Reporter, "New Enemy Attacks Hit Ben Het Camp," ____, 25 June 1969.
6. Staff Reporter, "B52s Saturate Ben Het Jungles," *Stars and Stripes,* 26 June 1969, Pacific edition.
7. Associated Press Reporter, "Allied Camp Defenders 'Desperate,' Reds Claim," *Lawton Constitution,* 27 June 1969.
8. Spec. 4 Bob Hodierne, "Ben Het: Sitting on a Bombarded Pinpoint," *Stars and Stripes,* 28 June 1969, Pacific edition.
9. Michael Lee Lanning and Dan Cragg, *Inside the VC and the NVA,* (New York: Ballintine Books, 1992), 194.
10. Ibid., 195.
11. Clark Dougan, Stephan Weiss, and the editors of Boston Publishing Company, *The fall of the South,* a volume of *The Vietnam Experience,* (Boston: Boston Publishing Company, 1985), 10.
12. Edward F. Murphy, *Dak To,* (New York: Pocket Books, 1993), 176-177.
13. Shelby L. Stanton, *Special Forces at War,* (Charlottesville: Howell Press, 1990), 290.
14. Ibid., 316.
15. Ibid., 290.

CHAPTER 12

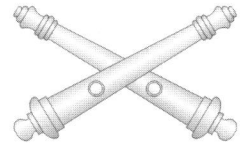

The Last Straw

*It doesn't take a hero to send men into battle.
It takes a hero to be one of those men
who goes into battle.*
General H. Norman Schwarzkopf, U.S. Army Retired

General William B. Rosson's 28 June 1969 visit to Ben Het was used to set the stage and trigger one of the most cleverly orchestrated propaganda moves of the entire Vietnam War. General Rosson was well experienced in affairs that "mouthed" the official line in order to keep the proverbial "waters calmed," as I have noted below:

> At midnight on 1 December 1967 General Rosson declared the battle for Dak To over. The MACV issued a press release lauding the great victory at Dak To, but General Rosson and the surviving participants knew better. Sure, the Americans had driven the North Vietnamese from the region, but the NVA had not been defeated; they'd be back someday. The Americans controlled some strategic hill tops, but they would soon depart, returning the hills to the jungle and the enemy.[1]

Note: FSB 12 (Ben Het) was among the strategic hills alluded to above.[2] During 1968 the site was converted by the 299th Engineer Battalion and the 5th U.S. Forces, 244th A Detachment, into the camp that still flourished and had survived the 59-day ordeal, unofficially dubbed "The Siege of Ben Het" during May and June, 1969.

Following General Rosson's visit, the *Stars and Stripes* newspaper featured a story that included facts on his visit, as well as some of the general's comments. However, in reference to the general's comments to me about an enemy withdrawal, records indicate that he based them on the following: "A high point took place on 25th-26. We noticed that the long-range artillery fire was lessening, and the VC/NVA were withdrawing. ARVN wasn't sweeping much."[3]

Note: The B-52 strike placed on the southeast end of Ben Het's airstrip was at 0300 hours on 25 June. It seems ironic to me that an NVA withdrawal was detected within 24 hours following that strike, unless there was an undisclosed reason, perhaps due to the effectiveness of the strike.

I cannot offer indisputable proof, however, the record does offer a margin of evidence to support my belief that the B-52 strike did major damage to the NVA command and control element conducting the offensive operation against Ben Het. One piece of evidence is provided in the remarks made by a senior U.S. Air Force field grade officer associated with providing U.S. air support, who said:

> From a DASC viewpoint, however, better coordination would have been accomplished if the Arc Lights were considered as tactical air and were included in the TACS operation.[4]

The DASC obviously liked the concept of the employment of B-52 bombers in the tactical role. The key players involved in providing the U.S. air support for Ben Het did not ever mention the one lone B-52 strike that I have explained. I believe that this was due to the fact that the strict policy covering the use of the strategic bomber was broken. It was a matter of CYA (cover your ass). The closest they came to disclosing the fact that they bombed so close was by disguising the strike as a routine CSS. The following documentation is provided below:

> The use of CSS was widespread around Ben Het, especially during bad weather conditions and at night. In early June, targets were hit about 1,100 to 2,000 meters away from the camp, and later the CSS strikes were flown as close as 500 meters ... In these cases, DASC Alpha would call the TACP at Dak To, who would then call the ground commander in Ben Het. The DASC would explain the limitations of CSS, and then ask if he would accept the responsibility. The ground commander answered in the affirmative in each case.[5]

I recall two such missions: One was when we used the USAF C-130 Daisy-Cutter drop, and the other was the lone B-52 close-in strike on 25 June. It must be noted that my references to specific dates in June may vary by 24 hours one way or the other. I could not keep a daily diary due to military restrictions prohibiting such actions; I would not have had the time to do so in any case. I most likely ignored the historical significance of our actions at Ben Het until after it was apparent that the enemy was withdrawing their besieging force.

Subsequent sorties were put in on new locations, which helped maintain an acceptable degree of accuracy and maximum effectiveness for CSS. With few exceptions, Arc Lights struck daily, some in the proximity of Ben Het. Frequent changes in Arc Light targets occurred, but this had been expected. According to Lt. Col. E.P. Callaway, SAC ADVON, Hq, 7AF:

> Our scheduling took place knowing full-well that there would be changes in the target boxes around Ben Het especially, because of the fleeting nature of the targets.
>
> From 21 to 27 June, we had 98 sorties around Ben Het. Every target box, except one, was changed. Some were changed two, three, and four times... Most were in close support—anything within three kilometers was classified as close support ... .[6]

Following General Rosson's visit, he returned to Dak To and took action that is reflected in the USAF records:

> G-3 Air and the Director, DASC Alpha, are constantly evaluating the tac air situation in the Ben Het area in order to place as much air as possible at the disposal of the ground commanders....
>
> During the same period, i.e., the last week of June, headquarters, 7AF, again made it plainly clear that Ben Het was to receive highest priority for air support .... The 7AF concern was further evidenced by communications between TACC and DASC Alpha, which included hourly updates of information from DASC and offers of more air from TACC. There was much command influence, as Col. E.W. Rosencrans at the TACC noted.
>
> On 28 June, special instructions were issued at the TACC relative to the situation at Ben Het. The Senior Duty Officers Official Activities Log contained the following entry:
>
> SDO—Lay it on Ben Het!
>
> ♦ Keep a Shadow or Spooky over Ben Het all night tonight. Take from other areas if necessary.
>
> ♦ I want two fighters every thirty minutes over Ben Het beginning as soon as possible on the morning of 29 June. Check with DASC Alpha to see how soon they can get the FAC there. All fighters are to expend!
>
> ♦ Lay on the COMBAT SKYSPOT tonight—as many as possible.
>
> ♦ I would rather be guilty of overkill than be blamed for another Dien Bien Phu!
>
> ♦ Ben Het sorties will be fragged (preplanned) beginning on Monday.
>
> ♦ Any questions—please call.
>
> S/Colonel Rosencrans[7]

One of my chief complaints to General Rosson had been immediately addressed. I had warned the general that unless we were given more control over the delivery of air assets, we might lose Ben Het. I remember saying, "When I determine that we need a certain amount or kind of fire power to attack a target, I want that fire now!" It would appear that the general took my words to heart. There was no way that even he could predict what the enemy's next move would be. Therefore, he did not declare the battle over just yet.

Not understanding the full implications of our perilous position at Ben Het, there were some at the TACC in Dak To who did not agree with additional air being ordered. The Senior ALO at Dak To, Col. Jack Cude, Jr. said:

> ... Toward the last, we had too much air ... we felt that we could have done a better job with one-half the sorties, if we could have gotten good confirmed targets and reasonable weather ... .[8]

Such thinking demonstrates to me that Colonel Cude did not understand where we at Ben Het were coming from. We had nothing but the deepest respect for the job that the Air Force was doing for us. But, I needed to have immediate response to my request for air support. To further demonstrate the misunderstanding of our situation at Ben Het, I offer the following example:

> We were being driven crazy by people trying to force the system to give them more support. They were in a heavily fortified position; they didn't take all that many casualties considering they were under attack. They were supplied and were given all that air support—*Arc Light right on the runway outside the perimeter*—all making sure that they killed those enemy close to Ben Het.[9]

As I have stated, my complaint was valid. Once you look up and see the enemy enmasse coming up the hill to get you, it's a bit late to complain about the flaws in the system. To the best of my knowledge, the enemy still had the capability to mass their troops and attack. It was my solemn duty to prevent this. To me it was a matter of survival.

In any case, General Rosson's visit to Ben Het was followed by a news release. On Sunday, 29 June, the following appeared in a featured story by the *Stars and Stripes*:

> General William B. Rosson, deputy commander of American Forces in Vietnam flew from Saigon headquarters to visit the camp, which has been under attack for 59 days.
>
> "I think the situation is exceedingly favorable," Rosson said after he arrived. "We've punished the enemy severely. The camp is intact, fully-manned, well-supplied, and the morale of forces very high."

Almost as he spoke, seven rounds of mortar fire slammed into the camp. There were no injuries, but shell fragments landed near the underground operations center where Rosson and his aides were discussing battle plans.

Three days earlier, U.S. artillery officers on the north hill of the camp said that morale was deteriorating because of the lack of fresh water, high casualties that were being replaced slowly and the slow movement of ammunitions and supplies.

The U.S. Command has apparently moved since then to correct the supply situation. In the past 48 hours, 20 new artillerymen arrived in the camp and fresh water had been air-dropped.

The article went on to note that "the U.S. Command is known to view the Ben Het/Dak To campaign as a test of the South Vietnamese army's capacity to fight it out against the North Vietnamese and Viet Cong." It also stated that "a new operation launched [...] over the weekend by seven fresh battalions of South Vietnamese troops flown from other areas in the Central highlands was underway."[10]

Note: The total time that Ben Het had been without fresh water was five days. However, we could either catch cordite-flavored rainwater in our ponchos or we could drink up the rest of our short supply of soda pop and beer.

On Friday, 27 June, we had gotten a convoy through to Ben Het and also a significant aerial resupply drop. The Saturday, 28 June, front page *Stars and Stripes* (Pacific Edition) headlines read: "ARVN Reopen Ben Het Road." This was in reference to the breakthrough of a heavily armed convoy on Friday. The move was a ploy by the ARVN designed to set the stage, making it appear that they were the ones who had broken "The Siege of Ben Het." The road was not open per se. That is why the ARVN launched the Sunday, 29 June, operation, which coincided with the following civilian VIP visit to Ben Het by South Vietnam's President Nguyen Van Thieu, an event that was not covered by American news reporters.

We got the word to prepare for Thieu's arrival. "Transportation for the SVN president and his entourage will be provided." Well, that was a laugh. We had no vehicles that were usable enough for the purpose, due to combat losses. All we had left was an M-8 full-tracked troop/ammunition carrier. We were also told, "No U.S. troops are welcome to attend the ARVN-run ceremony; this includes any attempt to greet the South Vietnamese president." In short, we were ordered to keep our distance. "A seen, but not heard" sort of a deal. That kind of treatment did not set well with most of us.

Thieu and his entourage, which included Vietnamese news reporters out of Saigon, arrived over there on North Hill, as many visitors as possible squeezed into the M-8 vehicle. The rest of the bunch had to slog along through the red clay mud as they trailed along behind. We laughed at the sight of those "shit-heads" in suits and ties slogging along as they followed the full-track vehicle over to Main Hill. Now, we were beginning to believe that the enemy had truly withdrawn. Otherwise, the whole kit and caboodle would have been blown away by enemy artillery fire. President Thieu decorated several ARVN during the ARVN-run ceremony that followed his arrival at Ben Het. Later it would be brought out that the ARVNS had been declared the victors over the NVA. It was said of them, "They met and defeated the best that the NVA had to offer."

As spelled out in the following newspaper article:

Ben Het battling ends

Ben Het—According to the commander of the South Vietnamese–U.S. task force operation in Dak To-Ben Het area, the North Vietnamese force which recently surrounded the Civilian Irregular Defense Group Camp at Ben Het has been defeated.

"The enemy has been smashed," said Col. Nguyen Ba Lien, commander of ARVN's 24th Special Tactical Zone ...

"The enemy's efforts were not successful. After three days of steady contact, which saw 214 of their troops killed, the NVA withdrew from the highway allowing two resupply convoys to reach the camp. ARVN losses during the fighting were 17 killed and 94 wounded, spokesmen said."[11]

This fight alluded to included the Friday 26 June convoy, not the ARVN Operation "Will Win" Dan Quyen 43 that was launched from Dak Mot bridge four miles east of Ben Het. The ARVN were not scheduled to make it to Ben Het until at least the next day. That night, the NVA hit the ARVNs in their night camp.

The newspapers on Monday, 30 June, carried the following story by David Hoffman, *Washington Post* Foreign Service, headlined "Ben Het used as 'Bait,' Officer Says:"

Kontum, South Vietnam, 30 June—"The South Vietnamese colonel commanding local allied ground forces claimed today that the beleaguered defenders of Ben Het Special Forces camp have been used to 'bait' a trap set two months ago for the enemy."

Since 6 May, North Vietnamese Army units encircling the hilltop outpost had pounded it with 5000 or more rounds of mixed mortar, rocket, and artillery fire. Among the camp's 1000-man defense force are approximately 200 American artillerymen and Special Forces advisors, who have endured considerable privation since the siege began in early June. South Vietnamese Marine Col. Nguyen Ba Lien; the ground commander, predicted today that four fresh South Vietnamese battalions advancing toward Ben Het about 50 miles north of here would break the Siege within three days. "I think the enemy is smashed," Lien said at his headquarters here. "The battle appears ended."

The youthful looking colonel, who commands the 24th Special Tactical Zone composed of Kontum and Pleiku Provinces, said he decided about two months ago to use Ben Het to bait the North Vietnamese forces—reportedly the equivalent of *two divisions*—operating near the juncture of Laos, Cambodia and South Vietnam.

By leaving the camp lightly defended, he said, he hoped to trick the enemy units into massing for an assault, thus exposing them to allied air strikes and artillery ... Asked to assess enemy strategy, Col. Lien said the Communists sought but failed to demonstrate that the South Vietnamese army could not be relied upon to protect American combat support units. But in no sense did Lien see the Ben Het fighting as a test of his army's capability vs. that of the enemy.

"The units were too small.," he said. South Vietnam has more than a million men under arms, "and only two or three thousand are involved here," he added.[12]

Following President Thieu's visit to Ben Het, nothing about it was to ever appear in the American newspapers. However, following that visit and before the ARVN arrived, we got another convoy into Ben Het. Colonel Bailey received a replacement jeep for the one that had been destroyed by enemy fire.

We had been hoarding water in a rain barrel that we had been able to half fill with monsoon rainwater that we had collected. Except for potable drinking water, there was no water available for such a luxury as a shower or bath. We intended to raffle off the rainwater to one of our people so that the lucky person could take a "bird bath." Well, I looked up to see a young lad from the convoy that had just arrived from the rear a short time before. His hair was wet, and he had a towel that he was using to dry himself off from the waist up. I let out a "war whoop" that scared the daylights out of the kid. He was lucky to escape with his hide. I still suffered from lack of proper rest, but I had a lot of required reports to file. I was busy compiling some of the facts. When I looked up from my work, I noticed a Lieutenant from the convoy walking out of the door of my S-2 shop with my folding canvas cot tucked under his arm. Once again, I let out an ear splitting bellow. "Hey Lieutenant!" I called to him, "Bring it back." He turned back to face me and said. "You're not using it, and I don't have a place to sleep." "Put it back," I said. "It's mine and I will be using it as soon as I get done with my reports. So I'll thank you to keep your 'shit-hooks' off of it." Before he could get himself in any deeper shit with me, someone pulled him aside and explained the facts of life to him. I had earned a lot of respect from my peers and colleagues.

I think it is appropriate here to add a few last remarks about air support at Ben Het. From an interview with Ltc. Jack Cude Jr., Senior ALO at Dak To:

> The reason that our BDA was low in this second period was that nobody was out looking at bodies. Most of the problems with air support we had during the Ben Het battle were caused by trying to work around the bad weather. For a couple of days, we couldn't get a FAC in the air, or fighters or airlift. The area was covered only by Bongo, from Pleiku, we could only use that one type navigational aid for radar bombing. If we had ARCLIGHT going in, we couldn't put in a CSS at the same time. Bongo is set up where they have a 'Sterile Period'—before ARCLIGHT. They run through equipment checks, make dry runs in preparation, so that there won't be mistakes. The strike itself will take 20–30 minutes to get off, so for each ARCLIGHT strike that went in, we lost an hour and a half.
>
> A lot of ARCLIGHTS were put in, and of course, we couldn't put in CSS. Also, a lot of the ARCLIGHT was close to Ben Het, so we couldn't put in TAC AIR, no matter what the weather, because we wanted to keep the aircraft about 10 kilometers away from the ARCLIGHTS.
>
> Most of the action was south-southwest and southeast of Ben Het, but a little in the north. In this limited area, it was difficult to work the multi-type (FACs, ARCLIGHT, Fighter) strikes. At night, we had Spooky and/or Shadow—when they were in the close vicinity of the camp, we couldn't put in any CSS near the camp. So we sent briefing people from the 14th Special Operations Wing to the Special Forces Camp (and ALOs) if they were going to use gunships, use them close to the camp and put the CSS out over the infiltration routes. If the weather got too bad for gunships or if there was no need for them, we would pull them away and use CSS around the camp.
>
> The CSS was accurate—in the initial parts of the battle we were talking about CSS 1100–2000 meters away from Ben Het; later it came as close as 500. Our method—when we put in CSS less than 1 kilometer, we go to the commander and make sure he realizes the seriousness and limitations of CSS and ask him if he would accept responsibility for bringing it in that close. In this case (Ben Het), Captain Noble, the senior advisor for the camp, did take it upon himself and we brought it in close.
>
> How close in to Ben Het did you bring hard ordnance? Right on top of the runway. The strip was not secure. I put bombs between the strip and the perimeter itself when the people at Ben Het were attempting to get out to sweep the area. What were around Ben Het to

start with were U.S. Army FOs for artillery, Special Forces/CIDG Recon patrols and a lot of [NVA] sappers getting ready to hit the base—we had to get these people out. They [the enemy] were giving us trouble and snipers. They shot at us several times. As a matter of fact, when the people from inside started a sweep around the perimeter on 27 June, I put in my last TIC. It was 700 meters north of Ben Het.

The only indication we had that they [the enemy] were leaving was from decreased activity. We would look for targets, and kept one man working the roads, we saw abandoned gun-positions. When they leave in a hurry, you can see this stuff, because they don't take care to camouflage it. We also uncovered a lot of stuff with the strikes—caves and such. But, there was just less activity.[13]

Note: I must give a quick critique of Colonel Cude's remarks above. I do not believe that the briefing people from the 14th Special Operations Wing nor any FACs came physically into Ben Het. If they did, we did not know of it. However, I do want to emphasize his point about close-in bombing. It ties in directly to what I have told you in reference to how close we brought in that single 30-ton load of 750-pound bombs, delivered by a lone B-52 bomber. I also want to insure that you (the reader) picked up on the point that there were times during the critical period of the siege that we lacked full air support capability. Also, please take note that the enemy made a very hasty withdrawal. This is an important point. The Allied command would soon release a joint communiqué that would indicate that they lacked any understanding for "Why the enemy made such a surprised and hasty withdrawal?" However, within a week they would do a "complete turn around." Last, I want to direct your attention to the fact that action from the north of Ben Het was very limited. The Allied troops from within who attempted a sweep to the north were the Mike Strike Force that I mentioned earlier. This was the force that bivouacked in the LZ made by the Daisy-Cutter mission.

A last ditch effort by the NVA command to provide some relief to the "besieging force" at Ben Het resulted in the following action:

> Meanwhile, the threat to Ben Het eased, but military spokesman said U.S. intelligence detected a new buildup of North Vietnamese troops farther south along the Cambodian border.
>
> Because of this, top priority for B-52 bombing strikes was taken away from the Special Forces camp 280 miles northeast of Saigon and given to an area 60 to 80 miles northeast of the capital and only three miles from the border.
>
> The spokesman said only a dozen of 50 B-52 raids flown Monday night and today were centered on Ben Het. The rest were aimed at troops of the North Vietnamese 7th Division gathered around the district town of the Loc Ninh, headquarters reported.

The same enemy regiment tried to take Loc Ninh in a week of heavy fighting in November 1967.

Spokesmen said the Stratofortresses dropped 750 tons of bombs on North Vietnamese troop concentrations, base camps, bunkers, and storage depots on four sides of Loc Ninh, which is 74 miles north of Saigon.

The above article appeared on pages one and four of the Lawton, Oklahoma, *Constitution,* Tuesday, 1 July 1969. It was titled, "G.I. Armor Rips into Red Troop Build Up, Kills 42."

The following is a brief report on troop withdrawal cited in a U.S. Air Force report:

> During the last week of June, both ABFs and sightings of enemy troops decreased around Ben Het and throughout the 24th STZ. Intelligence sources indicated that the VC/NVA were pulling back toward the west into Cambodia. Col. Cude, however, was not totally convinced the enemy had given up the siege. He related that his uncertainty was based partly on what had been happening during the latter part of May and early June.
>
> The U.S. Army advisors were also uncertain about the enemy's movements and intentions. It was not until 2 July that they were fairly certain the VC/NVA had gone, and the siege was declared officially over. Then the advisors wanted an end to the air support for Ben Het.[14]

As I recall, on Tuesday evening, 1 July, several of us at the TOC area were outside by the 81mm mortar pit. We were bareheaded for the first time in weeks. Standing around and "shooting the bull," I suddenly heard a faint "pop" sound from the west. "Incoming," I announced, and raced toward the TOC entrance to seek cover. Everyone else had been following my lead and had been close on my heels. Suddenly the others stopped. "False Alarm!" someone said. About at that very instant, Ker-blam! An 85mm gun shell splattered nearby. I heard one of the men say; "I ain't ever going to doubt Ole Sergeant Lamerson ever again." Hell, I didn't even bother to take any counteraction. Mr. Charles had just saluted us goodbye.

We all got a good night's sleep that night for the first time in weeks. I was in the tower on Wednesday morning, 2 July. I spotted the colonel's driver putting stuff in the colonel's jeep. I called down to him. "What's going on?" I asked. "Well, the ARVNs are coming down the road and they have one of our Forward Observation parties with them. Colonel Bailey and I are going out there to take them Kool-Aid and cigarettes," he said. "Not without me you ain't," I called as I came tumbling down the tower ladder. Once on the ground, I told the driver to be sure that they didn't leave without me and I raced off to get my gear. When I came running back, the colonel was there and very impatient to leave. I explained, "You're not going to go out of this camp without me riding shotgun, colonel," I half-joked. In actuality, I was serious. No one from our battalion had been out that front gate since our arrival at Ben Het more than a month ago. We had no assurance that there was not an enemy sniper still lurking about.

As we pulled through the camp's main gate and entered Highway 512, we turned east. A short way down the road, we had to pass an abandoned VTR that was setting along the side of the Highway. I asked the colonel if we could stop so that I could check the vehicle crew compartment out. I was able to recover two M-14 rifles and one receiver group for a 50-caliber machine gun. I then knew that the enemy had indeed withdrawn, otherwise those weapons would never have been passed up. Just a bit farther to the east, we met up with the ARVN lead element. Our F.O. party was with it. A full colonel led the ARVN force. Colonel Bailey, greeting the F.O. Lieutenant., bade him to follow as they both walked behind a small knoll nearby where they could talk in private. I stood near the jeep, while the driver remained at the wheel. I heard the report of a single shot from an AK-47 being fired about thirty-five or fourty yards to the south. Neither the ARVN colonel, nor anyone of his staff officers who were standing with him seemed to flinch. Within a couple of minutes, a couple of ARVN soldiers appeared. They had a third unarmed soldier sandwiched between them as if guarding a captive prisoner. He was obviously the culprit guilty of picking up and firing an abandoned enemy AK-47 weapon. They marched up before the ARVN commander and stopped. Words in Vietnamese were exchanged, and the two soldiers stepped off to the side, leaving their charge standing alone to face the Vietnamese colonel. The colonel spoke more words in Vietnamese. The ARVN soldier standing there alone, I noticed was sporting a very long fingernail on his left pinkie finger. That was a sign that he came from a well-to-do Vietnamese family, prior to being drafted. In any case, the soldier did an abrupt about-face and marched off a few paces to the west before stopping at a "freeze" position.

The Viet colonel, who was armed with an M-16 rifle, then ordered the soldier to run. The man had run no more than ten or fifteen yards before the colonel opened fire with the M-16. The rounds were kicking up chunks of dirt, spattering near the soldier's feet without hitting him, before the man flung himself to the ground. The soldier was saying something, perhaps pleading for his life to be spared. The ARVN colonel was not moved by the soldier's pleas. He ordered the man to his feet. He next commanded that he come forward once more. The soldier was allowed to come right up close to the ARVN commander, stopping at no more than one full pace away. The colonel again said something in Vietnamese, and someone with a radio handed the colonel the microphone. The colonel, talking to someone on the other end in Vietnamese, broke off the conversation by speaking in clear and distinct English, "You goddamn right!" he said, as he brought the M-16 rifle to full port before rendering a horizontal butt stroke to the soldier's mouth. The rifle butt tore away flesh and removed teeth in its wake. The soldier collapsed to his knees. About that time, Colonel Bailey and our unit F.O. reappeared on the scene. I asked the young American lieutenant to intercede. "Please ask the colonel (ARVN) not to kill this man in my presence," I said. The ARVN colonel, giving me a frosty look again, spoke English as he spoke directly to me. "He VC!" The colonel proclaimed. He then instructed the first two soldiers to produce some parachute cord, which they carried on their persons. He then instructed them to truss the soldier up in such a manner as to render him completely immobile. If he dared to move, no matter how slightly, his air was cut off so that he could no longer breathe. Within moments, as we loaded up in the jeep to leave, I looked back at the choking soldier. His eyes were starting to bulge. As we drove away I remember wondering to myself, "Are we fighting on the right side?"

The *Stars and Stripes* newspaper of Thursday, 3 July, reporting on the ARVN arrival at Ben Het on Tuesday, published their featured headline story which read: "Ben Het: All's Quiet—for Now." I quote the article verbatim.

> SAIGON (UPI).
> Communist forces have apparently ended their 56-day siege of the embattled camp at Ben Het as South Vietnamese troops moved through once-treacherous jungles without opposition and reached the area Tuesday.
> Government infantrymen leading a 3,500-man relief force reported no sign of North Vietnamese troop activity around the outpost 280 miles northeast of Saigon. For the first time since May 6, no Communist shells were fired into the base.
> South Vietnamese military spokesmen said troops of the ARVN 53rd Infantry Regiment linked the outpost with the central highlands city of Dak To eight miles to the east, traveling without resistance over a jungle road which had become known as "Suicide Run" because of frequent Communist ambushes in the past.

A spokesman declined to say, however, that the siege had ended. "I only know that the road is clear now," he said. It was the first time in six days that the base was accessible other than by air.

U.S. military sources said all indications were that an estimated 1,800 North Vietnamese troops operating in the tri-border area had withdrawn to nearby Cambodia—possibly only for a brief period in which to resupply and replace manpower losses.

U.S. Green Beret adviser Capt. Michael E. Taylor of Grenada, Miss., said, "It appears that things are pretty quiet now, but this time of year is bad."

"This area is a traditional trouble spot in the rainy season. And we're just starting to get into the rainy season now…"

Communist troops fired about 6,000 rounds of artillery, mortar, and recoilless rifle shells into the base during the siege. Casualties among Ben Het's 200 American and 450 South Vietnamese civilian irregular defensemen were reported light.

On Monday, Communist troops fired only eight artillery rounds into Ben Het. As of 10 P.M. Tuesday, no shells had hit the base, marking the first time since the start of the siege that 24 hours had elapsed without incoming fire.

"From the sound of yesterday's shelling it looks like Charlie was using up his ammo and getting ready to get out," one U.S. officer said. "He doesn't want us to find him."

But South Vietnamese troops sweeping toward the base reported finding numerous freshly dug fortifications, indicating the Communists planned to return to use them. The worsening of the monsoon weather added to the possibility the Reds would return.

"The B-52's can keep pounding them no matter what the weather is like," a U.S. Special Forces advisor said. "But for the close-in air support you need good ceiling and the enemy is well aware of that."

En route to the base Tuesday, South Vietnamese infantrymen reported finding the bodies of 30 North Vietnamese troops killed earlier by either air or artillery strikes. It raised to 1,630 the number of Communists reported killed in the region since the start of the siege.

I wish to make note of the fact that the newspaper article quoted above is not an official record, even though it is quite accurate. The official enemy death count was estimated to be well above 1900 killed, and that is debatable. We estimated enemy losses to be much greater, but that is irrelevant. The next day, Friday, 4 July, I was off somewhere enjoying some quiet time, when the silence was broken by some type of explosive devices being discharged. I knew from the sounds that the noise was not enemy incoming fire, but decided it needed investigation. As I looked around, I discovered that some of the troops were using pyrotechnic pistols to fire off flares. They were celebrating the Fourth of July. The *Stars and Stripes* article had an accompanying photograph;

it certainly represented "yellow" journalism. The picture was of the Army EOD people's destruction of a pile of "dud" artillery rounds that had been policed from the Main Hill compound. The picture was explained as enemy incoming artillery at Ben Het! I had watched the explosion set off by the EOD from a vantage point in the observation tower. Any U.S. artilleryman worth his salt would not be fooled by the caption.

Another newspaper article dated 4 July 1969 and headlined "U.S. Hit Reds in Cambodia to Save Ben Het" is also quoted verbatim because of its significant information relevant to Communist troop strengths during the siege.

> SAIGON (UPI) from 4 July 1969—American warplanes and artillery bombarded North Vietnamese gun positions in neutral Cambodia during the Communist siege of the Ben Het outpost, military spokesmen said Wednesday.
>
> "Everytime they shell us from Cambodia we do our best to knock out the guns that shell us," said Col. George A. Miller, the senior U.S. advisor at the Special Forces base.
>
> "We used artillery and TAC air (tactical air strikes) to knock out guns in Cambodia," Miller added. "We declare a tactical emergency when fired upon."
>
> Miller and his South Vietnamese counterpart, Col. Nguyen Ba Lien, disclosed that at least 12 Communist artillery positions were destroyed during the 56-day siege of Ben Het which ended Tuesday. Lien said the gun sites destroyed included "some in Cambodia, some in South Vietnam."
>
> U.S. casualties during the siege were at least 14 killed and 132 wounded, military sources said. South Vietnamese losses at the base were reported at 26 dead and 68 wounded. A U.S. advisor said about 300 other ARVN soldiers were killed in operations around the outpost, which resulted in a reported 1,850 Communist killed.
>
> The 200 Americans and 450 South Vietnamese Civilian Irregular Defense Group (CIDG) troops at the base were engaged in clean-up operations Wednesday. The outpost is located 280 miles northeast of Saigon in the jungle highlands eight miles east of Vietnam's joint frontier with Cambodia and Laos.
>
> Following 56 days of shelling which ended Monday, Communist gunners failed again Wednesday to fire a shot. U.S. intelligence officers believed an estimated 1,800-man North Vietnamese force which had been operating in the region withdrew across the borders to resupply and to replace troops.
>
> "They can come back at any time," Col. Lien said. "All they have to do is cross the border and they're here. One step."
>
> Lien said that at one point in the siege a *reinforced North Vietnamese division of some 10,000 troops was in the region.* He said that

the Communist planned to capture Ben Het, then take the city of Dak To eight miles to the east. [emphasis added]
    The colonel, commander of the 24th Special Tactical Zone, said South Vietnamese troops supported by U.S. B52 raids, tactical fighter-bomber missions and artillery *systematically "destroyed" elements of four Communist regiments before the Reds began to withdraw.* [emphasis added]
    "We have defeated the enemy at Ben Het," he said. "We have friendly forces on all sides of Ben Het. The enemy said the ARVN couldn't clear the road between Dak To and Ben Het. Now it is cleared."

My question after first reading this article was, "Where does Lien get off using the words we, and ARVN, when speaking of a victory at Ben Het?"

People were leaving Ben Het; it was rotation time for many of them. Master Sergeant Ralph Trout's, the senior A-Team sergeant, time was up. He introduced his replacement as he was preparing to leave. He told this newly arrived SF master sergeant, "Look out for this guy (referring to me); he is good, he knows what he is doing." I took this as a real complement coming from a higher enlisted grade Special Forces NCO. It was also time for LT. Col. Bailey to get back to Pleiku and reclaim his command, which was in dire need of his leadership. Our battalion was overdue for another command inspection by the I.G.'s Office.

We got word that Major Wadell, the Battalion Executive Officer's replacement, was in and on his way up to Ben Het. He was scheduled to take over from Bailey in order to finish up at Ben Het, a job that was expected to take a week to ten days, maybe more. "What's his name?" I innocently asked. "Major Huff," someone said. "What's his full name?" I queried further. "Roy P.," answered the colonel as he added a question. "Why? Do you know him?" he asked. "Yes, I know him," I said. "And unless he's changed, God help us," I answered. I decided to meet the chopper because it had our mail aboard, and I was curious to see how much the incoming major had changed over the years since I last served under him in Germany in 1964. He was a captain back then in charge of our artillery battalion's nuclear weapons program. I was his school-trained special weapons NCO. We did not see eye-to-eye. I transferred out to U.S. Army–Europe's Special Weapons School at Oberamergau.

    Captain Huff had been furious with me for leaving. Now I was standing bareheaded, down by the Main Hill Special Forces helipad, the same place I'd been mortar attacked just five weeks earlier. The Huey

Slick set down and out stepped Major Huff. Smiling, I greeted the major who said, "Sergeant! Where is your helmet?" And just barely pausing, he continued speaking in an icy tone, "Let's go get it, put it on, and don't ever let me catch you outdoors without it again." I saluted. Grabbing the mailbag, I raced ahead of the major, reaching the TOC well ahead of him. As I went past the colonel, I said, "He ain't changed a bit." The colonel, who had to return to Pleiku on the waiting Huey Slick, briefed Major Huff and told him, "Listen to Sergeant Lamerson and your job will be easy." At this, Colonel Bailey went to the chopper pad and departed Ben Het. He was no more than out of sight before the major informed me that he didn't need any advice from the likes of me.

That night, after I sent in my last daily SIT-REP to Nha Trang, the new Special Forces NCO invited me to his quarters in the Team House. It was the first and only time the privilege was extended to me. It was past midnight when we arrived at the team house, which sported a small bar. The sergeant went to his bunk where he dug down in his duffel bag and came out with a jug of good whiskey in his hands. Opening the bottle, he passed it to me. I turned it up and took an extra long pull. I'd bet I slugged down a triple shot in that one drink. We talked some before I took another slug before leaving. In the line units, hard liquor was prohibited on the fire bases. But the Special Forces team played by a different set of rules. I liked them. The next morning Huff gave me a ration of shit, so as soon as he was off doing some little detail, I sneaked a call into Pleiku. "Get me out of here," I pleaded. "I'm needed back there; I have an inspection to prepare for." A bit later, the RTO on duty in the S-3 received a message from Colonel Bailey. "Get Sergeant Lamerson back here on the next available," he instructed the major.

Notes

[1] Edward F. Murphy, *Dak To,* (New York: Pocket Books, 1993), 331.
[2] Ibid., 138.
[3] U.S. Air Force, *CHECO Report:* "Interview with Lt. D.A. Devilbliss, Assistant Highland Desk Officer, G-2, Hq. IFFV," (8 July 1969), 3.
[4] U.S. Air Force, Air War College, *Tactical Air Support and the Battle of Ben Het: A Professional Study,* by Thomas M. Crawford, Jr., No. 4029 (Air University: 1970), 44.
[5] U.S. Air Force, CHECO Division, *The Siege of Ben Het,* prepared by Ernie S. Montagliani, (1 October 1969), 14–15.
[6] Ibid., 15.
[7] Ibid., 23–24.

8 Ibid., 24.
9 U.S. Air Force, *CHECO Report:* "Interview with Major William Yenke, Pleiku Sector ALO, II Corps," (13 July 1969), 14.
10 Associated Press Reporter, "Benhet Shelling Eased," *Stars and Stripes,* 29 June 1969, Pacific edition.
11 Staff Reporter, "Ben Het Battling Ends," ____, 2 July 1969.
12 David Hoffman, "Benhet used as 'Bait,' Officer Says," *The Washington Post,* 1 July 1969.
13 U.S. Air Force, *CHECO Report:* "Interview with Lt. Col. Jack G. Cude, Jr., ALO 24 STZ," (13 July 1969), 12–14.
14 U.S. Air Force, CHECO Division, *The Siege of Ben Het,* prepared by Ernie S. Montagliani, (1 October 1969), 25.

CHAPTER 13

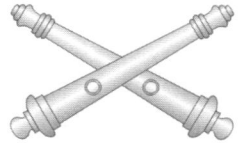

The Siege of Ben Het

They can come back at any time, all they have to do is cross the border and they're here. One step.
Colonel Nguyen Ba Lien 24th STZ Commander (ARVN)

ANALYTICAL REVIEW

As soon as the defenders of Ben Het were assured that the enemy had in fact withdrawn from the area, they came back aboveground. Their true intentions for future enemy actions planned against the area were unknown. However, we at Ben Het went right to work by patching up and reinforcing our shell-battered structures. You may recall my conversation with the IFFV Artillery command sergeant major about sending me a portable latrine or commode. As General Rosson had promised, "If you need anything, you just ask." A convoy came in, and off the back of one of the trucks, the truck driver and his assistant unloaded a small "outhouse." It only stood about five feet tall and had a door. It was painted battleship gray. Inside was a boxed-in area with a hole, around, which was mounted a conventional toilet seat. The bottom half of the back of the building was open. Inside was one-third of a 55-gallon drum with handles attached. The outhouse was designed so that the drum could be removed and the contents disposed of. To top off his work, the man who had designed and built it, included his last name. Neatly hand printed in red paint was the following: "Body by Fish." During the siege, our Main Hill Special Forces' latrine had been put out of commission early on. Bob Hodiern, a *Stars and Stripes* news correspondent, said in one article, "It's worth a Bronze Star just for going to the latrine at Ben Het."

    The next item on our "To Do" list was to execute a program of accountability, i.e., accounting for equipment lost or destroyed during the siege. A week or so had passed before I was to find myself at the

Main Hill helipad awaiting the arrival of air transportation back to Pleiku. As I stood there waiting, my mind was racing. I tried to understand the "dramatic conclusion" of the surrealism of the Ben Het battle. The question that lingered in my mind was, "Did it all really happen, or was it just a figment of my imagination? A nightmare, as it were." I did make one particular rationalization; I most likely would live to see my family again. The four little stair-stepped daughters and young beautiful wife that I had left behind eight long months ago would see me again someday. As I stood there lost in my private thoughts, the silence was broken by the wump-wump sound made by an approaching Huey Slick. As the Huey hovered close to the ground, I pushed my gear ahead of me as I was helped aboard. Once I was aboard, no words were exchanged between the crew and me as our flight heading took us directly over the southeast end of the Ben Het airstrip.

Looking directly down at the area, I could see the cluster of 750-pound bomb craters that were the result of the 30-ton bomb load delivered by a single B-52 bomber on 25 June. It was at that instant that all doubt in my mind was erased about why the enemy had made his hasty withdrawal. My mind did a reality check. It was not me who had evoked the spirit or ghost of Dien Bien Phu at Ben Het; I could give NVA Senior General Vo Nguyen Giap credit for that. However, it was I who cornered the dreaded "Ghost of Dien Bien Phu" on the southeast end of the abandoned airstrip there at Ben Het. With the help from the United States Air Force people, permission from Lt. Col. Bailey, the artillery commander, and Captain Noble, the ground commander, I was able to send the "Ghost of Dien Bien Phu" back into the monsoon-soaked ground of Ben Het. However, this time instead of winning a spectacular victory on the battlefield, Giap lost nearly all of a veteran NVA infantry regiment. The simple truth is that more than half of the 28th Infantry Regiment, officers and men, to the best of my knowledge, still lie there entombed alongside the "Ghost", never to walk on this earth again.

Unbeknownst to me when I boarded the Huey Slick at Ben Het, our destination was not Pleiku. The crew had been told to pick me up and deliver me to Dak To, not Pleiku. They were on a mission that would take them north. I was deposited on the tarmac of the Dak To airstrip. It was no longer the beehive of activity it had been during the siege; now it was too damn quiet. I had to wait out there in the blazing afternoon sun for two hours before another Huey Slick came along. This time, however, I took no chances as I asked the door gunner, "Is this chopper heading back to Pleiku?" The reply made me happy. "We have one short stop to make first, but, yes. After that we are heading back to

Pleiku." Realizing that our flight heading would take us directly to Ben Het once more, I became very nervous. Luckily, our stop was only to deliver a bag of mail.

Back in Pleiku late that afternoon, I was happy to get a haircut and to take a shower, the first in nearly six weeks. I received some very unpleasant news a few days later. Following the completion of flying a four-hour combat aerial observer mission, I returned to Artillery Hill from Camp Holloway. As was standard procedure, I stopped by the 52d Artillery Group Headquarters S- 2 Section in order to record my combat flight time. Fifty hours of official combat flight time earned one the air medal in Vietnam. As I asked the Group Intelligence sergeant for my flight records folder, he gave me the sad news. "I'm sorry Sergeant Lamerson, but they told me you had shipped out. We don't keep records on file once the man ships out. I've purged your flight records from the file. You're going to have to start all over from scratch." "But my certificate of A.O. training from the school at Camp Holloway was in that folder," I protested to no avail. Master Sergeant Boetcher, the Group Intelligence sergeant said, "I can let you fly without that, because I can vouch for the fact that you attended the school." But he informed me that I would have to start a new file from scratch, which I agreed to do.

We passed our big inspection with flying colors. Meanwhile, just five days following "The Siege of Ben Het," on 7 July 1969, B. Drummond Ayers Jr., a news correspondent and writer for the *New York Times,* filed a story for release.

PROPAGANDISTS CHANGE MIND
Ben Het: A 'Great Victory' or A Routine Engagement?
by B. Drummond Ayers Jr.
© N.Y. Times News Service

Saigon—Allied military officials have done an about face in less than a week over the meaning of the battle of Ben Het.

On Monday, they were portraying the struggle to free the besieged outpost as just a routine engagement in the Central Highlands.

But by Sunday, with the siege broken and a major public relations effort underway, they were boasting that the battle was a great Allied victory.

SOMEWHERE BETWEEN

The truth probably lies somewhere in between.

Certainly the battle was not a routine engagement. Each side committed at least 3,000 men in the seven-week fight that ended Saturday.

The problem in terming the battle a great victory is that no one knows whether the enemy actually was driven away from the camp or left voluntarily.

The disappearance of the enemy units coincided with the news that enemy troops near the Demilitarized Zone had also pulled back and that fighting elsewhere in South Vietnam was at one of the lowest levels of the year.

TEST OF ALLY?

Was the battle a good test of the ability of [the] South Vietnamese infantry? To take over combat when supported by United States Air Force, helicopter artillery and logistical units?

Only in the early weeks of the fighting was there much head-to-head contact between South Vietnamese and North Vietnamese infantry units. The government troops were outnumbered and suffered numerous casualties.

By the time the South Vietnamese command had put together a force large enough to fight the enemy on equal terms—at least on paper—the North Vietnamese had vanished.

TOOK TOO LONG

Some U.S. officers feel the South Vietnamese took far too long to form the Ben Het relief force. These Americans point out that the enemy's presence in the area was known as early as April and that the shelling of Ben Het began in early May.

The top South Vietnamese commander, Col. Nguyen Ba Lien, says that Ben Het was relieved slowly because he was using the camp as bait to lure the enemy into a trap.

Top American officers involved in the battle deny there was any "bait" plan. They say it was necessary to move slowly because the locations of some enemy units were unknown and over-all enemy intention was never clear.

The lack of intelligence information may be blamed in good part on the failure of Lien's Troops to patrol aggressively.

Despite the long period it took to relieve Ben Het, at no time point was the outpost on the verge of collapse. Its defenses always were strong and the enemy could not have overrun them without taking extremely high casualties.

The enemy gained much, however, simply by surrounding Ben Het. Once again the American public and the Allied negotiators at Paris were reminded that the foe in South Vietnam remains tough and resourceful.[1]

I wish to make a point before I make any attempt to critique Mr. Drummond Ayers on his news commentary. I believe that the enemy saw Ben Het as the first of a series of obstacles that would have to be overcome before they could push sizable maneuver elements far enough east into South Vietnam. It would be necessary to turn Highway QL-14 into a southern corridor that could be used to push their newly formed mobile and mechanized multidivisional force south for the purpose of capturing Kontum and Pleiku Cities during their summer offensive. Their intentions were clear as far as I can see. The enemy plan called for overrunning Ben Het, capturing or killing everyone they could. Certain prisoners would be important pawns; these they would and send to NVA prisoner of war camp 102, which was located just a few miles across the Cambodian border in the vicinity of Enemy Base Area 609.[2] The other obstacles that had to be overrun and captured before a serious move on Kontum City could be considered were the bridge at Dak Mot, the city of Dak To, and finally the city of Tanh Canh, which was the home base of the ARVN 42d Infantry Regiment.

I believe Giap and Dung thought that once a predawn attack was executed against Ben Het, with the cover of an early morning fog that would last until noon, NVA forces could overrun and capture the first obstacles by noon. With the ARVN in complete disarray due to the blitzkrieg-like attacks, the NVA would maneuver their attack forces into night positions from where they would overrun Tanh Canh the following morning. Again, with early morning fog conditions aiding them, they would move with lightning speed and have Kontum surrounded and under attack by noon of the second day. Keep in mind that according to my calculations, the NVA main attack force, now comprised of one reinforced mobile infantry division and a mechanized infantry division reinforced by an armor/artillery regiment, would, after taking Kontum City, link up with a major NVA infantry regiment of a 3d division of infantry forces just south of Pleiku. The 1st NVA Infantry Division did not need to be mobile to reinforce the other multidivisional attack force in their planned attack to seize Pleiku City.

Now permit me to critique seven of Mr. Ayer's points in his news commentary of 7 July:

1. The joint Allied military officials first described the enemy disappearance as a mystery, an enigma if you will.

2. One week later they declared a great victory for ARVN forces. They were careful to downplay the American support role. They were too busy touting the action as a test in favor for the Vietnamization program.

3. The fact that Ben Het was not just a routine engagement, I consider to be a true statement.

4. Even at first I was convinced, as I still am today, that I had the answer to the question in reference to the NVA sudden withdrawal. Even though I had personally briefed General William B. Rosson, the MACV deputy commander, on the situation at Ben Het, the question never came up in reference to an enemy withdrawal. He merely informed me that it was underway, not complete. It did not enter my mind to bother him with the details of the B-52 strike because I thought that he probably already knew that. Besides, he was primarily concerned about the negative publicity surrounding the situation at the outpost.

5. It was true that the Ben Het fortifications held up well, considering that the enemy poured 6,000 rounds into the camp during the siege. However, all the rest of the buildings were sagging from shrapnel and explosive damage from the incessant shelling. However, a frontal or pincer ground assault by overwhelming NVA forces could have very well made quick work of the fall of the camp and produced another whole story. As I pointed out early on, Giap had revealed the loss of 600,000 troops in the war to date. Is it likely that he concerned himself with the loss of a few thousand more? I think not! We, the true defenders of Ben Het, however, resented the thought of being used as guinea pigs, bait for a trap, or expendable cannon fodder—not that the NVA soldiers were all that much better off.

6. As for a test—the ARVN failed by a mile. However, Lien's intelligence sources were better than they were given credit for being. There is no doubt in my mind that he knew the true size of the enemy forces I have described. Too, he knew the enemy's true intention, but recognized that his forces were just too small to deal with the NVA forces without following a precedent that he had learned from watching the Americans. That is to say, since he was so far outnumbered, he decided to set up a giant killing field. When the enemy forces entered it, he would let the American firepower destroy the enemy. What better way, he thought, to hold down casualties (which he had been ordered to do) than to withhold his troops from doing battle with the NVA. In that sense, I think Colonel Lien was justified in taking the actions he did. However, the "bait" issue is another story. MACV should never have placed American support troops in a role in which an Allied troop commander could misuse them. Since it was obvious that Lien had no immediate plans to launch

a counteraction, MACV should have taken some bold step to guarantee the security of Ben Het. Basically, I am talking about a ground action supported by an air-mobile force. These forces could have been made up of ARVN Rangers, since this was touted as a test of the ARVN's ability to cope with equal sized enemy forces. My contention is that if the Dak To/Ben Het campaign was actually a test, then I say it was piss poor planning on the part of MACV. As for the American "official spokesmen" who were sitting back and making comments to the effect that Ben Het was a fortress that could not be taken, I will only reply by calling them "armchair commandos," REMFs,[3] who didn't know crap!

7. In reference to the comment by American officers who were quoted as saying they had to move slowly to relieve Ben Het because they didn't know the locations of all enemy forces involved nor of the enemy's intention: It seems clear to me that when a sizable enemy force takes a remote outpost under siege, his intentions as well as his present troop locations are fully disclosed. Such statements at best, can only be described as a cop-out.

The next news commentary appeared in the July 1969 issue of *Time Magazine*. The article is quoted as follows:

THE LESSON OF BEN HET

WHAT will happen when the U.S. withdraws ground forces from Viet Nam? The first trial run came at Ben Het, the embattled South Vietnamese outpost near Cambodia that was the well-publicized object of enemy pressure for 55 successive days. For the first time since the massive U.S. military buildup in 1965, South Vietnamese forces (ARVN) bore the brunt of a major ground action in difficult border terrain. Though the siege last week was lifted and Ben Het remained in Allied hands, the results were far from reassuring. "You can see it happening all the way to the beaches," said one U.S. general. "As we move back, they will inch right in behind us and smack hell out of whatever ARVN unit we leave in the way."

That may prove a premature and overly pessimistic prognosis, uttered in the midst of an engagement that left a sour taste in many an American's mouth. But there was no denying that Ben Het raised serious doubts about the military feasibility of American plans for orderly early withdrawal and disengagement in Viet Nam.

Like Khe Sanh and Con Thien to the north, Ben Het, which was completed in 1968, was an isolated fortification of bunkers and barbed wire that sits astride an important infiltration route. Inside its perimeters were 500 Montagnard irregulars led by a South Vietnamese Special Forces team of twelve and twelve U.S. Green Beret advisors. Initially, Ben Het could rely for added protection on the U.S. 4th Infantry Division, which was operating in the surrounding highlands. As part of a redeployment, U.S. infantry forces withdrew from the Ben Het area in April. The responsibility for the base passed to a South Vietnamese commander, Marine Colonel Nguyen Ba Lien of the 24th Special Tactical Zone. In accord with the U.S. policy of continuing to provide fire support for South Vietnamese forces, 500 American Artillerymen remained dug in at key points in and around Ben Het. The biggest U.S. concentration was at Dak To, ten miles to the east, where 500 American combat engineers were also stationed.

Ominously, the North Vietnamese in early May began to mass two regiments in the area and occasionally to shell Dak To and Ben Het. In the past, the U.S. would have rushed American infantrymen to the aid of the South Vietnamese. This time they did not. In an effort to head off an attack, Lien sent South Vietnamese battalions into craggy mountains around the two bases. At first the South Vietnamese fought well and aggressively. But after a month in the field, they wearied. Unfortunately, the South Vietnamese still seemed incapable of fighting a prolonged and bloody engagement with the more determined and seasoned North Vietnamese regulars. In action reminiscent of the ARVN's performance in the mid-1960s, the South Vietnamese retired to their forts, leaving the initiative and the countryside to the enemy.

* * *

The ensuing siege strained relations between the South Vietnamese and the American battalion at Dak To. As support troops, the U.S. engineers and artillerymen were counting on the South Vietnamese to provide the security force for their base. But Lien refused. As a result, the Americans had to do double-duty guarding their own perimeter, leaving the gun crews and work teams overworked and exhausted.

Far more serious was the situation on the road between the two bases. While working to keep the road open and in good repair, the American engineers could not depend on the South Vietnamese for protection. On several occasions, the South Vietnamese refused to respond to pleas by ambushed engineers. Four weeks ago, a 20-man ARVN guard detail deserted a U.S. working party when North Vietnamese ambushers opened fire. Cursing their allies, the surviving Americans finally managed to drag their dead and wounded to safety. Over an eight-week period, the U.S. engineers lost 17 men killed and 120 wounded, in part because they received inadequate protection from their allies.

In mid-June, the North Vietnamese completely surrounded Ben Het and cut off virtually all ground access to it. Though ammunition remained plentiful, Ben Het's defenders suffered from lack of fresh water and hot food. They also suffered from the lack of an on-the-spot commander. Directing the battle from his headquarters at

Kontum, 30 miles southeast of Ben Het, Lien rarely flew into the besieged outpost. As a result, he was unable to make the most effective use of massive U.S. air power and artillery that were put at his disposal. Communications between the various defending units were also poor. Meanwhile, communications to the outside world about Ben Het set cable and telex wires humming. Hard-pressed to find stories in an increasingly quiet war, the press corps in Vietnam seized eagerly on Ben Het. Some stories even warned that the outpost might be overrun, a threat the North Vietnamese encouraged by code-naming the base Dienbienphu.

* * *

Perhaps in an attempt to counter such bad publicity, Colonel Lien explained his strategy to newsmen in Kontum. In excellent English, the cocky colonel confided that he deliberately used Ben Het as "bait" to lure the North Vietnamese into a position where Allied firepower could destroy them. At Ben Het and Dak To, U.S. officers laughed openly at Lien's suggestion. U.S. headquarters in Saigon pointed out that General Creighton Abrams has specifically forbidden ever-using Allied men as bait.

Two days later after Lien's press conference, the Siege of Ben Het abruptly ceased, and the enemy faded away into Cambodia. A relief force of 1,500 South Vietnamese troopers last week encountered no resistance on their way to Ben Het. Why did the enemy withdraw? During the height of the attacks, North Vietnamese propagandist boasted that Ben Het represented a "humiliating failure for the U.S. in its plot to de-Americanize the war and use Vietnamese to kill Vietnamese." Having already lost 1,800 men in the battle, the North Vietnamese may have felt that they needed to waste no more lives to make their point.[4]

I will now present my critique of the above quoted article.

1. Ben Het was not a South Vietnamese outpost as reported in the opening paragraph. It was an officially recognized 5th U.S. Special Forces outpost. But it is true that the problem was that the South Vietnamese were failing to bear the brunt of the fighting there.

2. The plan for Vietnamization was flawed from the start, as I so aptly pointed out in the introduction to this book.

3. Let us examine some points of comparison between Khe Sanh and Ben Het.
    a. The approximate rate of fire by enemy artillery that slammed the base at Khe Sanh was 105 rounds per day. At Ben Het it exceeded 100 rounds per day, a very close comparison.[5]

b. Similarly, the trench and tunnel diggings at the two bases could be compared to a certain degree to those at Dien Bien Phu. However, no tunnels at Khe Sanh were discovered and the trenches did not get in as close to Khe Sanh as they did at Ben Het.[6] The closest the trenches got to the base at Khe Sanh was 320 meters from the base; since the enemy was averaging 90 meters per night, he was nearly four days digging time away from being able to create the same conditions as he had at Dien Bien Phu.[7]

c. The enemy never touched Khe Sanh's sole water source. At Ben Het they cut the supply route and kept it interdicted for the duration of the siege.[8]

d. Length of sieges: 77 days at Khe Sanh[9] and 58 days at Ben Het.

Note: *Time Magazine* reported 55 days for Ben Het.

e. Relief for both bases was very similar. Since the U.S. Marine command at Khe Sanh insisted all along that the base was not besieged, Operation Pegasus was planned and executed by General W.B. Rosson to relieve the base. Operation Pegasus, it was said, was to be as follows: "Not relief in the sense of rescue ... . But, relief in the sense of reopening ground contact (Highway 9) and eliminating the enemy with mobile operations."[10] As at Ben Het, the Pegasus relief forces only met with token resistance on the way into Khe Sanh.[11] A question lingered as it did following both sieges—why the enemy decided to withdraw remained a matter of conjecture.[12]

f. Airlift between the two bases differed markedly. Khe Sanh never lost the use of their airstrip. At Ben Het, the airstrip, being declared untenable, had to be abandoned. All told, 455 planes landed at Khe Sanh, which supplied 35 percent of the needs of the base. Helicopters brought in 465 tons of supplies to the main base. Additional supplies were parachuted in except when zero-zero conditions prevailed (zero visibility, zero ceiling), but helicopters could not land at Ben Het's Main Hill. However, some ammunition resupply was completed by helicopter deliveries at the North Hill compound. Due to the small "postage stamp" size of the drop zone at Ben Het, airdrop was considered to be difficult.

Ben Het was only 80 yards wide and 180 yards long. The whole complex at Khe Sanh was two miles long and one mile wide.[13] The airlift operation at Ben Het was considered to be the biggest in the war to date.[14] And 294.2 tons of supplies were dropped into Ben Het, taking 120 sorties.[15] However, remember that there were 6,000 Marines at Khe Sanh and only about 1,000 souls made up the population of Ben Het.

g. Both bases suffered by the following similar living conditions: "Buildings lay in pieces. Debris littered the perimeter. Everywhere were piles empty of shell casings, C-ration cans, splinters of wood, and chunks of shrapnel. Bunkers reeked of mold and decay, sweat, and urine. Rats skittered around, and sometimes crawled right on sleeping marines." According to one reporter's view, Khe Sanh "looked like a shanty slum on the outskirts of Manila."[16] Ben Het looked no better from my point of view.

h. General Westmoreland became concerned that at Khe Sanh, the enemy's trench system, which was being extended by 90 meters per night, might result in the enemy being able to tunnel underneath the base and blow it up as they did at Dien Bien Phu. At the end of February, there was a discovery of a network of trenches a mile or more long. They were leading toward the base and they ended within 320 meters from the base; but these branched out into Ts, usually the final stage of preparation before an assault when ramps are employed.[17] At Ben Het, the trenches were right on the outside of the perimeter. Tunnels led into North Hill and wire breaching demolition cache's were found in the close in trenches.

i. 35,000 tons of ordnance were dropped on Khe Sanh by USAF delivery systems,[18] while only 20,000 tons were used at Ben Het.[19] At least 135,311 rounds of Allied artillery were fired at Ben Het; 4639 enemy rounds were fired.[20] That equals an exchange of fire ratio of about 27 to 1. No figures were available to me on the number of artillery rounds fired at Khe Sanh.

j. In both cases, the number of bombs that fell was high, even by World War II standards, with total estimates ranging from 59,000 to 96,000 tons.[21] Close-in B-52 strikes at Khe Sanh edged close and it was said, "One hiccup, and we would have decimated the base."[22] The 500 Montagnards mentioned as part of the Ben Het defense force included the company from Plei Djereng that inserted in to Ben Het near the end of the siege.

k. Since I am in contention over the question of enemy troop strength, I can only say the record indicates that Ben Het was surrounded by the equivalent of at least one NVA Infantry Division.[23]

Based on my own research of the Vietnam War, I have come to the conclusion that the American military leaders were not fooled by the North Vietnamese, but were guilty of breaking the most basic principles of warfare. I explain the above comment in more detail in the epilogue. I do not wish to seem redundant, however, I believe it is necessary to spare a bit of space for the words of a few key military members of the team involved in the defense of Ben Het.

Near the end of the siege, Colonel E.W. Rosencrans, Chief Current Operations Division, in a document dated 30 June 1969, stated: "I would rather be guilty of overkill than be blamed for another Dien Bien Phu." This was, of course, in response to the complaint by other Air Force people that too much air power was being applied in the defense of Ben Het. Colonel Rosencrans finished his document with the following statement: "Ben Het is in a bad physical location—it facilitates an enemy victory—that is, a politically significant victory. It's ideal for the enemy, but we'll not lose it, if I can help it."[24]

Lt. Col. E.P. Callaway, SAC ADVON, in a 24 July 1969 interview said in reference to air support for Ben Het: "Also, we found out that the rules of Engagement in regard to T.E. were vague, that is, II Corps and MACV had different views. Another point, 4 Inf. Div. was operating out of their AOs in some cases."

Note: According to the words included in official documents in reference to Ben Het, the 4th Infantry Division had moved south in a redeployment movement. I have failed to point out that this was a sore point among the defenders of the Ben Het camp. Where was the 4th Infantry Division when we really needed them? We knew that units were still operating in the vicinity of Ben Het. We were never told that they had been prohibited from rushing to our defense. The first time we heard about a "test" was from the news media and by that time, the NVA was breathing down our necks as they prepared to launch a mass assault against our vulnerable position.

Lt. Col. Callaway continues as follows:

> We had a hell of a lot of TAC air around Ben Het. We're talking about an area about 15Ks by 20Ks. We had about 3 FACs covering this, which is about as many as you can cram into that air space. These FACs were busy all of the time, putting TAC air in about 60 sorties per day, I would guess. We were putting [ordnance] on old targets because we had no good intelligence.

Note: Do not misunderstand the "no good intelligence" statement. It is clarified in the following quotation.

> Also we sent up a massive CSS program around Ben Het. In most cases this was productive because the ground commander in the camp was providing us with good valid targets around the perimeter. However, as the threat was reduced around the camp, targets were provided by II Corps G-3 air, and these later targets were the ones that were not necessarily valid. I would say that generally targets provided by 24th STZ and from Dak To-Ben Het were good and valid. But, those provided by G-3 Air II Corps, to use up all of the sorties that they were getting, were not necessarily so. They were based on, in my opinion; old intelligence and they had none, which were current. So, they just dumped the bombs."[25]

Note: The ground commander at Ben Het was being advised by the U.S. Army Field Artillery gunnery team, collocated there in the Special Forces TOC. The target locations were within my purview. I could have made better use of air assets had I been given a free hand. This is my main contention with the system that existed. The "rear echelon people" were calling all the shots. Hell, at II Corps Headquarters in Pleiku, they were sitting in air-conditioned offices, as were the ones at IFFV in Nha Trang. My question concerned their abilities to call the shots for me, while I was located on the spot and knew the nature of the true enemy situation.

In an interview with Lt. T.A. Devilbliss, assistant Highland desk officer, G-2, Hq. IFFV, dated 8 July 1969, came the following enemy intelligence information:

> Highway QL-14 from Pleiku, Kontum, and Ben Het. The main position of the fight was planned in the northern portion of Kontum-Ben Het area, with diversions in the south. Mostly in the south there were to be interdictions against the roads. The enemy didn't want the allies to reinforce once the fighting started.
> The B-3 Front was running things, with the 66th and 28th NVA Regiments, and the 24th NVA Regiment around the Plei Mrong area.

Again, the major action was to be up north, with diversions in the south to keep the Allied units busy there.

Prior to the fight, we had lost some enemy units to III Corps. Starting in late April, however, and in early May, we saw a buildup in the Ben Het area. The 66th NVA Regiment and part of the 28th had been in the Plei Mrong area in the Plei Trap Valley to the South. Then, they started north and went to the Tri-Border area. We noted extensive logistical activity in the area.

We figured that the target was Dak To, Tan Canh (the 42d ARVN Regiment) and Ben Het. ... There were severe contacts to the south in May. ARVN paid heavily and sustained a large number of casualties. The 66th and 28th Regiment (NVA) was engaged from 8 May until early June.

Then, the emphasis shifted as the 66th NVA Regiment went to Cambodia and picked up new troops. The ARVN did not take up blocking positions to keep the 66th Regiment from coming back in country. The opposing forces were just about equal, but ARC LIGHT, TAC air, and some air cavalry were attempting to block.

All of a sudden, we started seeing them, 512 being interdicted by VC/NVA and it was discovered that the 1st Battalion, 28th Regiment had probably surrounded Ben Het. The 2d and 3d Battalions were along the road, and in the south, the 66th Regiment was coming back in. There was a psychological effort from the south side of the airfield. The enemy came in tight.

We think that the enemy was going to try to take Ben Het on the 23d June with sapper action. The FSBs in the south were attacked on the 23d, and that same day an action took place on the perimeter of B-H, but somebody (NVA) stopped it in a hurry. This shows a great deal of command flexibility on their part. After this, there was little action, but a highpoint took place on the 25th–26th. We noticed that the long range artillery-fire was lessening, and the VC/NVA were withdrawing ... .[26]

Note: The 25th and 26th are included in the period of the B-52 strike that I have already discussed in detail.

From an interview with Lt. Col. Thomas L. Crawford, Jr., Director, DASC Alpha, dated. 10 July 69:

In summary—I know that, had it not been for our B-52s and TAC air, Charlie would have taken Ben Het—and maybe even Dak To. With our whole effort, we stopped Charlie. With our airlift—the supplies we airlifted in, the interdiction of the enemy's LOCs into the area, the wonderful air support that we gave the ground people, I'm sure that we convinced the VC/NVA to pick up whatever they had left and retreat back across the border.[27]

Note: What Lt. Col. Crawford said ties in with my contention. I base my claim on the following:

> Brigadier General J.S, Timothy, in a message to General George S. Brown, Seventh Air Force Commander, dated 12 October 1969, revealed the effect of the B-52 air strikes on one NVA unit that had taken part in the action around Ben Het:
> "Prisoner Duong Than Ban ... stated that he was in the B-3 Front headquarters area in Cambodia (Base Area 609) when the 28th NVA Regiment returned from the May–June 1969 battle near the Ben Het SF Camp. He said that the regiment had been hit by a series of B-52 strikes in the immediate vicinity of the Ben Het camp, then had been hit by another series of B-52 strikes as they pulled back to their base area in Cambodia. These strikes caused major damage to the regiment. There were only two companies (200 men) left of more than 1,000 men that had entered the battle area ... ."[28]

Note: I was part of a "Phantom Gunnery Team" that inserted into Ben Het during a critical time. We had no knowledge at that time of the enemy's intention in reference to Ben Het. As Colonel Kenneth R. Bailey, U.S. Army Retired, told me back in the mid-nineties, "We went where we were sent, and we did what we were sent there to do." However, since my name was never formally, nor publicly, associated with the fighting, I have taken literary license in calling myself, "The Phantom of Ben Het." The closest I came to public notice was when *Stars and Stripes* news correspondent Bob Hodiern snapped my picture, which he used in the paper with the caption: "Weary GI Takes Break During Lull in Shelling." I know why the NVA withdrew.

There is no doubt left in my military mind that most of the 800 or so 28th Regiment deaths were the result of a single 30-ton bomb load from a B-52, delivered on the southeast end of the Ben Het airstrip on 25 June 1969.

To close my overall analysis and critique of the subject, I wish to add one more observation made by Mr. Crawford.

> By itself, however, the defense of Ben Het had no major impact on the war in Vietnam, but it did offer a prime example of the useful effect of air assets ... viewed in the tactical sense, the use of air at Ben Het might have been a precursor of things to come. Such employment of U.S. airpower could spell the difference between victory and defeat in ARVN versus VC/NVA ground battles.[29]

I find myself in contention once more with Thomas M. Crawford Jr.'s assessment. I base this on the following:

"You know you never defeated us on the battlefield," said the American colonel. The North Vietnamese colonel pondered this remark a moment. "That may be so," he replied, "but it is also irrelevant."30

My point is: Which, if any, of America's battles made a significant impact on the war in Vietnam? Does not the Siege of Ben Het stand alone as one of the most "epic" battles of the war? If it does, then shouldn't it take its rightful place alongside other epic battles, such as Con Thien, the Battle of Dak To, and the Siege of Khe Sanh, in the annals of American warfare? I think the evidence speaks for itself!

Notes

1 B. Drumond Ayers Jr., "Ben Het: A Great Victory or a Routine Engagement?" *New York Times,* 7 July 1969.
2 Clark Dougan, David Fulhum, Stephan Weiss, and the editors of Boston Publishing Company, *A War Remembered,* a volume of *The Vietnam Experience,* (Boston: Boston Publishing Company, 1986), 93.
3 Staff in higher headquarters who were perceived not to understand the difficulties of any fighting soldiers duties. Hence REMF, Rear Echelon Mother Fucker! was used liberally by the troops in the field. See: Linda Reinberg, *In the Field: The Language of the Vietnam War,* (New York: Facts on File, Inc., 1991), 182.
4 Staff reporter, "The Lesson of Ben Het," *Time Magazine,* 11 July 1969, 28.
5 Clark Dougan, Stephan Weiss, and the editors of Boston Publishing Company, *Nineteen Sixty-Eight,* a volume of *The Vietnam Experience,* (Boston: Boston Publishing Company, 1983), 55.
6 Ibid., 55.
7 Ibid., 55.
8 Ibid., 55.
9 Ibid., 57.
10 Ibid., 51.
11 Ibid., 51.
12 Ibid., 51.
13 Ibid., 49.
14 U.S. Air Force, *History of the 834th Air Division,* vol. I, (1 July 1968–30 June 1970), 28.
15 Ibid., 28.
16 Clark Dougan, Stephan Weiss, and the editors of Boston Publishing Company, *Nineteen Sixty-Eight,* a volume of *The Vietnam Experience,* (Boston: Boston Publishing Company, 1983), 49–50.
17 Ibid., 50.
18 Ibid., 48.

19 See: U.S. Air Force, CHECO Division, *The Siege of Ben Het,* prepared by Ernie S. Montagliani, (1 October 1969), ____. (exact tonnage of 19,553)
20 U.S. Air Force, Air War College, *Tactical Air Support and the Battle of Ben Het: A Professional Study,* by Thomas M. Crawford, Jr., No. 4029 (Air University: 1970), 54.
21 Clark Dougan, Stephan Weiss, and the editors of Boston Publishing Company, *Nineteen Sixty-Eight,* a volume of *The Vietnam Experience,* (Boston: Boston Publishing Company, 1983), 48.
22 Ibid., 42.
23 U.S. Air Force, Air War College, *Tactical Air Support and the Battle of Ben Het: A Professional Study,* by Thomas M. Crawford, Jr., No. 4029 (Air University: 1970), 50.
24 Colonel E.W. Rosencrans, U.S. Air Force, Document 11, 30 June 1969.
25 U.S. Air Force, *CHECO Report:* "Interview with Lt. Col. E.P. Callaway," (24 July 1969), 2.
26 U.S. Air Force, *CHECO Report:* "Interview with Lt. D.A. Devilbliss, Assistant Highland Desk Officer, G-2, Hq. IFFV," (8 July 1969), 1–3.
27 U.S. Air Force, *CHECO Report:* "Interview with Lt. Col. Thomas M. Crawford, Jr.," (10 July 1969), p. 5.
28 U.S. Air Force, Air War College, *Tactical Air Support and the Battle of Ben Het: A Professional Study,* by Thomas M. Crawford, Jr., No. 4029 (Air University: 1970), 43–44.
29 Ibid., 51.
30 Harry G. Summers, Jr., *On Strategy: A Critical Analysis of the Vietnam War,* (New York: Dell Publishing Co., 1982), 21.

CHAPTER 14

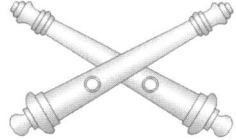

Aftermath

"You know, you never defeated us on the battlefield," said the American colonel. The North Vietnamese colonel pondered this remark a moment. "That may be so," he replied, "but it is also irrelevant."
Harry J. Summers, Jr.
Colonel of Infantry

PART I

The most significant thing that happened immediately following the Siege of Ben Het was the commencement of a public relations program to misconstrue and misrepresent the facts. Tentacle's reached behind the scenes at every level of command. Personal interviews were conducted. Key people involved at command level during the siege were queried. The one notable exception was the American ground support units, which were by either intention or design, ignored. The desired bottom line was that by using clever deceptive practices, the public relations people portrayed Ben Het in a light that would reflect very favorably on the ARVN's ability to move successfully forward with the newly touted "Vietnamization" program. Therefore, a situation was created whereby the official record was skewed to reflect the desired picture.

Because of this public relations program effort directed from the top level of command, the true heroes of Ben Het did not receive the recognition they deserved for the great American victory that they won—official recognition for the gallantry, valor, and joint heroism which they displayed. The records were stamped "CLASSIFIED SECRET," the books on Ben Het were closed and sent off to the various military historical records centers, where they were to lay hidden behind a screen of secrecy for decades. The records were virtually swept into the "dust bin" of history, insulating the perpetrators from public scrutiny in the years that were to follow.

A prime example of how the figures were manipulated is presented below:

I. Friendly Forces Deployed:

42nd ARVN Regiment
47th ARVN Regiment
53rd ARVN Regiment
3rd ARVN Cavalry Squadron
14th ARVN Cavalry Squadron

2nd MSF Battalion
5th MSF Battalion
22nd ARVN Ranger Battalion
404th ARVN Scout Company

6 Camp Strike Force Companies:
3 from Ben Het
1 from Plateau Gi
1 from Dak Pek
1 from Plei Djereng

Adding up all tolls, the total ARVN Force was presented as 6,500 men strong. This is where I am in contention with the recorded figures. Up until the enemy made his sudden withdrawal, ARVN Forces available for deployment in the immediate area of the 24th STZ, Dak To/Ben Het/Tanh Canh, numbered no more than 3,000 men. And even they were not deployed during the last four weeks of the overall 58-day siege of Ben Het. The battle was actually identified by a misnomer. It should have been divided into two distinct parts: "The Battle of Dak To II," and "The Siege of Ben Het," because that's how it all unfolded—the ARVN fighting the Battle of Dak To II, and the US/CIDG with a small sprinkling of ARVN help fighting the Siege of Ben Het.

II. Enemy Strengths:

24th NVA Regiment
40th NVA Artillery Regiment
28th NVA Infantry Regiment

66th NVA Infantry Regiment
K-20 Sapper Battalion
304th Local Force Battalion (VC)

The enemy was reported to have had a 5,340-man force deployed and engaged against the ARVN forces of the 24th STZ. The commanding general, First Field Force, Vietnam, along with G-2 and G-3, failed to consider reports that indicated that the North Vietnamese Army, in addition to the forces listed above, had a reinforced 10,000-man division operating in the vicinity of Ben Het during the siege, as was alluded to by ARVN Colonel Nguyen Ba Lien, the commander of the 24th STZ. The reports were also very careful to avoid mentioning the 1st NVA Division, whose traditional stomping ground was Pleiku Province. Perhaps they were purposely ignoring the fact that General Vo Nguyen Giap, along with General Dung working in his shadow, had long sought to obtain a spectacular victory by using a three infantry divisional force, striking out of the Central Highland border provinces as indicated below:

> General Giap intended to gain a spectacular victory—a Southern Dien Bien Phu with all the trimmings—by slicing South Vietnam in half on the line from Pleiku through An Khe to Qui Nhon. Between October 1965 and April 1966, he planned to commit three full North Vietnamese divisions along that axis.... ...As Giap analyzed the situation, his three divisions, jumping off from secure bases in Cambodia and closely supported by Viet Cong units native to the area being invaded, would be superior to any countering force the Americans and South Vietnamese could employ. Strong holding attacks in the vicinity of Saigon and populated areas near the Demilitarized Zone would tie down reserves, while the tough terrain itself would limit the employment of such reaction forces as Saigon could muster.[1]

I believe that even though there had been some important changes made to their overall military fighting machine, Giap and Dung revised their original attack plan for use by the NVA in the spring/summer offensive of 1969.

Note: The 28th and 66th NVA Infantry Regiments are carried in "the Order of Battle" making up the 10th NVA Infantry Division. The 202d Armor/Artillery Regiment's presence in the area lends credence to the fact that they were there for the purpose of reinforcing an unidentified NVA force. I contend that it was the NVA 325 C Infantry Division.

The first United States unit I wish to mention in reference to official recognition is the 6th Special Operations Squadron, located at Pleiku AFB, Pleiku Province:

> As a result of their valor under enemy fire during the Ben Het and Dan Quyan 38A operation, seven A-1 Skyraider pilots were recommended for the Silver Star Medal. Because of the outstanding support rendered by the pilots and ground support personnel of the 6th Special Operations Squadron, the Army of the Republic of Vietnam (ARVN) recommended all members of the unit, plus attached flying personnel, for a Vietnamese decoration. The decorations had not been approved at the end of the April–June 1969 Historical reporting period.[2]

Since none of the U.S. Army Support Unit personnel (including artillery) were interviewed in relation to the siege, the U.S. Army failed to document some of what I believe to be very important war history.

We were required to execute a quarterly report, through the appropriate channels, entitled "Lessons Learned in Vietnam." Our battalion staff was not available during the siege to write up the documentation for the April–June quarter of 1969. Because there were no provisions made for making a late report, the U.S. Army Historical Documents Department at Carlisle Barracks, Pennsylvania, does not have a report on record for my unit during the April–June 1969 time period. Regrettably, I am unable to travel to Carlisle Barracks myself to verify this.

In the meantime, a trickle of information reached us, Lt. Col. Bailey and myself, in Pleiku.

One rumor I heard was that I had been put in for an award; the person who told me implied that it was to be the Silver Star Medal for heroism in ground combat. I received word from Ben Het that during sweeping operations southwest of Ben Het, there were thirty-odd NVA dead, along with three South Vietnamese prisoners. These prisoners were discovered in a cave up on top of a hill that we knew as Old FSB 29, an abandoned 4th Infantry Division fire base that the 40th NVA Artillery used as a FSB during the siege against Ben Het. I was also told that SFC. Scoppa, Buddha, whom I had written up for the Silver Star Medal, had, in fact, received it. Lt. Colonel Bailey told me that he had heard that a special team of so called military tacticians, "experts" in their field, had visited the Ben Het site and declared it to be untenable. After that, I heard that the U.S. Army engineer people had come in and bulldozed one-third of the height of North Hill in order to destroy the enemy trench and bunker system that they had constructed around and dug out under the hill during the siege.

The day arrived for our own 6/14 people to receive their awards for Ben Het. Several of our people in Pleiku received their MOPH's (Purple Hearts); some received multiple Purple Hearts. I was singled out of the formation and called forward where the Bronze Star with V was pinned on my chest. I was a bit disappointed, but I have always been proud of my award.

It seems that it is within the purview of an artilleryman's duty to perform crater analysis while under intense bombardment from the enemy's big guns or mortars and, therefore, makes him ineligible to receive a higher award. In my book, I never worried about the bullet with my name inscribed on it. What always had me worried was one of those big enemy shells—those "Sons-of-bitches" with "to whom it may concern" written on them! I was just thankful that I got out of Ben Het alive and unwounded. Medals are nice to receive, but not worth dying for. Hell, when I went to Vietnam, I was only authorized to wear the Good Conduct Medal, 4th Award and the National Defense Service Medal 2nd Award; and that, after nearly 18 years of military service. See Figure 14-1. The line-firing batteries involved in the siege held their own awards ceremonies. As for Lt. Colonel Bailey, as well as others at various levels of command within the IFFV Artillery, DEROS, the Date of Expected Return from Overseas, was approaching.

FIGURE 14-1   Author, John D. Lamerson, following the Siege of Ben Het, July 1969

Meanwhile, Major Huff returned from Ben Het. As he settled into his routine duties, my daily contacts with him helped me to build a tolerable working relationship with him. However, the Headquarters and Service Battery troops took an immediate dislike to the major.

The Service Battery troops owned a little monkey as their mascot. One day one of them asked me if I wanted to see something funny. When I agreed to look, he brought out this little monkey. His head had been shaved (Major Huff was bald), and around the monkey's neck hung a set of dog tags dangling from a chain. They were stamped with the name "ROY P." As I stood there snickering, who comes walking down the path but Major Huff. "Oh what a cute little fella!" he said as he reached out to pat the monkey. I moved quickly to prevent him from coming any closer. "Sorry Sir, but he bites!" I said, pushing his hand aside. The Major was content to continue on his route.

At Pleiku, I had a collection of captured enemy weapon ammunition and enemy shell shrapnel that I used as training aids. All new incoming personnel were required to receive a two- or three-day orientation program. The 52d Artillery Group, using instructors that were experts in their fields, taught the course of instruction as needed, which was about once every four to six weeks. When I returned from Ben Het, I brought some new items to add to my collection. The most important item was the small fist-sized chunk of bomb shrapnel or fragment that had lodged in a sandbag just above my head during the much-touted B-52 strike that I have previously talked so much about. I added the bases of two 120mm enemy mortar shells. They were the ones I had recovered following the incident when the enemy shelled us and destroyed the Special Force's ammunition magazine.

It was time to say good-bye to Lt. Col. Bailey, who was rotating back to "The Real World,"[3] following which he would move to his new PCS[4] after taking military leave. Colonel Bailey's next duty assignment was the Tactical Evaluation Division, Supreme Headquarters, Allied Powers, Europe, in Brussels, Belgium.

We NCOs of the Headquarters Battery 6/14 decided to throw a going-away party for the Colonel. Prior to the event, Command Sergeant Major Ski (Shrap-a-zin-ski) approached me. "Sergeant Lamerson," he said., "We want to give the colonel an SKS[5] as a going-away present. However, the only one we have has a bullet-damaged stock. Now I know that you have one with a nice stock, so will you exchange stocks?" Of course, my answer was yes. So we fixed up the rifle with a nice engraved brass plate. On the night of the party, we presented the colonel with it. It was a nice party with steaks and booze, etc. Next, the Headquarters Battery personnel had a party for the colonel, which was held in the unit mess. Again, we had a steak dinner, followed with a wine toast. We were all in a pretty good mood until Major Huff interrupted the party by saying, "All right guys, let's get back to work."

During the change of command ceremony, I was given the honor of receiving the Battalion Colors from Colonel Bailey and passing them to the new commander, as Lt. Colonel Bailey relinquished his command to Lt. Colonel Billy G. Seale from Birmingham, Alabama. Lt. Colonel Bailey, a West Point graduate who demonstrated a high degree of military bearing and who stood "ramrod" straight, differed from Lt. Colonel Seale in that Lt. Colonel Seale appeared much older, in a fatherly sort of way. Although he did demonstrate good military bearing, it became clear that he was no Bailey. That is not to say that he was not a good commander, because he proved to be very proficient in his duties.

The medals Lt. Colonel Bailey received during the ceremony were: the Bronze Star Medal, the Vietnamese Cross of Gallantry with Silver Star, the Legion of Merit with one Oak Leaf Cluster, an Air medal with two Oak Leaf Clusters, and the Army Commendation Medal with one Oak Leaf Cluster. It was said of Lt. Colonel Bailey:

> While serving as commander, Lt. Colonel Bailey went far beyond his call of duty. His concern for the men of the 6th Battalion, 14th Artillery made him an exceptional commander. He made daily trips to the firing batteries to see that everything was functioning properly. During the siege of Ben Het, he exposed himself to enemy fire, when he personally directed artillery fire and air support fire upon the enemy.[6]

Upon entering the Army, on 4 June 1954, Colonel Bailey attended the U.S. Military Academy at West Point, NY.

As an extra historical note I wish to make mention of a test that 6/14 Artillery participated in. My summary is as follows:

General Sidle, accompanied by Colonel Alan R. Toffler, commanding officer of the 52d Artillery Group, used a 50-foot lanyard to fire the first projectile through one of the new tubes, followed by a short lanyard used to fire the second round. The new tube alluded to was the M113E1 auto-frattaged (process used by army ordnance people) gun tube that was to be tested for several weeks before it was to replace all presently used tubes (gun barrels). The first rounds fired by General Sidle, the commanding general of IFFV Artillery, was fired at C/6/14 at Lz Mary Lou on the 22d of June (or thereabout), 1969. This new gun tube for the 175mm guns was designed to double or triple the life of the older model tubes that were only good for 400 rounds.[7]

I feel that, in addition to what I have already written in reference to the Siege of Ben Het, I must include the following article to support my contention that Ben Het U.S. Artillery defenders received next to no recognition for their efforts, while all the credit went to an undeserving ARVN.

THE BATTLE OF DAK TO-BEN HET

(Editor's Note: This is the second in a two part series on the recent battle of Dak To-Ben Het.)

The swift enemy build-up was confirmed By ARVN and Mobile Strike Forces (Montagnard) elements screening Ben Het to the west. After the MSFs detected the enemy and initiated several small contacts, ARVN infantry and ranger battalions were moved up about May 6 to launch offensive actions for which they are trained.

This move reflected a change in tactics. Newly-manned forces concentrated on destroying an NVA regiment between Ben Het and Dak To. Heavy contact resulted throughout the area southwest of Ben Het and continued through June 1. In the last week of that period, ranger units killed more than 500 NVA.

On June 1, ARVN units partially pulled back from the battlefield to allow for extensive B-52 strikes in that area. Another phase of the battle began on June 3 when ARVN infantry units reentered the B-52 strike areas, this time to assess the results.

ARTILLERY SUPPORT

United States and ARVN air and artillery support characterized much of the fighting from the beginning of the battle on 5 May.

Throughout their search for the enemy, The ARVN infantry, MSF and Ranger units used B-52 strikes to prepare areas they planned to search and to protect their rear. Whenever contact was made, U.S. gunships teamed up with tactical bombers from both the U.S. and RVN air forces to support the ARVN units on the ground. At night, Shadow and Spooky gunships fired their miniguns almost continuously on known or suspected enemy locations around Ben Het.

ARVN and U.S. artillery, based at Ben Het and on Rocket Ridge, also supported ground action on a round-the-clock basis. After June 5, with the enemy showing decreasing willingness to close in sustained battle with ARVN forces, the character of the action turned to artillery duels between NVA and allied units. The camp at Ben Het received an average of 100 rounds of mixed artillery, mortar and rocket fire nightly for several nights during the last week of June, and they countered with even heavier fire of their own.

The turning point in the Ben Het-Dak To area occurred on May 26. During the period May 6—May 25, there were thirteen major engagements. The ratio of enemy to friendly losses resulting from these battles was approximately six to one. On 26 May, however, at the end of an eight-hour engagement between the 11th ARVN Ranger Battalion and a reinforced NVA unit southwest of Dak To, 262 enemy had been killed. Friendly casualties totaled 11 killed—a ratio of more than 23 to one. From then on the enemy avoided a major engagement with ARVN forces and resorted to standoff attacks in the area. During this lull in ground activity, friendly forces were repositioned in preparation for extensive search and clear operations in an area southwest of Dak To. Emphasis was on blocking enemy ammunition supply and infiltration routes to their standoff positions.

NVA PULL BACK

During the period June 1—June 25, ground contact around Dak To remained light to moderate, while the enemy standoff attacks was met by equally intense numbers of friendly air strikes and artillery fire. With the multi-battalion-size operation, involving ARVN infantry, ranger, and CIDG still in progress, the number of rounds from enemy standoff attacks continued to diminish.

Results thus far have shown that, with artillery and helicopter support buttressed by tactical air support, an independent ARVN infantry force has successfully launched an offensive operation and defeated the best the NVA has to offer.

The enemy has been seriously hurt. He has lost more than 1,750 killed in the Battle of DakTo-Ben Het.[8]

To my readers, I ask a rhetorical question. "Does the above quoted article present a fair summation of the battle that I have just spent several chapters describing?" Of course it doesn't. It is a shameful attempt at legitimizing the newly touted Vietnamization program, by stealing a U.S. won victory and handing it to an undeserving ARVN, who did not "join" the battle during the Siege at Ben Het.

Another article in the IFFV *The Wrap Up* heaped additional praise on the ARVN. Using past action to put the ARVN in the spotlight, IFFV took one more step to legitimatize the ARVN fighting capacity:

42nd INFANTRY REGIMENT CITED

TAN CANH (II CTZ IO)—The U. S. Presidential Unit Citation for extraordinary heroism was presented recently to the 42nd Infantry Regiment, 24th Special Tactical Zone, Army of the Republic of Vietnam.

The Regiment was honored in ceremonies here for [its] part in Operation Hawthorne in the Central Highlands in June of 1966. General Creighton W. Abrams, commander of U.S. Forces in Vietnam, made the presentation on behalf of the President.

After placing the Presidential Unit streamer on the regiment's colors, General Abrams told the men of the 42nd that, "It is because of your efforts on the battlefield that the people here are now secure, and we can hold this ceremony here today on this valley floor in Kontum Province."

… When the smoke cleared, it was obvious that the enemy offensive had been smashed. More than 1,200 NVA dead were counted on the battlefield and the 24th North Vietnamese Army Regiment was all but destroyed as a fighting unit.

The men of the 42nd will be most recently remembered for their role in the DAN QUYEN-QUYET THANG series in the Dak To-Ben Het area last May and June in which the 42nd helped to eliminate more than 1,600 NVA troops."[9]

> *Author's Note:* Another example of the extensive and ongoing public relations program pursued in promoting "Vietnamization" of the war.

In addition to the above, Brigadier General Winant Sidle was cited for "Visionary Leadership" during a change of command ceremony in

Nha Trang, prior to leaving Vietnam to assume the duties of Deputy Chief of Information, Department of the Army, in Washington D.C.[10]

A final touch was added to the big post-Ben Het public relations program that the Allied commands were using to promote the much-acclaimed Vietnamization program. In a special edition of the Sunday *Pacific Stars and Stripes* newspaper dated 13 July 1969, a series of feature articles was run that tended to draw all public attention away from Ben Het once and for all. The following headlined stories were included in a 24-page special Vietnam issue. In part, I borrow a few words from the *Stars and Stripes* Editor's Note before I list the featured stories below:

VIETNAM NOW

It was too much to hope for—and so some did not hope at all. Even in the face of the screaming headlines that swept across Vietnam like a monsoon rain: "PULLOUT OF 25,000 ORDERED BY NIXON," there was as much skepticism as rejoicing.

There have been too many "lights" at the "end of the dark tunnel" in the past 11 years for those involved for any time in the Vietnam war to hope for too much too soon—what with the rockets still falling, the Claymores still exploding, the human waves still piling up on the barbed wire.

Nevertheless, a new American president had made a dramatic move to end a long and costly war. Troops were going home.

But it did not mean the end of the war. It only represented an effort, a start, and a hope, to bring the war to an honorable conclusion.

Those, who were going back to their world would leave behind thousands in the foxholes, bunkers, and steaming jungle who would fight on in defense of the principles for which Americans and all free men have died for centuries—and will continue to die for if they are to remain free men. ....

IN THIS ISSUE

3	In The Beginning, by Hal Drake
5	Massacre at Hue, by Horst Faas
7	The Air War, by Bill Collins
10	The ARVN Grows, by Al Kramer
12	Young Kentuckians, by Hal Drake
14	The Defector, by Hal Drake
15	The Big Lift, by Al Kramer
18	Diary of a GI, by Spec. 4 Horace Cassels
19	Pacification, by Hal Drake
21	Fighting Priest, by Hal Drake
23	Death and Taxes, by Hal Drake[11]

Author's Note: The above intriguing and compelling stories fit in too well with the political aims of the Washington-based public relations people to be viewed as coincidental.

Meanwhile, during the summer of the 1969 Public Relations Campaign, the 6th Battalion 14th Artillery endured a new and inexperienced commander, along with a new battalion executive officer. Even before a change in command took place, I had been assured that my duty assignment as the battalion S-2 was to remain, despite the fact that a new captain specially trained in the Artillery Intelligence field had come aboard. Captain Calvin Maxwell, like his predecessor, was assigned to be the OIC of the CFSCC, at 24th STZ Headquarters in Kontum City.

Lt. Colonel Seale, the new battalion commander, was a typical "old southern boy." He had a severe case of lumbago or some such thing in one of his feet and often attended the daily briefing carrying one of his boots as he gave relief to his sore foot. Each evening following dinner "chow," we traditionally held a battalion staff briefing. Going back just three months before, Colonel Bailey had changed the daily briefing to the first order of business, prior to breakfast. I, for one, hated the schedule. My rational was simple, breakfast is the most important meal of the day and since it was simple to prepare, it was likely to be more edible than many of the other meals served. Our briefing sessions were traditionally too long. By the time I would get to chow, there was nothing for me to eat. I had my reasons for not complaining to the commander, as I was the only enlisted man on the staff. I had to live with the other NCOs, whereas the officers did not. I did not want to create dissension within the ranks of our Headquarters Battery NCO cadre.

One morning, as I had the habit of doing, I injected into my portion of the daily briefing the following information that I had taken from a classified document received in the form of a teletype message: "… little bitty pieces of bodies lying all around and pieces of shredded clothing hanging in the trees …" (See chapter 8) "… is all that a BDA (Bomb Damage Assessment) team found as they inspected the site of a recent B-52 strike," I reported with a smile on my face. Following this, Colonel Bailey asked me, "Sergeant Lamerson, did it really say 'little bitty pieces of bodies'?" I answered, "Yes Sir! Would the Colonel like to read the message?" He replied, "No, that's OK." However, following that day's briefing, Colonel Bailey announced that the daily briefings would return to the traditional evening sessions. I was happy with his decision.

So here we were operating under a new commander and we found ourselves in attendance at the evening daily briefing. The S-3 was not present nor was one of his assistants. Standing in for the S-3 was the battalion assistant operations sergeant, Staff Sergeant Pate, who had little experience in doing the S-3 portion of the briefing. He gave a report in reference to a shipment of supplies that had been sent to Ben Het by way of convoy that day. Addressing the staff, Sergeant Pate explained, "We sent gravel to Ben Het today." Colonel Seale held his hand up as a signal to halt all further discussion. Interrupting Sergeant Pate's report, he said, "Now, I know how all you fellers use all that slang and stuff, Sergeant Pate. But what in the hell is gravel?" Sergeant Pate, caught off guard by the Colonel's question, but never cracking a smile, answered the Colonel. "You know Sir. Little rocks!" Colonel Seale brought his balled-up fist down hard on his other open palmed hand. "God damn, Sergeant Pate, you got me on that one!" he laughed, as did the entire staff.

Another comical incident also happened during a staff briefing. I do not recall whether it was during Bailey or Seale's tenure. We were at the evening briefing when—Ka-Boom! An explosion was heard coming from the direction of our battalion's Artillery Hill section of the perimeter defense area, which lay alongside Highway QL-14 on the extreme outskirts of Pleiku City where it stretched in a northerly direction toward Kontum City. I knew instantly that an accidental firing of a Claymore mine most probably resulted from a battalion perimeter guard making a faulty hook-up. Hooking up the Claymore for electrical ignition was his duty upon taking up his post. The perimeter was unmanned during the day, so when the guard came on for the first shift, the Claymore mines had to be armed. I ran outside and down to the perimeter guard bunkers. I called out to the newly posted first evening guard shift occupying a section covered by a bunker-protected guard post. "OK?" I called out. "Who the hell did it? Who fired off a Claymore?"

"No one Sarge!" someone answered. "It came from out there," said one of the guards pointing in the direction of a disabled tank sitting alongside the highway.

I called out to the tank crew. "What happened? Did you guys hit a mine?"

"No Sir," one of the tankers answered. I saw that one of the tank tracks of the tank headed south was off on the roadside. So, scratching my head, I looked for another possible explanation. Suddenly, I noticed small bits of fresh looking paper clinging to a large section of our perimeter wire. I entered the inner perimeter wire area and walked across the open area to the edge of the outer wire. I picked up some samples of the paper, which weren't much larger than one-quarter the size of a standard letter envelope. I was able to determine upon close examination that the pieces of paper were the remains of some recent letters, all received from the same girl. I was now within easy earshot of the tank crew. Knowing that the tankers often carried their duffel bags tied to the outside of the tank gun turret, I questioned them once more. "All right," I said. "Who has a girlfriend named…?"

A crewman spoke up, "It's me, why do you ask?"

"Did you have a hand grenade in your luggage?" I asked. Sheepishly the man explained that he had been carrying his girlfriend's love letters around in a tin box, which he kept stored in his duffel bag. He also had an M-26 concussion grenade stored with the letters.

"Well," I said. "There you go. When your tank was being towed in with a missing or broken track, the tremendous vibration caused the pin in the hand grenade to come loose and fall out, thus blowing up the letter container and further destroying your duffel bag." All the tank crew could do was to shake their heads, as I did mine.

As in the past, I found Major Huff, the Battalion XO, a bit over zealous in the pursuit of his assigned duties. I was never guilty of demonstrating any disrespect for him or his Field Grade Officer position. We got along pretty well. As the month of August approached, I looked forward to taking my six-day R&R down in Sydney, Australia. My schedule called for me to catch a C-130 out of Pleiku AFB on 5 August.

Flying into Cam Ranh Bay, we R&R people were assigned quarters for the night. We were authorized to eat in the Replacement Company mess. Our flight to Sydney was scheduled to leave Cam Ranh Bay early in the evening hours of 6 August. The previous evening, I was having a drink at the NCO club where I met an older sergeant first class, who was a proud infantry soldier doing his third tour in Vietnam. He was at Cam Ranh for medical reasons. In any case, we struck up a fleeting friendship. When the hour for our departure approached, we were told that there was an unexpected flight delay. When pinned down, the OIC admitted it would be an hour or two delay, so we all took off for wherever. I ended up back over at the NCO Club. To make a long story short, they continued delaying our flight several times over until the hours rolled over to midnight.

At a few minutes after midnight the big jet engines came to life, our pilot taxied out to the end of a runway, and we were soon airborne. It was only minutes past midnight on the 7 August 1969. A few minutes after taking flight, our plane crew received a message, which they passed on to us. The VC had just attacked at Cam Ranh Bay with a sizable sapper action. Those defenders received severe casualties in the area of the North Post, in the vicinity of the U.S. Army 22d Replacement Company from which we had just departed a short while ago. As it turned out, the main damage and casualties were actually across the camp at the 6th Convalescent Center.[12] We were thankful to have escaped when we did.

My six days and nights in Sydney were marked by overindulgence in good food and good booze. I hit the restaurants and pubs during the day and the nightclubs at night. I was not aware of the fact that a place called "The Texas Tavern" was a known whorehouse. All I knew was that their restaurant served damn good T-bone steaks, their bar served good booze, and there was a bevy of young girls who liked to dance. I made that my second home during the evening hours. I ordered a second T-bone steak every night just before the kitchen closed. I would then stay on until the 2 P.M. closing. My hotel room was only a block or so away.

When I first got to Sydney, I was in a pub late one afternoon drinking beer. Some little ole barfly called out, "Incoming!" I hit the deck before realizing that it was a joke. Everyone else at the bar laughed or squealed with delight. Picking myself up from the prone position, I did not crack a smile. That little joke did not set well with me.

My R&R came to an end. I made my final visit to my favorite watering hole. Not looking forward to going back to Vietnam, I drank my blues away and ended up half-smashed. After the bar closed, I found myself out on the street with no place to go since I'd checked out of the hotel earlier that evening. As I staggered around looking for a cab, which was hard to find, I ran into a couple of whores who propositioned me. "You can have us both, if you like, and it will cost you only the price of one."

I explained to them that I had no interest in sex. However, I was interested in making them an offer 'that they could hardly refuse'. "I'll give you every cent that I have left, which is twenty-three Australian dollars and a pocket full of change, if you will just keep me awake and deliver me to the airport by 5 o'clock in the morning!" (My flight was less than three hours away.)

I made my flight, and on the way back to Darwin we could look down at the countryside below. I found it fascinating. About halfway across the continent, I spotted a herd of wild animals that was so large they were raising a large cloud of dust, as if they were stampeding. I've always had a secret urge to return to Australia; however, it is not likely that I ever will.

Back in Vietnam, I had another night's stay at Cam Ranh Bay. I returned to the NCO club where I ran into the "Old Sarge," who was recovering now from wounds received while he was hospitalized. He was sure ticked! "Them 'young-uns' over there in the medics didn't know how to load their weapons. I had to show em, right in the middle of that sapper attack. As I tried to give them some quick instructions, when the sappers hit, I got wounded. Can you imagine that? Three tours and not wounded once. I had to catch it while trying to get me some well-earned medical bed rest. Damn it all to hell! Some damn war, hey, Sarge?" I had to agree with him. It was a shame the way things went sometimes.

Back in Pleiku once more, I resumed my routine duties. I was back to flying some reconnaissance, and it looked like I might have enough flight hours before long, which would qualify me for the air medal. An incident happened that won Major Huff my admiration. While standing near the Senior NCO hootch one evening, I heard the sound made by a low flying "Loach." Directly across the road from our compound's southern side, lay a "tank farm," which included an unguarded security fence to protect the five large fuel storage tanks within. Directly to the east of the tank farm was a large ditch. The Loach nosed into the ditch and crashed, right before my eyes. I yelled up the hill to a jeep driver to drive down and pick me up. However, before he could act, Major Huff came running up, jumped in the jeep and they sped off toward the front compound gate. Once out of the gate they traveled directly to the crash site. Both men in the chopper were seriously hurt and required medical attention, however, they were pinned inside. There was always a chance that the helicopter would catch fire or, worse yet, explode. Major Huff, without regard for his own safety and well-being, rushed in and pulled the two injured men to safety. I had a new kind of respect for Major Huff following that heroic deed.

On 3 September 1969, North Vietnam's Ho Chi Minh passed away at 9:47 A.M.[13]

In early October, or maybe it was late September, Major Huff called me into his office. Smiling at me, he made note of the fact that I had nearly achieved getting the necessary hours to qualify me for that elusive air medal. He stated that he was prepared to see to it that I got the missions necessary to put me over the hump, so to speak. I explained to the major that being a "short timer" I had no more desire to fly. "I don't fly just to get a medal, so thanks, but no thanks." And that was that.

One of the most controversial programs of the Vietnam War, "Phoenix," was an "intelligence-gathering, sharing, and coordination effort designed to identify individual members of VCI, so that armed Vietnamese forces—regular troops, RF and PFs, National Police, and Provincial Reconnaissance Units—could take action against them."[14] The program controversy stemmed from alleged misuse by program members to get rid of innocent people. Captain Calvin Maxwell, 6/14 Artillery officer assigned as the OIC of the CFSCC at 24th STZ in Kontum, also had ties to the Phoenix program.

Therefore, I was surprised to hear that a mission to fly an aerial observation mission up north had been assigned to him. Now word reached us that the plane, an L-19 Headhunter from the 219th Aviation Company carrying Captain Maxwell and the Headhunter pilot, was missing. I knew in my own mind that I was lucky to have turned down volunteering for any future missions on my tour. After a few day's, the following results were recorded. My source document is full of glaring errors, which I shall disclose following my quotes from it.

Name:	Calvin Walter Maxwell
Rank/Branch:	03/US Army
Unit:	HHB, 6th Battalion, 14th Artillery "Warbonnets," 52nd Artillery Group, I Field Force Vietnam Artillery
Date of Birth:	06 November 1943 (Atlantic City, NJ)
Home City of Record:	Eddy, NM (Or Carlsbad, NM)
Date of Loss:	10 October 1969
Loss Coordinates:	1500554N 1074835E (ZB043728)
Status (In 1973):	Missing in Action
Category:	2
ACFT/Vehicle/Ground:	O1G
Other Personnel in Incident:	Franklin Weisner (missing)

REMARKS:

SYNOPSIS: The Cessna O1 Bird Dog was an indispensable craft for forward air controllers in the early years of the war in Indochina. The aircraft, cruising at highway speeds, could fly close enough and slow enough to detect things a higher and faster flying aircraft could not. When the targets were found, they were marked with rockets and air strikes called in. Smoke from carefully placed rockets brought swift destruction upon the enemy and also prevented accidental bombing of friendly troops.

In the early years of the conflict, the O1 patrolled the roads over which friendly truck convoys passed, searching for ambush sites. For a time, the mere presence of one of these planes served as a deterrent, since the enemy was reluctant to open fire, reveal his location, and invite fighters controlled by the slowly circling Bird Dog. The Viet Cong and North Vietnamese soon grew bolder, however, and any group that believed it had been sighted would open fire, trying to bring down the forward air controller and reduce the accuracy of the impending strike.

By October 10, 1969, the Vietnamese were trying to knock the vulnerable Bird Dog out of the air. On that day, they successfully downed the craft flown by Franklin L. Weisner and Calvin Maxwell in Quang Nam Province. Capt. Weisner was the pilot and Capt. Maxwell the observer in the "high aircraft" (serial #51-11942) in a flight of two O1G aircraft on a high/low search mission on that day in Military Region 2 (MR2), South Vietnam. The aircraft flew from the "Headhunters" 219th Aviation Company, 17th Aviation Group, while the observer was an artillery man from 14th Artillery, 6th Battalion. A high/low search involved a "low" aircraft moving slower and close to the ground doing the looking for target locations (in this case, undoubtedly for artillery targets), and a "high" aircraft doing the location identification and conformation.

The low aircraft made radio contact with Capt. Weisner as they were proceeding down a valley. About 10 or 15 seconds after this radio contact, the low aircraft picked up a radio transmission in which, after a few minutes, they heard screams and moans. No further contact could be made with the high aircraft. (Note: there are discrepancies in the records of Weisner and Maxwell—on some records, they are coded as a helicopter crew lost in Kontum Province. All records indicate the aircraft type as O1G. Additionally, various records place the loss in Kontum, Quang Nam, or Binh Dinh provinces, but coordinates are in Kontum Province, about 5 miles northeast of the city of Dak Pek. In addition to location and aircraft type discrepancies, each man has two home cities of record listed in different records.)

On October 13, search aircraft found the wreckage of the Weisner/Maxwell aircraft lying inverted in a fast-flowing river. Ground search teams were brought into the area the next day and confirmed the tail number as that of Weisner and Maxwell. They reported that the aircraft had hit a cliff above the river and had slid into present position.

Barefoot tracks of four people were found in the area, but no bodies were located. A scuba team was brought in, and reported that both seat belts and shoulder harnesses were still hooked together in the cockpit, but no seat pads remained in the aircraft. One seat pad and an aviator's helmet were located about 100 meters downstream of the crash. An 8 inch thick tree had been carried to the site for unknown reasons. Two 30-caliber holes were found in the aircraft, but they would not have caused the malfunction and would not have wounded either crew member. All searches were terminated on October 18 with no remains recovered, and no further information as to the fate of Maxwell and Weisner.

> Weisner and Maxwell were classified Missing In Action, with a strong probability that the enemy knew their fates. Whether they survived to be captured is unknown. When 591 Americans were released from prisons at the end of the war, they were not among them. But, as thousands of reports have indicated, neither were hundreds of others who survived and were captured. Many of them, according to many authorities, are still alive and held captive today. Weisner and Maxwell could be among them. It's time these men were brought home.[15]

I wore an MIA/POW bracelet for years for Maxwell; however, it got so old and beat up, I exchanged it for a gold one which I still wear. Captain Maxwell is listed on the National War Memorial, "The Wall," as Major Maxwell. His name appears on Panel 17 West, line #63 and ironically, Lt. Ditullio, 6/14 is on Panel 23 West, line 63, also.

I was shocked to see all the discrepancies that are alleged to exist in the records. Therefore, I can only testify to what I know to be true, based on my indirect involvment just prior to my late October 1969 rotation home. The aircraft was an L-19, flown from the "Headhunters" as claimed. However, Weisner and Maxwell were said to have been flying alone, not with a low aircraft as claimed. They were looking for another L-19 from the "Headhunters" that was lost the previous day. The search team sent in was allegedly led by members of a 4th Infantry Division Dog Team. The mystery could have been tied to Captain Maxwell's association with a highly classified mission. But, I shall leave that to others to sort out. I have carried a good dose of guilt with me for more than three decades, because if I had accepted the mission instead of Maxwell, he might still be alive and accounted for. Instead, I blame myself for the loss of Calvin Maxwell.

Late Entry

After the Battle of Ben Het, the enemy terminated his unsuccessful Summer Offensive. By mid-July, all NVA forces which had participated in the offensive, had withdrawn to sanctuaries in the Tri-Border area to refit. Previous experience, however, indicated that the enemy is a creature of habit; therefore, our attention became focused on Darlac and Quang Duc Provinces, since the enemy had deployed to these areas following the Summer Offensive last year. By mid-August, intelligence reports indicated that major B-3 Front enemy forces were moving south from the Tri-Border area. At the end of August, intelligence had confirmed presence of these B-3 front units in Cambodia opposite the II Corps Border … along with the arrival of their support elements by late August.[16]

Note: The 28th NVA Infantry Regiment began their preparations for attacks against objectives in Quang Duc Province. CG, IFFV promptly reinforced the Bu Prang CIDG Camp with two MSF Battalions. CO, 23d Division (ARVN) dispatched a battalion of the 45th Regiment to the Duc Lap area and made plans to counter the expected enemy offensive, which has become known as "The Bu-Prang-Duc Lap Campaign." The 4th U.S. Infantry Division assumed the major role in the defense of Ban Me Thout by replacing the 23d Division battalions.

About mid-October, the headquarters battery commander, in confidence, told me that he had just finished writing me up for the second award of the Bronze Star Medal for Meritorious Service. I stopped him in mid-sentence. "Captain" (I do not recall his name), "I don't want a Bronze Star, the one I have is for valor. To give me one for meritorious service seems to diminish meaning in reference to heroism. Hell, the people only count the rows and numbers of medals, so I'd just as soon get the ARCOM, if you don't mind." He seemed dismayed at my request, but said, " OK, if that's what you want."

When I was getting ready to leave for Vietnam in October 1968, I accidentally dropped and broke my upper partial plate. "Don't worry," I was told. "They have dentist in Vietnam." Well, here I was getting ready to ship home and still no partial plate. As I prepared to leave, I'd gotten a one-week drop (a program that allowed the soldier to leave Vietnam earlier than his exact rotation date, while still receiving credit for his full tour of duty). The battalion command sergeant major, whom I considered to be my only really close friend in Vietnam, said to me. "Sergeant Lamerson, here is a little gift for you." Handing me the very first Department of the Army's E-8 promotion list, he said, "Congratulations, you're on it. Now promise me that you will do this other favor for me when you get home."

I asked him "What would that be?"

He answered. "Get them goddamed teeth fixed." I promised. I had decided to pass my weapons collection down to others staying behind. This included my collection of shrapnel, fuze fragments, and so on. The only thing I was intending to carry back was the SKS Chicom carbine with the bullet-damaged stock. The morning I was to depart Artillery Hill, a three-quarter-ton truck pulled up close to the senior NCO hootch to pick up me and my luggage. KA-Boom! Ka-Boom! Ka-Boom! A 122mm rocket attack hit Artillery Hill. As I took cover, I could see some more rockets hitting over at Pleiku AFB or nearby. After the attack was over, I placed my duffel bag in the truck and returned to the hootch to get my SKS. As I was returning to the truck, one of the young battery E-4s came running up. "Sergeant Lamerson," he begged me one more time. "Please, please sell me your SKS." I said, "Well, how much you got to spend?" He said, " All I have to my name is sixty-eight bucks."

I said, "Sold!" I handed my SKS over and he forked over the sixty-eight dollars. As I boarded the truck, I sucked in my breath, gave a sigh of relief, took one last glance around, mounted up, and told the driver, "Move her out!" Following a few days of out-processing at Cam Ranh Bay, we ate midnight chow and departed by bus to the air base where we loaded up on a big commercial jet that was soon climbing off into the midnight sky. I felt good.

Notes

1. Harry G. Summers Jr., *On Strategy: A Critical Analysis of the Vietnam War*, (New York: Dell Publishing Co., 1982), 182.
2. U.S. Air Force, *History of the 633d Special Operations Wing*, vol. I, (April–June 1969), 18.
3. Slang for the Continental United States.
4. Abbreviation for Permanent Change of Station, usually meaning a transfer out of Vietnam. See: Linda Reinberg, *In the Field: The Language of the Vietnam War*, (New York: Facts on File, Inc., 1991), 164.
5. A 7.62 bolt-action carbine (rifle). See: Linda Reinberg, *In the Field: The Language of the Vietnam War*, (New York: Facts on File, Inc., 1991), 200.
6. SP5 William F. Lesch, "LTC Bailey Accorded 5 Awards," *The Artillery Review*, 4 August 1969.
7. SP5 Richard Kimball, "6/14th Test New Expanded Life 175mm Tube," *The Artillery Review*, vol. 1 no. 12, 22 June 1969.
8. Staff reporter, "The Battle of Dak To-Ben Het," part II, *The Wrap Up*, 1 August 1969.
9. Staff reporter, "42nd Infantry Regiment Cited," *The Wrap Up*, vol. 2 no. 18, 16 September 1969, 2 and 8.
10. Staff reporter, "Col. Hawthorne Assumes Arty Command," *The Wrap Up*, vol. 2 no. 18, 16 September 1969, 1.
11. Forest L. Kimler, editor, "Vietnam Now," and "In This Issue," *Stars and Stripes*, vol. 12 no. 29, 13 July 1969, Pacific edition.
12. Edward Doyle, Samuel Lipsman, and the editors of Boston Publishing Company, *Fighting for Time*, a volume of *The Vietnam Experience*, (Boston: Boston Publishing Company, 1983), 59 and 63.
13. Ibid., 40.
14. Ibid., 78–79.

15 Print out synopsis obtained through Task Force Omega, an organization formed to determine MIA fates and to gain release of any known POWs still held in captivity.
16 U.S. Department of Defense, *Senior Officer Debriefing Report: December 1968 to December 1969,* (Washington: 1970), 25.

CHAPTER 15

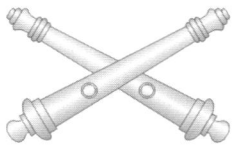

Aftermath

No matter how prepared South Vietnam was to assume the burden of its own defense, it would not be enough to stop the North from winning the war sometime in the foreseeable future ... .
The Vietnam Experience, South Vietnam on Trial

PART II

Shortly after take-off, the civilian stewardesses on the big commercial jetliner served us a second breakfast. Too excited to sleep, I lay back in my seat and reflected on my recent tour of duty. As a sort of "common man's philosopher," I mulled the meaning of war over in my mind. I had just experienced an event that was filled with drama, tragedy, comedy, and mystery, all rolled up into one big ball of surrealistic action. These private thoughts forced me to ask myself a rhetorical question, "Was my experience within the realm of reality?" I rationalized that it certainly was, based on the fact that somewhere buried within my record folder were several sheets of paper. One was a hand-penciled sketch of the Special Forces TOC and Tower back at Ben Het. The others contained poetry that I had written in conjunction with my Ben Het experience.

Note: I will include my self-composed poems at the end of this chapter. My sketch of Ben Het under siege is used on the book cover.

Yes, I concluded it was all too real. By the normal breakfast hour we were landing at Yokohama AFB in Japan. Following yet another breakfast break, we boarded up for take-off. Once airborne again, we would fly nonstop to McChord AFB in Washington State. Enroute we were served breakfast once more.

We arrived at McChord AFB at about midnight. We were put aboard buses and transported to nearby Fort Lewis. The buses dropped us off at a mess hall at Fort Lewis for yet another breakfast. We were then taken to the replacement company for a session of in-processing that included being reissued a complete set of military uniforms. The only thing not replaced was the authorized set of military underwear (OD). Authorized medals were available for purchase and there was a tailor shop open that offered "while you wait" service. Patches, stripes, hash marks, overseas bars, and trouser lengths could all be done in just minutes. They gave each one of us a ticket that was good for a "Free" steak dinner over at the replacement company's mess. We were told that if we wanted to skip the steak dinner, we were free to sign out and leave. Several senior NCOs and I decided to take that route. However, I stopped by a Dempsey dumpster, where I threw away all of my jungle fatigues and boots. Except for my dog tags and chain, the only items of wear I had held over from Vietnam were several sets of underwear, one of which I was wearing. We shared the cost of a taxicab for the trip to Sea-Tac International Airport. By the time we got to Sea-Tac and bought our tickets to our various last stop destinations, we had enough time on our hands to catch one more breakfast before our flight departure. My destination was Lawton, Oklahoma; however, I would have to change planes at Dallas International Airport in Texas.

A short while after taking off from Sea-Tac, the Braniff Airlines stewardess came around with (You guessed it!) breakfast. After changing planes about noon in Dallas, Texas, my flight to the Lawton, Oklahoma, Municipal Airport got me into Lawton at about 2 P.M. By the clock, it had only taken 14 hours for me to get home from Vietnam, counting the seven breakfasts.

The 24-hour period from midnight to midnight did not count on the calendar, due to the time zone changes involved, e.g. going to Vietnam we lost a day on the calendar, coming home, we gained a day.

As I made my appearance, Mavis and the four girls rushed forward from the waiting airport crowd to welcome me home. Knowing from her letter discussions that Mavis would feel intimidated by me if she were driving, I accepted her offer by taking the car keys from her. However, I also realized that my driver's license had expired. Mavis asked that I stop to get the children something to eat at one of the local drive-in restaurants. She had a friend who had volunteered to keep the girls overnight. We still had a couple of hours, during which I could visit with the girls before delivering them to the home of the volunteer babysitter.

Much later that night, Mavis created an interlude in our romantic session by asking me: "Johnny! What's that horrible smell?" After a bit of self-examination by sniff, sniff, sniffing of my person by Mavis and me, it was determined that the horrible odor was coming from my moldy monsoon-affected underwear. Needless to say, I finished out the night by sleeping in the raw.

Following breakfast that next morning, the first thing on my day's agenda was a trip to the Sears men's clothing department. I stopped by the Oklahoma State Police operated driver's license bureau to pick up a driver's manual. I could not afford to be stopped for driving without a valid driver's license, so I was "chomping at the bit" to get requalified by taking the Oklahoma State driver's test.

Mavis, following my instructions by telephone from Sea-Tac airport, had accepted a final offer to sell our home in Lawton. We were scheduled for an almost immediate closing. We had to make a trip to Fort Sill and arrange to have our household goods shipped. Because of weight limits by the Army, I decided that my wife's beautiful old upright grand piano had to be sold. I felt fortunate to get rid of it for the paltry sum of seventy-five dollars. Too, they told me that government quarters were available at Fort Carson, Colorado, so as much as I dreaded it, our beautiful big German Shepherd guard dog, Tim, had to go. I gave him to a home-building contractor that I knew. His mother lived out on a farm. I realized too late that his mother was a cat lover. Tim hated cats and was headed for real trouble out there on that man's mother's farm.

The second day home started out badly. The youngest of my four daughters came into the bedroom to wake her daddy up with a gentle poke to the head, I came up to a setting position, flailing the air with my arms and hands. My poor little defenseless daughter was scared out of her wits and had to be calmed by her mother, who told her, "Daddy didn't mean to scare you." The third morning I was home, I was awakened by a "hard poke" delivered by the same little daughter with the end of a broomstick.

The only shabby treatment that I was to receive, based on my military uniform and Vietnam Veteran status, took place when I went for my driver's license test. The state trooper had a problem. He tricked me into making a safety violation during the driving portion of my test. Protesting his remark, "You just failed your driving test," I produced my military driver's license that qualified me to drive everything in the U.S. Army up to and including tanks. The guy flatly refused to give me a break; I had to have my wife pull some strings with the wife of a high official in the Oklahoma State Highway Patrol. The laws of Oklahoma stated that failure of the driver's test would require a minimum of one week before one could retake the test. Though warned that the test would be severe, I was allowed to retake it the following day, but not with the same trooper who had failed me the day prior. I passed with flying colors.

After our house closing, furniture pickup, and so on, we packed up the old 1966 Plymouth nine-passenger station wagon, with me at the wheel; and we departed Lawton, Oklahoma. This was on Friday, 14 November 1969. Mavis was still a bit nervous at the wheel, so I would be doing all the driving.

During my absence, she had driven no more than was absolutely necessary. There were two possible routes to follow when traveling to Fort Sill from Lawton. One entered the post on the west side, and the other exited the post on the east side. By taking this route to the post for medical appointments and commissary shopping, Mavis was only required to make right turns during her periodic trips to the post.

Unbeknownst to me, some water had gotten into the gas tank in our car prior to my overseas assignment. The damage it did was not so serious as to affect the engine's performance enough to become noticeable to the driver. However, it caused the tank to rust from the inside out, creating hundreds of pin-sized holes in the gas tank. These holes caused a major leak. Shortly after reaching our new post, I would have to have it replaced. En route, we stopped overnight.

Special Insert

Meanwhile, the following documented incident was taking place on the other side of the world. During the month of November 1969, in the vicinity of NVA Base Area 609 and in a POW Camp designated by the enemy as Camp 102: following nearly two years as a Prisoner of War, held in captivity by the NVA, Michael Benge, previously an agriculturist assigned to South Vietnam with the Agriculturist Agency for International Development Central Highlands, 1962–1968, who was taken prisoner during TET, 1968 was now being moved. He was taken from POW Camp 102 and moved into Laos and from there on to North Vietnam, where his final stay was to be in the infamous "Hanoi Hilton."[1] (I insert this to bring the reader's attention to the fact that a major enemy POW camp existed right under our noses, and our B-52 bombing apparently was not harming the camp's existence. I refer to Nixon's Operation Menu.)

Colorado

After a nearly uneventful trip, we pulled into the suburbs of Colorado Springs, Colorado, at about 1:00 P.M. on Saturday afternoon, 15 November 1969. I followed the signs that directed me to Fort Carson's B Street Gate by way of South Academy Boulevard. At Fort Carson, I was able to find my way to the "Red Diamond Inn," where I obtained quarters for my family and me for the remainder of the weekend. The Red Diamond Inn, named after the 5th Infantry Division, Mechanized, was overcrowded and depressing.

I got on the phone and contacted some friends we had made while stationed in West Germany. Retired Army Master Sergeant Sydney G. Johnson, his wife Gladys, and two of their three daughters lived nearby in Manitou Springs. We were invited to come out and join them for supper, and of course this included our whole family. We were only too happy to accept their gracious invitation. We had a delightful evening, reminiscing about old times. Sergeant Johnson, an old WWII Vet and Korean War era Vet, retired in 1968. While our daughters played with the Johnson girls, Mavis and Gladys visited. Sid Johnson and I each enjoyed a couple of after-dinner cocktails and a good cigar as we related our war experiences to each other. Following our very enjoyable evening, I called the family together; we loaded up in the old station wagon and headed back to Fort Carson and our dismal rooms. Sunday morning, following breakfast at the post snack bar, we attended the Episcopal church services at one of the post chapels. The rest of Sunday was spent touring the suburbs of Colorado Springs.

Monday, November 17 was a "Day of Reckoning." That is to say, it was a "Murphy's Law" day. Anything that could go wrong, did. Leaving my wife and kids at the Red Diamond Inn, I traveled over to the 10th Rocket/Field Artillery's Headquarters Battery (Honest John) and signed in, off military leave. I then reported to the battalion command sergeant major. To make a long story short, the battalion did not want me in their organization. They offered me an undesirable duty position that was not commensurate with the rank that I was about to be promoted to. Despite the warning I gave to the battalion command sergeant major (that using a staff sergeant E-6 to hold down the position of battalion intelligence sergeant, an E-8 duty position, was unfair to the man and to myself) he refused to honor my duty assignment. I made it easy on him. I told him, "Sergeant Major, I am holding you responsible for finding me a new home. Otherwise, you're not going to like my solution to the problem." The sergeant major made a telephone call. I was given new directions: I was to report to Command Sergeant Major John Bailey's office at Division Artillery Headquarters. I was assigned on paper as the assistant division artillery intelligence sergeant, an E-8 position. It was a bogus assignment. In reality, I was sent to the S-3 Operations Center to act as "The Plans NCO" another non-TOE position. Not one to make unnecessary waves, I bowed and accepted my new duty position. I then asked for time to get my family settled.

At Post Housing, I got another rude awakening. "Your government quarters will not be available for at least two weeks." I was stunned. I said, "I've got a wife and four kids over there in the Red Diamond Inn who are already climbing the walls. Hell, I can't afford to move to a motel. Now damn it, I want some action and I want it now!" Some housing authority figure, a woman, appeared. "What's the problem sergeant?" she asked. When I was finished telling her the situation, she asked me a question. "Have you considered Government Leased Housing?" "What's that?" I asked. "We rent homes from military personnel on overseas assignments who have elected to take their families with them. We then authorize "Active Duty" personnel to move into these homes in lieu of government quarters." I said, "Sounds great! How do I apply?"

To make a long story short, she had a four-bedroom home available in a nearby housing area. As it turned out, it was just around the bend from the home of the division artillery command sergeant major. By the time I signed for my quarters and prepared to move my family from the "Red Diamond Inn," it was mid-afternoon and a snow blizzard was in progress. I had been given instructions on how to locate the Post Family Lending Facility, where people in our position (because our furniture and household goods were not available yet) could go to borrow the essentials for setting up housekeeping, e.g., pots, pans, dishes and silverware, drinking glasses, G.I. mattresses w/covers, and bed sheets and pillowcases. I lost my way in the storm, although, I finally found the facility and was successful in getting what we needed. We stopped by the Post Commissary Annex, bought some basic food supplies, and drove back to our new home. Neighbors, seeing us move in, under such spartan conditions came to our aid by lending us a couple of chairs, a card table, and two canvass folding cots (military type), for Mavis and I. The home was equipped with a stove and refrigerator, but our "loaners" were the only other pieces of furniture we had. We used some of the borrowed sheets as window blinds. We were thrilled to be home, where we could cook, eat, and sleep as a family again with a bit of genuine privacy.

Three of our school-age children had to be registered and re-entered into school. I, on the other hand, had a session of "In-Processing" to complete. In conjunction with my 38th birthday, we celebrated the Thanksgiving holiday before I settled in for what was to be my last military stateside Tour of Duty. My name was near the line number required for promotion. My orders promoting me to Master Sergeant E-8, was effective 29 December 1969. See Figure 15-1.

By some time in January 1970, my newest award was received for presentation. The awards ceremony was conducted in the Division Artillery Gymnasium. Colonel Montague, the Division Artillery Commander, conducted the presentation. I was pinned with the Army Commendation Medal for Meritorious Service in Vietnam. The troops stood by to hear the following General Orders and Citation read:

FIGURE 15-1 Promotion to Master Sergeant 29 December, 1969, Fort Carson, Colorado

Dept. of the Army, HQ. IFFORCEV Arty. APO San Francisco 96350, dtd 12 November 1969.

General Orders Number 1013

AWARD OF THE ARMY COMMENDATION MEDAL

1. TC 320.
LAMERSON, JOHN D. (SSN) Sergeant First Class, United States Army, Headquarters and Headquarters Battery, 6th Battalion, 14th Artillery, APO San Francisco 96318
Date action: November 1968 to November 1969
FOR MERITORIOUS SERVICE

CITATION

SERGEANT FIRST CLASS JOHN D. LAMERSON DISTINGUISHED HIMSELF BY EXCEPTIONALLY MERITORIOUS SERVICE IN THE REPUBLIC OF VIETNAM DURING THE PERIOD NOVEMBER 1968 TO NOVEMBER 1969, WHILE SERVING AS <u>ACTING INTELLIGENCE OFFICER</u> WITH THE 6TH BATTALION, 14TH ARTILLERY. SERGEANT LAMERSON'S COMPETENCE WAS REFLECTED BY THE FACT THAT THE POSITION HE HELD CALLED FOR A <u>CAPTAIN</u>. HIS RELIABILITY AND DILIGENCE WERE WELL KNOWN TO THE ENTIRE UNIT. NOT ONLY DID HE KEEP THE BATTALION WELL INFORMED ON CURRENT INTELLIGENCE MATTERS, BUT THE INTELLIGENCE SECTION ALSO ACHIEVED OUTSTANDING RESULTS ON NUMEROUS INSPECTIONS. SERGEANT LAMERSON COORDINATED ALL FORWARD OBSERVER PARTIES AND ALL AERIAL OBSERVER MISSIONS FOR THE BATTALION, AS WELL AS OVERSEEING THE PERIMETER DEFENSE. HIS EFFICIENCY WAS EVIDENT TO ALL WHO SERVED WITH HIM. HIS DEVOTION TO DUTY WAS FURTHER SHOWN BY HIS HEROIC ACTIONS DURING THE SIEGE OF BEN HET. SERGEANT LAMERSON, WITHOUT REGARD FOR HIS OWN SAFETY, CALLED FOR ARTILLERY FIRE ON ENEMY POSITIONS FROM AN EXPOSED OBSERVATION TOWER LOCATED WITHIN THE BEN HET COMPOUND. HIS ACCOMPLISHMENTS DURING HIS TOUR OF DUTY IN VIETNAM WERE EXCEPTIONAL. SERGEANT LAMERSON'S MERITORIOUS SERVICE IS IN KEEPING WITH THE HIGHEST TRADITIONS OF THE MILITARY SERVICE AND REFLECTS GREAT CREDIT UPON HIMSELF, HIS UNIT AND THE UNITED STATES ARMY.

CAMBODIA, March 1970:

A crisis was created for North Vietnam during the month of March. To understand the situation, it is necessary to set the stage.

> ... When the American bombings, starting in 1965, constricted the flow of material transported down the [Ho Chi Minh] trail, Chinese

Premiér Chou En-lai personally asked [Prince] Sihanouk [of Cambodia] to permit the completed Cambodian port of Sihanoukville to be used as an alternate supply conduit 2

... Furthermore: With coastal infiltration blocked, North Vietnam diverted shipment of arms and other supplies through international waters to the Cambodian Port of Sihanoukville. War material and supplies, including rice purchased on the Cambodian market, were moving into South Vietnam along a complex of dirt roads called the Sihanouk Trail that linked up with the Ho Chi Minh Trail in an area where Laos, Cambodia, and South Vietnam meet 3

... The overthrow of Prince Sihanouk in March 1970 by pro-American General Lon Nol threatened Hanoi with the loss of sanctuaries and closed the Port of Sihanoukville to the Communists, thus disrupting the supply lines to the sanctuaries. The ability to move supplies through Sihanoukville to NVA troops along South Vietnam's border was essential to carrying on the war in the South 4

... Reacting to Cambodian crisis, Hanoi, in March 1970, had hastily planned and begun to execute what it termed "Campaign X." It deployed <u>four divisions</u> from South Vietnam and the border sanctuaries to perform a three-part "emergency mission" deep in Cambodia: protection of the vital LOCs, expansion of Communist liberated zones, and expansion of the insurgent Cambodian Liberation Army. The Front Unifie Nationale de Kampuchea (FUNK) was to carry on the fight against the Lon Nol government, as the Vietcong had carried on Hanoi's fight in South Vietnam in the early years of the war. Campaign X amounted in effect to an invasion of Cambodia by some 60,000 soldiers and cadres—the 5th and 9th VC Divisions and the 1st and 7th NVA Divisions—and the creation of an organization similar to the one it had put together in South Vietnam years before.

In short, while the United States was "Vietnamizing" the war in South Vietnam to permit its own withdrawal, Hanoi was attempting to "North Vietnamize" the widening war in Cambodia to insure its own continued use of the eastern half of that country.

To set up an organization similar to the Vietcong in South Vietnam during the early years of the war, 60,000 soldiers and cadre, (literally an invasion force), from the 5th and 9th VC Divisions and the <u>1st</u> and 7th NVA Divisions as North Vietnams answer to America's "Vietnamization" program.5

But with the withdrawal of four NVA Divisions from the South Vietnam battlefields, it meant that (On the Allied side) "Vietnamization" and pacification could proceed virtually unimpeded in the Southern part of South Vietnam. The North Vietnamese, however, knew, more surely than ever before, that <u>Time</u> was still their main ally. No matter how prepared South Vietnam was to assume the burden of its own defense, it would not be enough to stop the North from winning the war sometime in the foreseeable future 6

In reference to the above extracts, I point out that at least in part, I have proved my hypothesis that the NVA did indeed have access to the tools of war, supplies, POL, and whatever else they needed, to field their first fully mobile mechanized and armor supported divisions. One main point I present is: we Americans, from day one, in the 2nd Indochina war broke some of the most basic "Principles of War." That is to say, we allowed Giap to establish his bases close to the battlegrounds he selected. We further allowed the enemy to establish an elaborate logistical system to support Giap on these selected fields of battle. As if that were not enough, we, in effect, placed him in the position whereby he could practice "Economy of Force." NVA Base Area 609, established as early as 1959, had never been threatened in the past by either U.S. Army or ARVN ground forces. Neither had the Allies against the sanctuaries posed a serious air power threat. It becomes quite obvious to any armor-experienced tactician, that without any route into South Vietnam's Central Highlands other than the Ho Chi Minh Trail, the North Vietnamese war against the South would have posed an insurmountable obstacle.

Too little too late, the Americans and the ARVN moved to pose a serious threat to the NVA sanctuaries in Cambodia. Too, Nixon authorized U.S. strategic bombing of the known Cambodian sanctuaries and base areas. However, without BDA, the total effects of such bombing cannot be determined. Obviously none of the efforts just stated above were effective enough to cause any major effect against the enemy's ability to carry on their war unimpeded. If the Allied attempts to deal with the border sanctuaries and enemy base areas had any major effect, it was all in vain due to the reckless action committed by the American Congress when they passed the Cooper-Church Amendment.[7] One additional point worth calling attention to is the fact that of the four divisions pulled away from the South Vietnam battlefields, the 1st NVA Infantry was of particular significance. The 1st NVA Division was a veteran fighting machine. It was directly responsible for providing the regiments that executed the enemy fighting in the 1965 Battle of the Ia Drang Valley. It provided part of the offensive force that drove the fighting during the 1967 Battle of Dak To, and finally, 24th NVA Infantry Regiment was involved in the fighting at Ben Het/Dak To during May–June 1969. Please note that the four-division force mentioned above should be estimated to be 60,000, all told. This indicates that a VC/NVA Infantry Division at full strength equaled 15,000 men. In any case, the North Vietnamese, using those four divisions, were able to impose their own form of Vietnamization in Cambodia as well as use the lessons learned at Ben Het as a first formal dress rehearsal for a battle yet to come—the 1972 Easter Offensive.

Sometime during 1970–1971, I found the time and had the desire to put together my newspaper clippings, saved for me by my S-2 clerk in Vietnam during the Siege of Ben Het, into a scrapbook. (Years later, I added to the collection, made possible through the efforts of sharing between Colonel Retired, Ken Bailey and me.) I had promised my S-2 clerk that I would send him his share of the news clippings sometime in the near future. Due to the misplacing of his address, and eventually forgetting his name, I must offer my most sincere regrets and apologize for my carelessness. One must keep in mind that this story goes back more than three decades, I have aged, and furthermore, my memory of names was affected when I suffered a fairly severe stroke on 22 June 1995. I do not, however, use that as an excuse for not doing the proper thing. In addition to the scrapbook, I used my penciled drawing to conjure up a small acrylic painting of "Ben Het under Siege," shown in Figure 15-2.

FIGURE 15-2 Ben Het under Siege

I also took the time to make readable copies of two short poems I wrote in reference to the siege.

"Medevac" was written in tribute to the Special Forces soldier WIA, while working with me in the tower at Ben Het. With our knees locked together to gain extra leverage while pulling up 50-caliber machine gun ammo, an enemy mortar round impacted below the tower entry hatch. Red-hot shrapnel struck the soldier removing a large part of his kneecap.

MEDEVAC
During "The Siege of Ben Het"

Patching up the wounded, WIA, call in the "Dust off" to carry him away!
Wump! Wump! Wump! Hear the mercy bird come—It lands on North Hill,
Two hundred yards to run.
Through barbed wire entanglements and mud, we run like hell,
with our wounded comrade and the good old U.S. Mail.[8]
Now a Damn gook observer spots us, have mercy oh God please!
As we face the deadly "Incoming" enemy artillery.
Thud! Ker-Boom! One splashes on the ground—
death and destruction—spreading all around.
Then, Ker-Blam! Another one, explodes in the air—
"Red Hot" shrapnel, falling every stinking where.
Push onward soldiers, only yards to go.
Run the "Gauntlet of Death!"
Run the "Gauntlet of Death!"
With a middle finger we salute you! Uncle Ho.

J.D.L.

Just days following my return to Pleiku, I wrote the following tribute to the Red Legs[9] of Ben Het.

The Ballad of Ben Het

In the war-torn land of Vietnam, at the Ben Het Camp of the Green Beret, The Big Guns of the Central Highlands changed the minds of the NVA.

Three Regiments had us surrounded—swore that none would get away—but the Big Guns spoke, the siege was lifted—Nguyen Charlie just faded away.

Now to all men who were there with us: You did your job in a mighty fine way, but it was the Big Guns of the Central Highlands that caused the retreat of the NVA.

All who know the Big Guns respect them, and some say that they are up there to stay. Away up there in the Central Highlands, at the Ben Het Camp of the Green Beret.

J.D.L.

Notes

1. Clark Dougan, David Fulhum, Stephan Weiss, and the editors of Boston Publishing Company, *A War Remembered,* a volume of *The Vietnam Experience,* (Boston: Boston Publishing Company, 1986), 94–99.
2. Edward Doyle, Samuel Lipsman, and the editors of Boston Publishing Company, *Fighting for Time,* a volume of *The Vietnam Experience,* (Boston: Boston Publishing Company, 1983), 127.
3. Terrence Maitland, Peter McInerney, and the editors of Boston Publishing Company, *A Contagion of War,* a volume of *The Vietnam Experience,* (Boston: Boston Publishing Company, 1983), 130.
4. David Fulghum, Terrence Maitland, and the editors of Boston Publishing Company, *South Vietnam on Trial,* a volume of *The Vietnam Experience,* (Boston: Boston Publishing Company, 1984), 12–13.
5. Ibid., 13–14.
6. Ibid., 14.
7. Ibid., 9.
8. We used any and every way we could to move our mail. In this case, on a "Dust off."
9. Alluding to the red piping worn on the early day artillery-mans trouser leg. See: Linda Reinberg, *In the Field: The Language of the Vietnam War,* (New York: Facts on File, Inc., 1991), 182.

CHAPTER 16

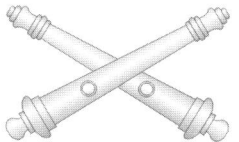

Ben Het

The Final Chapter

As an American fighting man, "a lifer," I am proud to have served in America's longest war—the only war America has ever lost.
John Lamerson

Somewhere along the way, Master Sergeant Pye, an acquaintance from Vietnam and the assistant 4th Infantry Division artillery operations sergeant, came down on orders to Korea. I was put into his duty position. The 4th ID colors were returned from Vietnam, following the division's deactivation as part of the troop withdrawal. The 5th Infantry Division Mechanized was deactivated and the exact same people were kept in place to reactivate the 4th ID. Thus, we were now the 4th ID (the Ivy Division). I was subsequently selected to attend the three-month long operations and intelligence course taught at Fort Sill, Oklahoma. I finished very high up in the class, as did the other men from the Division Artillery who were taking the course with me. We were rewarded with a stipend upon our return to Fort Carson.

While down at Fort Sill, I was fortunate to run into John Horalek, the A/3/6 Battery commander from Ben Het, his six gun 105mm battery fired in excess of 40,000 rounds during the six-week period ending with the siege. After bragging me up to several commissioned officer students who were with him in the snack bar the morning we met, he asked me if I could come back to the snack bar during the lunch hour. I answered in the affirmative. During lunch, Horalek came over to my table accompanied by a few others from his class. Present were at least two officers I knew from out of the past. Captain Horalek (he may have been a major by then, I don't recall) reached in his pocket and brought out a Valorous Unit Award (medal) and pinned it on the right chest side of my uniform. I mildly protested. "I'm not sure that I'm entitled to wear this," I said. "Nobody is more deserving than you," he said. "I know of nobody more than you who should wear this award. Now I don't want to hear another word." I have worn it with pride ever since. The award ranks alongside the Silver Star in importance or standing. In this case, this award was to be worn by all of the U.S. defenders of the Camp who had served there during the Siege, irrespective of unit.

To qualify for the operations and intelligence course, I had to guarantee in writing that I would stay on active duty for at least thirteen months following graduation. However, as things often go in the military, a letter crossed my desk in October 1971. In it was a statement that nullified my active duty lock-in. The very next day, I submitted my retirement papers.

On 1 February 1972, I stood as part of the thirty other retirees in front of the Post Headquarters flagpole. During the Retreat Ceremony that followed, the visiting Under Secretary of the Army who pinned the Meritorious Service medal on my chest singled me out. I was very proud to receive the award, since I was one of the first, if not the first man at Fort Carson to receive the fairly new award. (The original purpose was that it be given to enlisted men in lieu of the Legion of Merit.) My wife and four daughters were present. Following the ceremony, Sergeant Major Thomas Weaver, the Division operations sergeant, and my immediate boss, along with Colonel Palmer, Division Artillery Commander (later Major General Palmer, who came back to command at Fort Carson) praised me for being the sharpest dressed NCO and the one displaying the highest standards of military bearing during the ceremony. I was "Gung Ho" to the very end. I was proud to have been called a "fucking lifer" by the everyday soldiers.

Just after two months following my military retirement date, the shocking news came out of Vietnam: "Exactly at noon on Holy Thursday an incoming artillery round hit the 3rd Division's headquarters at Ai Tu Combat Base just north of Quang Tri."[1] It was the beginning of the much-publicized Easter Offensive of the Vietnam War. During the 1972 Easter offensive, the third of the three major offensive operations launched was destined to strike in the Central Highlands. Nationwide, the North Vietnamese used fourteen 10,000-man strong divisions in their attempts to bring down the ARVN and finish the war.

> The final prong of the Easter offensive struck into the central highlands on April 12. The NVA took a complex of outposts at Dak To and the survivors fell back toward Kontum. Failure of the NVA to

advance quickly on Kontum allowed the ARVN time to reinforce the city with the 23rd Division and stop the Communist drive.2

This time around there was no doubt that the B-52s of the USAF saved South Vietnam one more time. Ben Het was spared the fate of Dak To until October 1972, when on 13 October 1972, the following newspaper headlined article screamed out at me. As seen in the Colorado Springs, Colorado, *Gazette Telegraph:*

Another Border Camp Overrun by Red Forces
by George Esper

Saigon (AP)—North Vietnamese forces today overran the Ben Het border camp in the central highlands, a legacy from the Green Berets that had withstood years of assaults. A two-day attack drove South Vietnamese forces from the camp for the first time in the war. This coupled with increased attacks in other parts of the highlands apparently signaled a renewal there of the offensive the North Vietnamese launched 6-1/2 months ago.

The Saigon command said that two days of heavy shelling in which at least 1,500 rounds of heavy artillery rounds, rockets and mortar rounds hit Ben Het, destroyed the defenders' artillery and ammunition and a food warehouse.

Radio contact was lost with the camp Thursday night after units of the 320th North Vietnamese Division launched a ground assault, the chief spokesman for the Saigon command, Lt. Col. Le Trung Hien, said.

More than 100 strikes by American and South Vietnamese fighter-bombers and U.S. B-52 bombers failed to drive off the North Vietnamese.

Hein said about 140 of the camp's 300-man garrison were spotted by observation planes southwest of the base and contact had been made with them.

There was no word yet on the fate of the other troops. Initial reports from the field said that more than 60 of the Ben Het garrison were killed and more than 120 wounded.

Most of the men were Montagnards (mountain tribesmen) and many had their families living in the camp.

The mountain camp is 30 miles northwest of Kontum City and just east of the tri-border region where the frontiers of South Vietnam, Cambodia, and Laos meet. It was established as an observation post to track North Vietnamese infiltration along the Ho Chi Minh Trail in southern Laos.

Ben Het has been virtually surrounded by the North Vietnamese for years, and periodically the enemy has laid siege to the camp, but this is the first time it has fallen.

When the Green Berets of the U.S. Special Forces were in Vietnam, they led and trained the camp's garrison of Montagnards. The camp was turned over to the South Vietnamese on 4 January 1971, but most of the Montagnards signed up as rangers and stayed on at the camp.

Fighting around Ben Het and Dak To in the spring of 1969 was considered the first major test of the South Vietnamese forces to defend themselves without massive American infantry support, although they still had U.S. artillery aid. The camp held through three months of fighting, and Saigon claimed nearly 2,000 North Vietnamese was [sic] killed and more than 1,000 South Vietnamese were wounded.

Two American advisors had been at the camp most of the summer, but they were pulled out during the past two weeks, the U.S. command said. It explained that advisors are being withdrawn from the lower levels of command such as the battalion-size unit at Ben Het.

Another article in reference to the fall of Ben Het appeared in the 14 October *Gazette Telegraph;* however, it would be redundant to quote it. So ended a saga. The Giap strategy stated many years earlier had worked. The outcome of two wars had primarily been achieved by applying Giap's "Grand Stratagem."

Notes

1 David Fulghum, Terrence Maitland, and the editors of Boston Publishing Company, *South Vietnam on Trial*, a volume of *The Vietnam Experience*, (Boston: Boston Publishing Company, 1984), 136.

2 Ibid., 152.

CHAPTER 17

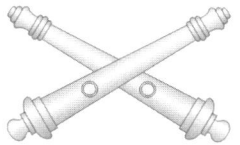

Summation

The senior general of the North Vietnamese Army revealed his "Grand Stratagem" in 1946. "To seize and control the highlands" Giap concluded, "is to solve the whole problem of South Vietnam."[1]

With the 1954 division of Vietnam at the 17th Parallel, "The Two Vietnams" was created. The false peace following that era lasted just under five years. The North Vietnamese made the fateful decision to make a significant military move against the sovereignty of South Vietnam in 1959. Following one of the basic principles of war, General Vo Nguyen Giap and his Army Chief of Staff, General Van Tien Dung, picked a strategic location to establish their base. The location picked lay in the area identified on military maps as the Tri-Border. Base Area 609 was established in the very farthest southeast corner of Laos and the very farthest northeast corner of Cambodia. The strategic battlefield site chosen lay just across the two borders of Laos and Cambodia, inside South Vietnam. A preexisting highway led east out of the newly established base area. Highway 512 once crossing the SVN border, ran only about twenty miles east, before intersecting with SVNs National, North-South axis, highway QL-14.

Following the preliminary action of establishing his base, the enemy, during May 1959, established a new infiltration/logistical support organization, subsequently identified as Group 559. The mission assigned to Group 559 was to expand and improve "The Old Man's Trail." This very strategically important infiltration/supply corridor, later to become known as The "Ho Chi Minh Trail" was developed over a period of the next six years. By 1965, the Ho Chi Minh Trail terminated at Base Area 609.[2]

During July 1959, a second North Vietnamese infiltration/logistical support group was formed. Group 759 was established for the purpose of creating a maritime conduit to South Vietnam. The 1,000-mile rugged irregular coastline of South Vietnam invited such a move. Once again, the North Vietnamese were successful in their endeavors, especially along the coast of Binh Dinh Province in SVN's ARVN II Corps area. At the peak of use, this enemy maritime route was responsible for supplying VC/NVA forces in the south with 70 percent of their necessary supplies. However, with U.S. Naval interference by 1966, the supply effort was cut to receipt of no more than 10 percent of supplies by the VC/NVA in the South.[3]

Because of the success of the U.S. Navy in curbing the maritime flow of logistical support goods to the south, North Vietnam was forced to divert all of the shipments supplied by Communist allies to international waters. The ships were diverted to the Cambodian port of Sihanoukville, where they were unloaded. From Sihanoukville, the necessary sustaining war materials flowed freely once more to the VC/NVA forces in South Vietnam. Thus a new ground conduit, "The Sihanouk Trail" was established.[4]

Meanwhile, the NVA's two tactical masterminds, Generals Giap and Dung, were keenly aware of the fact that future victory in their war could only be brought about by the introduction of mechanized divisions supported by armor, mobilized artillery, and troops. Before this could come about, it would be necessary to construct a POL (fuel) pipeline to the southern battlefield. There is no existing information available to me as to when the construction of the pipeline commenced, but that is irrelevant, since it was constructed. It ran, when completed, from the port city of Vinh in North Vietnam, over into Laos, where it snaked its way south to Cambodia. Once crossing the Cambodian border it continued south, then cut back east until it intersected the SVN border just above Loc Ninh. Final terminus was located at Loc Ninh, just northwest of Saigon.[5] As the pipeline construction progressed, it is certain that spur lines were added, and fuel was diverted to the various base areas as needed. The fuel to run the tanks that attacked Lang Vei on the night of 6 February 1968, obviously came from such a spur line. The fuel for tanks used in the nocturnal attack against Ben Het on 3 March 1969, most likely, too, came from such a source. Because of the obvious availability of POL by the NVA, I am able to present my hypothesis that Giap and Dung not only possessed the capability to launch a mechanized attack during June 1969, but also were planning to do so.

Neither NVA generals being "Pattons," they were both excited at the prospects. They needed a valid test result of this newly acquired capability. With high expectations, Giap and Dung launched their Spring/Summer Offensive of 1969.

Even though their battle plans failed, a valuable lesson was learned. The Siege of Ben Het lessons would be used, in part, as a full dress rehearsal for a major battle yet to come. Meanwhile, under the scenario for modernizing the PAVN and the construction of the fuel pipeline reaching the critical areas of the Central Highlands, truck convoys carrying war materials and soldiers soon moved to the front faster and in greater quantities. Pausing to refuel at jungle filling stations, tanks, armored personnel carriers, and soon 130mm long-range artillery, mostly supplied by the Soviet Union, cruised toward the southern battlefield. During this time, tank crews were receiving up to five months of training at the Soviet armor school at Odessa, USSR (now Ukraine). By Easter Sunday 1972, some 25,000 NVA troops received training abroad, most in the Soviet Union and Eastern Europe. Three thousand tank crews had been trained at Odessa.[6]

On Easter weekend, 1972, following a long-range bombardment with new Soviet-made 130mm artillery, North Vietnamese troops invaded South Vietnam across the DMZ. To Hanoi it was the 1972 strategic offensive. South Vietnam called it the Easter Offensive. With subsequent attacks against the central highland towns of Dak To and Kontum, … PAVN ultimately threw fourteen divisions into the greatest military offensive the world had seen since the Korean War.[7]

The third phase of the offensive began when North Vietnamese troops attacked ARVN outposts near Dak To in the central highlands, locales familiar to Americans who fought in pitched battles there in late 1967. First Rocket Ridge fell, then Ben Het, then Dak To itself. PAVN troops then swung south down highway 14 to attack the provincial capital of Kontum.[8]

Do these tactics sound familiar? Notice the absence of any reference to "The Siege of Ben Het." The NVA used three divisions in their attacks on the Central Highlands during the 1972 Easter offensive. The NVA Easter offensive signaled a failure of the much touted Vietnamization program as well as the ending any hopes for a U.S. "Peace With Honor."

As an American fighting man, "a lifer," as I was referred to by the troops, I am proud to have served in America's longest war. The only war America has ever lost. Lest we forget, remember the "Lessons Learned" in Vietnam, lest the past, all too soon, becomes the future.

Notes

1. Edward Doyle, Samuel Lipsman, and the editors of Boston Publishing Company, *Setting the Stage*, a volume of *The Vietnam Experience*, (Boston: Boston Publishing Company, 1981), 39.
2. Edward Doyle, Samuel Lipsman, Terrence Maitland, and the editors of Boston Publishing Company, *The North*, a volume of *The Vietnam Experience*, (Boston: Boston Publishing Company, 1986), 32 and 46.
3. Ibid, 32.
4. Ibid., 5.
5. Clark Dougan, Stephan Weiss, and the editors of Boston Publishing Company, *The Fall of the South*, a volume of *The Vietnam Experience*, (Boston: Boston Publishing Company, 1985), 10.
6. Edward Doyle, Samuel Lipsman, Terrence Maitland, and the editors of Boston Publishing Company, *The North*, a volume of *The Vietnam Experience*, (Boston: Boston Publishing Company, 1986), 134.
7. Ibid., 138.
8. Ibid., 144

EPILOGUE

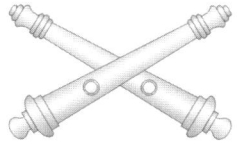

The Phantom of Ben Het

*We went where we were sent, and
did what we were sent there to do.*
Kenneth R. Bailey
Colonel, U.S. Army Retired

The employment of guerrilla tactics by General Vo Nguyen Giap, who was an ardent student of the teachings of Tran Hung Dao, an ancient master of guerrilla warfare, had little to do with the fact that North Vietnam won their war against the United States of America and our South Vietnamese ally. It is true that Tran Hung Dao's teachings are as revered today as they were in the thirteenth century when he defeated five hundred thousand Mongol invaders. His tactics also became a classic feature of North Vietnamese military strategy during their war with France, and then against the Americans and South Vietnamese. These tactics merely complicated the war rather than leading to an NVA victory.

What did beat the allied forces is plain and simple.

> VC/NVA logistical support of the war probably would not have been successful except for the unusual method by which the United States fought the conflict ... The United States and the government of South Vietnam did little to impede the continuous logistical stream originating outside North Vietnam ... Just as important, but less known at the time or since, was the landing of Soviet and eastern bloc shipping at the Cambodian port of Kompong Son, also known as Sihawoukville ... [From 1966 until 1970, 80 percent of the supplies used by the VC/NVA in the southern half of South Vietnam flowed through Kompong Son.] ... As the war progressed and the tactical situation changed, the Soviets provided more sophisticated weapons ... Larger caliber rockets and artillery arrived, as did soviet PT-76 tanks to be used by the NVA against ARVNs and Americans at Lang Vie in February 1968 and Ben Het in 1969. By the Easter Offensive of 1972, the NVA were equipped with the soviet T-54 tanks ... In preparation for these armor operations, the NVA began establishing petroleum pipelines from the north to the south as early as 1968. The first pipeline

reached from Vinh to the Mu Gia Pass. In 1969, this line was extended to Muong Nung and onto the A Shau Valley.[1]

Because it is unknown by anyone but the North Vietnamese, I feel that it is safe to say that the petroleum pipeline construction was commenced long before 1968. When completed, North Vietnam's General Van Tien Dung boasted that it totaled 5,000 kilometers; all 5,000 kilometers traversed over some of the roughest terrain in the world. Considering the fact that the enemy road construction also traversed over the rugged Truong Son Mountains, all completed while fighting a war, I very much doubt that the job was completed in the short time we have given the North credit for.

During 1969, it was noted that large shipments of weapons and ammunition into the II Corp Tactical Zone were arriving via Sampan and were being trucked through Cambodia. "The main Sampan route was from Stung Treng to Bo Kham, which is near NVA base area 702 on the border of Pleiku Province. A truck route also originated at Stung Treng and went via Bo Kheo to Bu Kham. The other truck route originated at Kratie and terminated at Camp le Rolland near Bu Prang in Quang Duc Province."[2]

I must mention here that NVA Base Area 609 was also a terminus for the logistical flow coming north up the Sihauouk Trail.

The main objective of my story is not to rewrite the history of the Vietnam War, nor to explain all of complicated issues. Rather, it is to prove that "The Siege of Ben Het" deserves a revered place in the annals of American warfare. In addition, it should be recognized by history as a classic battle. The defenders of Ben Het should receive formal recognition for their valor, gallantry, and heroism displayed during the battle.

Harry G. Summers, Colonel of Infantry, in his book, *On Strategy: A critical analysis of the Vietnam War,* recalled his conversation in Hanoi with an NVA colonel during the peace negotiations. "You know, you never defeated us on the battlefield," he said.

"That may be so," the NVA colonel replied after pondering Colonel Summer's remark for a moment. "But, it is also irrelevant."

I think that the NVA colonel's philosophy supports the fact that not one U.S. troop-fought battle against the North, held more or greater importance than any other, as to the war's final outcome. To leave "The Siege of Ben Het" out of the history books is a travesty. As an old Red Leg warrior, I am proud to have played a key role in the action as "The Phantom of Ben Het."

Notes

1 Michael Lee Lanning and Dan Cragg, *Inside the VC and the NVA*, (New York: Ballantine Books, 1992), 120–121.
2 Department of Defense, *Senior Officer Debriefing Report: December 1968 to December 1969*, (Washington: 1970), 8.

GLOSSARY

The glossary of terms, acronyms, and slang is designed to help the reader follow the story. However, the glossary is absent of some of the colorful language that we used in our day-to-day operations in Vietnam. By deleting most of the vulgar language from this work, I wish to insure that the book is suitable reading for all "students" of history.

A

AA Anti-Aircraft

AAA Anti-Aircraft Artillery

ABF Attack By Fire

AEL Acquired Enemy Location

Airstrike Bombing attacks by planes

AFB Air Force Base

AK/SKS Soviet or Chinese-built semi-automatic rifles used by the enemy in SVN

ALO Air Liaison Officer

Ammo Ammunition

AO Area of Operations

ANGRY-109 Slang for the AN-109 radio used by the Special Forces units for long-range communication

A-1E The Douglas Skyraider, a propeller-driven single-engine attack aircraft, used for ground support. (The 6th SOS call sign Spad. Thus, they are referred to as Spads.)

Ap Bia Mountain Hill 937, site of the May 1969 "Battle of Hamburger Hill"

Arc Light Code name for B-52 bombing operations

Artillery Gunpowder weapons too large to be hand carried. The weapons are classified as (1) Light, up to and including 120mm, (2) Medium, 121 through 160mm, and (3) Heavy 160mm upward. (The correct spelling for Artillery fuses as opposed to Engineer Ordnance Demolition fuses is FUZE.)

ARTY Slang for Artillery

ARVN Regular forces of the Army of the Republic of Vietnam, includes airborne and ranger units

ASAP As Soon As Possible

A-Team The basic 12-man team of Special Forces that led and trained the irregular units, such as the CIDG

Azimuth A bearing or magnetic direction from North, given in degrees (except for the Field Artillery, which used the mil 1/6400th of a circle measurement, e.g. 180 degrees = 3200 mils).

B

Bangalore Torpedo Wire breaching explosive device. The TNT-loaded pipe has a time fuse that when lit allows the user time to walk quickly away to a safe distance prior to the explosive device going off.

Base Area Enemy Base Areas are described as territory having installations and defensive fortifications, supply depots, hospitals, and training areas.

Battalion A military unit composed of a headquarters and two or more companies or batteries

Battery Company-sized artillery unit, normally 100 men including officers

BDA Bomb Damage Assessment

209

Bunker A fighting position with overhead cover to protect from enemy fire

C

Camp Enari A camp near the city of Pleiku at the foot of Dragon Mountain, it was the Headquarters of the U.S. 4th Infantry Division.

Camp Holloway U.S. Army airfield. Home of the 17th Aviation Group's 219th Aviation Squadron (Headhunters)

Canopy Overhead foliage in the jungle. Usually described, because of the layers of growth, as a double or triple canopy.

CAR-15 The Colt Automatic Rifle (carbine)

Carbine A short-barreled, lightweight automatic or semiautomatic rifle

CEL Confirmed Enemy Location

CFSCC Combined Fire Support Coordination Center

CG Commanding General

CH-54 The Tarhe, AKA Skycrane. It was the largest American load-carrying helicopter used in Vietnam.

Chi-Com Abbreviation for Chinese Communist

Chieu Hoi The open arms program promising fair treatment to enemy soldiers whom voluntarily stopped fighting

CIDG Civilian Irregular Defense Group

CINC PAC Commander in Chief, Pacific (fleet)

Conex Large corrugated metal packing crate that measured 6×6×6 feet. A hasp on the large door allowed them to be padlocked.

Cooper-Church Amendment Adapted by the U.S. Senate to control or prohibit spending funds on U.S. military operations in Cambodia after 1970

Crater Analysis Method used by the Field Artillery to determine the location of enemy gun emplacements so that counterfire could be returned on the enemy's artillery

CSS Combat Sky Spot

CTZ Corps Tactical Zone

D

DASC Direct Air Support Center

DEFCON Defensive Concentration (A type of pre-planned fire)

DEROS Date of Expected Return from Overseas (Rotation date)

Division A U.S. Division consists of two or three regiments/brigades that have a total average strength of from 15,000 to 20,000 men when adding in support units. The VC/NVA Infantry Division, not counting support units, averaged from 8,000 to 10,000 troop strength.

Duster M-42 full-tracked vehicle armed with two 40mm AA guns. In Vietnam, U.S. forces used them for ground support as well as for convoy escort support.

Dust-off Medical evacuation by helicopter; radio call sign for Medevac-helicopters.

F

FAC USAF Forward Air Controller

Fast Mover Nickname for a jet fighter-bomber, e.g., F-4 and F-100.

FDC Fire Direction Control Center, Artillery

Field Force U.S. Army corps-level tactical control headquarters element

FFV Field Force, Vietnam

Fire Base Self-contained and self-defended artillery base that was usually fortified or reinforced with infantry support units

Fire Mission Authorized artillery fire

F-100 Super Sabre; USAF fighter-bomber that supplied Tac Air Support for ground troops

FSB Fire Support Base

FWMAF Free World Military Assistance Forces

H

Helipad A helicopter landing area prepared specifically for that purpose

Hoi Chanh A VC/NVA defector who was protected under the Chieu Hoi amnesty program.

H-34 The U.S. Army version of the CH-34 Sikorsky helicopter, a medium-sized transport. SOG teams during my tour were using them.

Hootch or Hooch A hut or simple dwelling that the soldiers in SVN built at the semi-permanent camp sites. They were built out of a host of different materials. However, they were usually reinforced with sandbag protective walls and roofs.

Howitzer An artillery piece (cannon) capable of firing high angle fire as well as the more traditional flat trajectory fire. The M-110, 8-inch gun tube could fire nuclear ammunition, which was not used in Vietnam. Conventional, accurate maximum range of 17,000 meters made it a very important part of the U.S. Artillery arsenal.

Huey Nickname for the Bell UH (utility helicopter) series of helicopters. Huey evolved from its previous name, HU for helicopter, utility. AKA Huey Gunship, Huey Slick, and Dust-off. "Slick" referred to unarmed except for the door-guns, mounted, and manned for self-protection of the craft.

I

ID Infantry Division. Also Identification or Identification Tags (dogtags).

IFFV First Field Force Vietnam (comparable to U.S. Army Corps)

Insert To be dropped into a tactical or combat area by helicopter or parachute, usually in secret. Also, Insertion.

Intelligence Any information about the enemy that is useful in planning a mission. Information regarding troop movements, strength, weapons, weather, and terrain, all useful in planning strategy.

Interdiction Interference with enemy movement and communication by using gunfire, bombs, or shells, with the purpose of making the enemy less mobile—H&I fires (Harassment and Interdiction) preplanned targets that are fired on at intervals all during the night, etc.

Irregulars Persons and/or groups in Vietnam who were armed and trained to fight, but not physically inducted into the armed forces (ARVN). Regional Popular Forces, CIDG, etc. They served mainly as defense forces.

J

June 8,1969 The date of President Nixon's announcement of the first planned 25,000 American troop withdrawal from SVN.

K

KBA Killed By Air

KIA Killed In Action

Kill Ratio A MACV term for keeping body count score during the Vietnam War

Kilometer 1,000 meters

Kontum City Capital city of Kontum Province

Kontum Province One of the 44 provinces of South Vietnam located in II Corps

L

Lifer Slang for career soldier, often used in a derogatory manner

Light Observation Helicopter See OH-6.

LLDB Abbreviation For Luc Luong Dac Biet, the South Vietnamese Special Forces. Many were minority group tribesmen including Nung Chinese, Montagnards, and others.

LOACH See *LOH.*

LOC Line Of Communication

LOH Abbreviation for light observation helicopter (pronounced loach), specifically the Hughes OH-6

L-19 The U.S. Army version of the Cessna C-37, an unarmed spotter plane used for carrying a specially trained aerial observer who could call in and adjust artillery fire on enemy targets. AKA O-1 Bird Dog. Used by USAF FACs.

LRRP Long-Range Reconnaissance Patrol commonly referred to as "LURP," also the rations specifically designed to be carried by them. Requiring only the addition of water to be added prior to preparation, they were called Lurp Rations or MREs (Meal, Ready-To-Eat).

Lt. Col. Lieutenant Colonel

LURP See *LRRP.*

LZ Landing Zone

M

Machine gun, .50 caliber, M-2, A belt-fed, recoil-operated, air-cooled automatic weapon, weighing about 80 pounds. It could fire 450 to 550 rounds per minute and had an effective range of 1,450 meters.

Machine gun, 7.62 mm, M-60 A belt-fed, gas-operated, air-cooled automatic weapon. Rate of fire was 100 rounds per minute with a range of 1,450 meters.

MACV Abbreviation for Military Assistance Command Vietnam (pronounced macvee). Headquarters of the general staff, American Expeditionary Corps Vietnam. Located at Tan Son Nhut air base 1962–1973.

Magazine The spring-loaded metal ammo clip that holds bullets and feeds them into the weapon. It is also the term used to describe an ammunition storage area that has been fortified against enemy fire.

Main Force Unit Regular NVA Infantry Unit

Malaria A disease commonly contracted in a jungle environment. There are two types falciparum and vivax common in Vietnam. The disease, if not treated, can cause death.

Master Sergeant U.S. Army, a senior NCO in the pay grade E-8

Maximum Range The absolute distance that an artillery shell will travel when fired by an artillery piece.

MEDEVAC Abbreviation for the medical evacuation of a soldier from the battlefield by medical helicopter (dust-off).

Mess Hall Military dining facility

Meter 39.37 inches or 1.09 yards

M-41 Tank American-built light tank issued to the ARVN. When the Americans first used the M-41 tank, it was used by Reconnaissance Forces.

M-46 A Soviet-made 130mm field gun used by the NVA

M-14 A standard issue U.S. rifle that was eventually replaced by the M-16. The M-14 fired the standard NATO 7.62mm round of ammunition.

MIA Missing In Action

Mike Force or MSF *See Mobile Strike Force.*

Mil An angular measurement of 1/6400 of a circumference of a circle, or about 1/18 of a degree. U.S. Field Artillery gun sight settings are in mils.

mm Millimeter (1/1000 of a meter). Designation for the size of an artillery shell.

Mobile Strike Force Units made up of indigenous personnel and used primarily for reinforcement duty. Trained by the U.S. Special Forces.

Moi Derogatory Vietnamese reference to Montagnards, meaning savages

M1911 A1 The Colt .45-caliber automatic pistol, a standard issue weapon for U.S. Army commissioned officers, however, exceptions were made.

M13 A1 155mm towed howitzer, weight 13 tons. In Vietnam they were lifted into hilltop positions by the CH-47 helicopter nicknamed "hook."

M-102 The 105mm howitzer that replaced the M-101 A1.

M-107 Self-propelled, full-tracked prime mover for the 175mm gun. The gun is mounted on the vehicle chassis.

Mortar, 81mm American mortar that was a smooth-bore, muzzle-loaded, single-shot, high angle of fire weapon. It fired many types of rounds.

Mortar, 82mm VC/NVA version of American 81mm mortar, as described above.

Mortar, 120mm NVA used this size mortar as a siege weapon. Because of fuzeing, it could penetrate to a depth of 10 feet, e.g., Fuze Delay.

Mortar, 60mm VC/NVA used this size weapon.

M-16 The standard U.S. 5.56mm military rifle used in South Vietnam. It fired on semi- or full-automatic—user's choice.

MTOE Modified Table of Organization and Equipment

M-26 Fragmentation grenade

N

Napalm An incendiary fluid named for its ingredients, naphthenic and palmitic acids. Jellied gasoline incendiary used in flamethrowers and bombs; it sticks to anything it touches, including human skin.

Nape Nickname for napalm

NCO Non-commissioned officer (Noncom)

Night Observation Device Same as traditional starlight scope, except for size. The medium range could detect enemy soldiers up to three kilometers away.

NSAM National Security Action Memorandum. This referred to presidential policy statements on determining how to handle national security issues.

NVA North Vietnamese Army—aka PAVN, VC, and VPA

O

OE-1 The Cessna single-engine observation plane, aka O-1B

OH-6 The Hughes Light Observation Helicopter (LOH)

OIC Officer In Charge

OPCON Operational Control

P

Perimeter Outer limits and defensive line of any military position, beyond which lay the enemy

PF Popular Forces (militia)

Phantom Nickname for the USAF F-4 fighter-bomber

Phoenix Code name for Phuong Hoang—a long-running program to identify and destroy the Viet Cong (controversial).

Piss-Tube A vertical metal or plastic tube (pipe) buried with two-thirds of length underground, used to urinate into. Also, nickname for a mortar.

POL Abbreviation for petroleum, oil, and lubricants

PRC-77 Similar to PRC-25, except it had a scrambler device for security, which added a lot of weight.

PRC-25 Portable radio communications, Model 25 (pronounced Prick-25). Back-packed FM receiver transmitter used for short distance communications. Average range 5–10 kilometers, depending on weather, terrain, etc. With a special antenna, range could be extended to 20 or 30 kilometers.

Psychological Operations The planned use of propaganda to influence the enemy's thinking. Dropping leaflets, making loudspeaker broadcasts to lower the enemy's morale, and the use of clandestine radio broadcasts.

PT-76 A Soviet amphibious reconnaissance vehicle (tank). U.S. intelligence determined that the enemy armor posed no real great threat in South Vietnam.

Purple Heart U.S. military decoration awarded to any member of the armed forces wounded by enemy action.

PW Prisoner Of War (POW)

Q

QL Designation for a national highway in Vietnam

Quad-50 Four .50-caliber machine guns mounted as one unit. A single gunner fires them all at the same time.

Quarters Living space

R

R & R Rest and Recuperation

Recoilless Rifle A lightweight artillery weapon in which the rearward movement (recoil) resulting from firing is essentially eliminated by a compensatory charge forward. Gases escape from orifices in the breach of the weapon. Nicknamed "Ricky Rifle."

Recoilless Rifle M-106mm U.S. weapon mounted on a Jeep, because of weight and size (as opposed to enemy 57mm and 75mm that were shoulder fired)

Recon Patrol A patrol whose function or mission is to gather facts about the enemy strength, location, and movement.

Red Haze Reconnaissance flights detecting heat emissions from ground located-enemy forces, e.g., camp fires, troops smoking cigarettes, etc.

Red Legs During the Civil War, artillerymen wore red piping up the outside seam of the trouser leg. Thus, they become known as "Red Legs." The term is still used in reference to artillerymen.

Regiment A military unit consisting (normally) of three battalions. In South Vietnam the ARVN used the regimental designation, as did the NVA. However, U.S. forces used the brigade designation. In all cases, a division normally consisted of three regimental-size infantry units. Support units were added to make up the complete division.

REMF Primarily, staff of higher headquarters who were perceived not to understand the difficulties faced by the soldiers in the field. (My name for them was, "Armchair commandos.") Vulgar term for troops or support people in the rear areas that did not know the true meaning of battle. "Rear Echelon MF's."

Revetment A wall constructed to protect against explosives, made of earth and reinforced with sandbags, etc. (No overhead cover was necessary to meet the classification standards.)

RF Regional Forces (Militia)

Rocket 122mm A heavy NVA weapon capable of being fired by several methods. The NVA regulars used precision fire control instruments mounted on manufactured launchers, which increased accuracy over the other methods employed.

RPD Soviet- or Chi-Com-made light machine gun, 7.62mm bipod mounted and belt fed. It is similar to the U.S. M-60 machine gun.

RPG-2 Rocket launcher, handheld and fired. It was capable of firing a 40mm antitank round used by the VC/NVA as an assault weapon. The RPG-7 was a highly improved version of the RPG-2.

S

Sapper VC/NVA commando, usually armed with explosive charges, referred to as satchel charges. These highly trained demolition experts were also used during ground assault operations, as they were experts at penetrating allied defenses.

Satchel Charge A canvas bag filled with explosives and a detonating device that the sappers could throw into target areas

SASI Seventh Air Force Special Interdiction (program). SASI Zulu refers to Zone covered by the program.

Scramblers A piece of communication equipment that could change radio transmissions sent in the clear, so that they could not be understood by the enemy. The user could talk in the clear to anyone who had a compatible receiver.

SEA Southeast Asia

SEL Suspected Enemy Location

Seventeenth (17th) Parallel The line dividing North and South Vietnam; it contained a 15-mile buffer zone referred to as "The DMZ" (Demilitarized Zone).

SF Special Forces (Green Berets)

Shadow C-119 aircraft carrying a search light and armed with four miniguns.

Shrapnel Pieces of sharp, jagged, hot metal sent flying through the air when a shell explodes

Sky Spot Radar directed and controlled bombing, effective during darkness and bad weather against enemy targets that had been pinpointed by map coordinates

SLAR Side Looking Airborne Radar

Small Arms (SA) Handguns and rifles

Smoke (Grenades) Colored smoke grenades used for signaling. Also smoke bombs that can be airdropped to set up a smoke screen to hide ground activity from the enemy.

SOG Studies and Operations Groups. These people were normally involved in secret operations dealing with the unconventional side of the war.

Squadron U.S. Army unit of cavalry. USAF unit of aircraft, e.g., Fighter Squadron.

S-3 Officer in Charge of the operations and training section of a brigade or smaller sized unit. A Battalion in the U.S. Army is the smallest unit authorized a TOE position of S-3.

Strafe To fire machine guns or cannons from low-flying aircraft at targets on the ground

Strobe A handheld flashing light used for signaling to incoming aircraft by marking the LZ at night. Special teams that are ready to be extracted use strobe lights to signal the pilot. Green means safe to come in, red means danger, keep out.

S-2 Officer in Charge of the military intelligence section of a unit

STZ Special Tactical Zone

SVN South Vietnam

T

TAC Air Abbreviation for Tactical Air Support. It can be directed by troops on the ground, however, it is usually directed by a highly trained USAF pilot flying in an observation aircraft. The position is designated as a FAC (Forward Air Controller).

TIC Troops In Contact; also Target Information Center

TOC Tactical Operations Center

Topside Upstairs or aboveground

Trajectory The path of a projectile traveling through space. A gun is fired; the path the bullet travels to reach the target is the trajectory.

Tri-border Area in SEA where the borders of Laos, Cambodia, and South Vietnam all come together at a common point on the map.

T-34 Russian-built light or medium tank, in the arsenal of the NVA

Tube Artillery Gun barrel of artillery pieces is referred to as the gun tube.

II Corps The second allied military region that extended through the Central Highlands as well as through some of the Central Lowlands

---
U

Uncle Ho Ho Chi Minh (slang)

V

Vinh A small port in North Vietnam

Vivax One of the two types of malaria found in Vietnam; the other one is falciparum.

VT-Fuze Variable Timed artillery fuze that allows the projectile to explode at a desired height above the ground. Primarily used against enemy troops in the open.

W

War of Attrition Theory of war that aims at destroying enemy forces faster than troops, material, and equipment can be replaced.

Whispering Death Nickname for B-52 bombers (the Arc Light)

WP Rocket White phosphorus rocket rounds carried by observation aircraft for the purpose of marking the target for the fighter-bombers

X

XO Executive Officer

Y

Yards Nickname for Montagnard tribesmen

Note: This glossary is compiled from experience (memory), from the 7AF CHECO Report dated October 1969, and from In The Field: The Language of the Vietnam War *by Linda Reinberg.*

BIBLIOGRAPHY

Books

Dorr, Robert F. *Skyraider: The Vietnam War.* New York: Bantam Books, 1988.

Dougan, Clark, Weiss, Stephan, and the editors of Boston Publishing Company. *The Vietnam Experience: The Fall of the South.* Boston: Boston Publishing Company, 1985.

_____. *The Vietnam Experience: Nineteen Sixty-Eight.* Boston: Boston Publishing Company, 1983.

Dougan, Clark, Fulghum, David, Weiss, Stephan, and the editors of Boston Publishing Company. *The Vietnam Experience: A War Remembered.* Boston: Boston Publishing Company, 1986.

Doyle, Edward, Lipsman, Samuel, and the editors of Boston Publishing Company. *The Vietnam Experience: America Takes Over.* Boston: Boston Publishing Company, 1982.

_____. *The Vietnam Experience: Fighting for Time.* Boston: Boston Publishing Company, 1983.

_____. *The Vietnam Experience: The North.* Boston: Boston Publishing Company, 1982.

_____. *The Vietnam Experience: Setting the Stage.* Boston: Boston Publishing Company, 1982.

Fulghum, David, Maitland, Terrence, and the editors of Boston Publishing Company. *The Vietnam Experience: South Vietnam on Trial.* Boston: Boston Publishing Company, 1984.

Karnow, Stanley. *Vietnam: A History.* New York: Penguin Books, 1986.

Lanning, Michael Lee and Cragg, Dan. *Inside the VC and the NVA: The Real Story of North Vietnam's Armed Forces.* New York: Fawcett Columbine, 1992.

Maitland, Terrence, McInerney, Peter, and the editors of Boston Publishing Company. *The Vietnam Experience: A Contagion of War.* Boston: Boston Publishing Company, 1983.

Moore, Harold G. and Galloway, Jospeh L. *We Were Soldiers Once ... And Young.* New York: Random House, 1992.

Murphy, Edward F. *Dak To: America's Sky Soldiers in South Vietnam's Central Highlands.* New York: Pocket Books, 1993.

Page, Tim and Pimlott, John, eds. *Nam: The Vietnam Experience 1965–75.* New York: Barnes and Nobles Inc., 1995.

Reinberg, Linda. *In the Field: The Language of the Vietnam War.* New York: Facts on File, 1991.

Summers, Harry G. *On Strategy: A Critical Analysis of the Vietnam War.* New York: Dell Publishing Company, 1982.

Stanton, Shelby L. *Special Forces at War.* Charlottesville: Howell Press, 1990.

Zaffiri, Samuel. *Westmoreland: A Biography of General William C. Westmoreland.* New York: William Morrow and Company, 1994.

Government Publications

All material appearing in this book with wartime restriction stamping has been declassified in accordance with routine Group 4 twelve-year declassification schedules. To the best of the author's knowledge they have been cleared by the Department of Defense for open publication.

Crawford, Thomas M. *Tactical Air Support and the Battle of Ben Het: A Professional Study.* No. 4028. U.S. Air Force, Air War College: Air University, 1970.

DA Headquarters, 52nd Artillery Group, APO 96318 to Commanding General, U.S. Army Vietnam, APO 96375, letter: *Recommendations for Meritorious Unit Commendation.* Department of the Army, 8 August 1968.

Rosencrans, Colonel E.W. Document 11, U.S. Air Force: 30 June 1969.

U.S. Air Force. *CHECO Report:* "Interview with Lt. Col. E.P. Callaway." 24 July 1969.

———. *CHECO Report:* "Interview with Lt. Col. Jack G. Cude, Jr., ALO 24 STZ." 13 July 1969.

———. *CHECO Report:* "Interview with Lt. Col. Thomas M. Crawford, Jr." 10 July 1969.

———. *CHECO Report:* "Interview with Lt. D.A. Devilbliss, Assistant Highland Desk Offcier, G-2, Hq. IFFV." 8 July 1969

———. *CHECO Report:* "Interview with Major William Yenke, Pleiku Sector ALO, II Corps." 13 July 1969.

———. CHECO Division. *The Siege of Ben Het,* prepared by Ernie S. Montagliani. 1 October 1969.

———. *History of the 633d Special Operations Wing,* vol. I. April–June 1969.

———. *History of the 633d Special Operations Wing,* vol. III. January–March 1969.

———. *History of the 834th Air Division,* vol. I. 1 July 1968–30 June 1970.

U.S. Department of Defense. *Senior Officer Debriefing Report: December 1968 to December 1969.* Washington D.C., 1970.

Newspapers, Magazines, and Periodicals

The Army Reporter. 7 July 1969.

The Daily Intelligencer Journal. (Lancaster, PA) 28 June 1969.

The Artillery Review. 22 June–4 August 1969.

The Independant Times. 23 June–28 June 1969.

The Lawton Constitution. 27 June 1969.

The New York Times. 7 July 1969.

The Stars and Stripes. 21 June–13 July 1969.
Time Magazine. 11 July 1969.
The Washington Post. 1 July–1 August 1969.
The Wrap Up. 16 September 1969.

Miscellaneous

The Green Berets. Prod. and dir. by Ray Kellogg and John Wayne. 135 minutes, Warner Brothers, 1968 (videocassette).